# The tears of Happy Jake

an inspiring story of discovery ... and hockey

## Andrew Bajda

White Horse Press

*"This book is dedicated to all those who suffer in silence from the trauma of physical, mental, or sexual abuse. And to all my hockey brothers who I had the honor of going into battle with for nearly two decades of competing in this wonderful game."*

**Jacob Newton**

**Also by Andrew Bajda**

***Captured in Liberation***

ISBN 979-8-9947234-0-1 (pbk)     979-8-9947234-1-8 (digital)     979-8-9947234-2-5 (hbk)

# Contents

# Preface

I first met Jacob Newton on a morning walk through the scenic Cleveland Metroparks. It was springtime. The anticipation of a hike through nature heightened even further with the escape from COVID-19 restrictions which had closed most work and social gathering activities. With my coffee in hand, it was exhilarating to feel the morning sunshine as I entered a wooded path that snakes along the banks of the Rocky River. Appearing from an opening I spotted a family enjoying their own walk, two playful children circling their father with a middle- and younger-aged woman chatting close behind. I raised my cup to greet them.

"Good morning. What a beautiful day."

A confident-looking man returned the greeting with a warm smile and genuine acknowledgement.

"Good morning, Sir. Yes, isn't this just beautiful?"

Something about the greeting perked me up even further. After being locked in for so long from the restrictions and extended winter, it seemed as if nature and that response had further awakened the senses. Strolling down the familiar path into thickening foliage, I began wondering about the backgrounds of the family I just passed. Who was that young man? Certainly not an ordinary civilian. He had a powerful presence, from his clean appearance and tall athletic stature to the confidence and warmth that he exuded. I deduced that he was likely a highly trained military personnel home on leave and spending time with his family. Judging by his lean muscular build, wouldn't be surprised if he was a Navy Seal or part of some Special Ops force.  Who else appears that way and addresses you as "Sir"?  And his kids were so visibly proud and happy to be with him.  They likely hadn't seen him for some time and were enjoying the bonding.

I continued the walk, content that I'd never have an answer to my question but intrigued nonetheless.  But then, returning to the same spot about an hour later, there was the family gazing out at the river from an open grassy area.  The same inviting smile and mutual recognition of serendipity in crossing paths again.

We easily broke into conversation and soon learned answers to questions that it seemed we were both contemplating.  I was wrong about his profession but accurate in the assessment of *not an ordinary civilian*.  Jacob was a professional athlete.  A hockey player who had spent the past six years overseas and was now back in familiar Cleveland following season-ending COVID, having played one year for the Lake Erie Monsters.  With every revelation came more questions. How did a kid growing up in the California desert end up playing hockey?  Of all the places you've been, why did you bring your family to Cleveland?  He introduced me to his loved ones: mom, sister, son and daughter, and an aura of light and brightness never left the surroundings.

Jacob was equally interested in my story: college professor, book talks on the adventurous story of my father, spending time abroad with my fiancée while waiting for her to join me from China.  Although on much different paths, we shared a common theme of enjoying travel and reaching out to help or educate others.

A month later, we picked it right back up.  Meeting at the same spot, we walked for hours in lively conversation that revealed a most intriguing life story and left us shocked upon realizing just how far we'd hiked.  We decided we'd best turn around and head back before it turned dark.

I didn't see much of Jacob after those enjoyable hikes.  Life has a way of changing the best intentions.  The seasons swept by as I retired from teaching full time to focus more energy in helping care for my aging father and arranging the fiancée visa to bring my Zhen to the United States.

The year 2024 proved to be a most difficult year in my personal life, but was not without several meaningful milestones. One of which took place in the same Metroparks where I first met Jacob, although in a different location from our original meeting.

Zhen and I hiked along the Rocky River Reservation, reflecting on the difficult year while searching for opportunities which lay ahead, when we approached the "magical stairs". The magical stairs is my affectionate reference for this picturesque setting, based upon the title of a story that I created and videotaped with my four daughters when they were little.

*Jacob (far right) with son Nash and his workout buddies,*

These magical stairs are made up of 165 steps, engineered and constructed to wrap around a steep cliff which takes you from the nearby Rocky River Nature Center to a scenic overlook above Fort Hill. The steps are a popular attraction for fitness enthusiasts, from beginners looking to complete one challenging lap to more advanced athletes using the steps to complement rigorous training for their own personal goals.

As we approached the steps, I viewed a group of young men and felt the gaze of their obvious leader with his unmistakable smile. These guys were serious about their conditioning. Thick sets of metal dumbbells aligned neatly at the base of the steps and they all congregated around their shirtless leader who stood in a relaxed manner as if holding court. As we got closer, I realized it was Jacob. He approached with a warm embrace, "Hey Brother, I've been thinking about you!"

I introduced him to Zhen and he couldn't hide his joy and enthusiasm. He then introduced us to his buddies who all showed much respect and courtesy. And then it came to me as if the revelation that I'd been searching for suddenly awakened.

"Jacob, let's meet up. I've got an idea for you."

"Any time, Brother.  I've got some of my own and have been wanting to share with you."

From the time I first met Jacob, I have been intrigued with his story.  A bright young man who overcame the most hideous abuse as an innocent child to achieve professional and later personal success in reaching out to help others.  A professional athlete who came so close to reaching the highest pinnacle, before experiencing a colorful journey of highs and lows in multiple countries across two continents.  An inside look of the exciting and violent sport of hockey, the hectic lifestyle and unique challenges which professional athletes endure that go unnoticed to their wide base of adoring and critical fans.

The timing was perfect to move on from the challenges of 2024 and begin a new journey.  I'd often reflected that the years writing the story of my father were among the best of my life, and further enhanced with the joy, recognition, and travel it allowed him to experience in his final years.  And I'd been approached and considered writing several other stories, but the combination of subject and timing was just never quite right to undertake such a project.

Would Jacob be interested in having me write his story?  Was this something that he'd be open to undertaking with me?

We met for lunch at the Hoof and Ladder restaurant in Olmsted Falls, and just like with every other encounter, we were on exactly the same page. He had also been approached over the years to have his story written, but the situation and timing never quite lined up.

With every follow-up meeting came more surprises, twists and turns, life lessons, a gamut of emotions, inspiration.  I typed up my outline and ideas were exploding in my head.  I reached for my phone.

"Jacob, this is an incredible story.  So much more even than what I originally anticipated!"

"Let's do it, Brother."

So began our journey into *The tears of Happy Jake.*

# Part 1

# Chapter One

# Ice Mirage on the Desert

## May 2002 – 2004

The distance between the San Jacinto desert and the Honda Center in Anaheim can be measured in many ways, depending on one's perspective of space, dimension, and travel. In terms of land mass, one can travel between the two locations anywhere between an hour and a half by train or car to three hours by bus. In terms of hockey, the separation is measured by 17,000 screaming fans and a group of kids playing a pickup game using roller blades on a desolate street. And in terms of competing between those two venues, the separation can be as fine as a General Manager's rash decision or an untimely injury.

Or, can it be explained by a haunting voice which lands a chilling effect. A voice which not only has the power to create the separation, but destroy a life, setting off a chain reaction to destroy many more.

This is the story of one person who sought the light to banish his demon and silence the voice, in pursuit of a colorful life filled with acceptance, love, healing, and inspiration.

As with every good story, this one is challenging to pinpoint a precise beginning. Everything that we experience in life is shaped by our actions and events from the past. So, for this story, it seems that as good a place to start as any is the cramped spot in the back seat of a well-worn Chevrolet Suburban, where the haunting voice was deeply hidden in the subconscious of thirteen-year-old Jacob Newton who was feeling on top of the world.

The sparkling serene waters of Lake Shasta viewed from State Highway 5 lined in total synch with his emotions. Was it the connection with nature that caused such a euphoric state? The fun-filled road trip? The exhilaration of success on the ice following his very first experience with much older, and even international, players? Whatever it was, it was a feeling that he embraced and didn't wish to end.

The road trip alone was a highlight that Jacob would never forget. For weeks, the anticipation grew when it was learned their applications were approved to compete in an annual Hockey Showcase held in Langley, British Columbia. Jacob, along with his older brothers Josh (19) and Andrew (17) and close friend Russell (14) were given an opportunity to compete with skaters from around the world. Jacob's excitement overcame any angst regarding how unknown skaters from their impoverished town in the California desert could compete against such stiff competition. The families, meanwhile, had a very legitimate concern. How do we get them there, from both a travel and financial standpoint?

From a travel perspective, Russell's mom proudly stepped up. Mrs. Anderson's Chevy Suburban would be sufficient to carry the boys and their equipment on the three-day trip. She arranged to get the car prepped and cleaned for the journey. Meanwhile, Jacob's family met to discuss and make the required sacrifices to generate enough income to allow the boys to go on this important trip. As excitement grew in their circle, so did the travelling party. After Russell's older brother Brian (20) asked to join, his mom relented, also allowing her youngest son Eric (6) and close family friend Mikey (14) to squeeze in. The travel party had grown to eight and the trip was on.

Jacob's reverie from the back seat was momentarily interrupted with the exchange between his brothers Josh and Andrew. Andrew, seated in the window seat in front of him, had just beat Josh in their NHL matchup on the Xbox, and was repositioning to the middle seat to compete against Brian. Throughout the journey, the boys spent much of their time competing against one another in their own tournaments of Xbox hockey. When not competing, they watched among several popular movies and there was also plenty of time for good-natured bantering and teasing. At one point, when driving over a long bridge entering Seattle, Jacob stuck his head outside the window and looking down screamed that you could see the water from openings under the bridge. Following much laughter, Jacob was reminded and asked after every bridge crossing if you could see the water below.

Now with the middle row of seating resettled and a new game underway, Jacob happily got back to reminders of the journey. Apparently, Russell and Mikey were feeling the same because for one of the few times on the road trip, there was silence in the back row. On the fifth day of travel, sandwiched around three days of hockey and event formalities, the boys were understandably tired.

Reflecting again on the trip, Jacob was amazed at just how fast and enjoyable the drive was. Between playing games, watching movies, and playful chatter, the time had just flown by. Observing the landscape change around them was equally enjoyable and entertaining. They would occasionally stop to take a walk in nature, and the cities offered their own fun experiences. How amazing was that when driving through Seattle, Jacob's brother Josh spotted a Hooters restaurant and convinced Russell's mom to stop there for lunch. Jacob was saucer-eyed as they sat to dine and enjoy the attention heaped upon from all the pretty waitresses clad in their iconic, skimpy attire.

"Oh my! What an attractive group of handsome men!"

"Well, lookey here! What do we owe the pleasure to have such charming young men come to visit us?"

Jacob couldn't help but feel warmth and gratitude towards Mrs. Anderson and was reminded of his own mother. Russell's mom was always smiling, never complained, and seemed to genuinely enjoy watching her sons and their friends having such fun time together. Everything was always organized with no yelling or stress. From the meals to the room arrangements at the roadside motels

*Andy, Josh, Jacob, Russell, Brian, and Eric (seated) posing with Hooters girls.*

where they stayed, packing and unpacking of bags loaded in the back of the Suburban and even tied to the roof, she was in control, getting them all to help out and content at just letting the boys be themselves and have a good time.

As amazing as the road trip was, Jacob realized that there was something else that contributed to his euphoric feeling. The hockey! For the first time in his life, despite experiencing success in competing against his older brothers and local skaters, he began to believe that there was maybe something special in his own personal skill level that would allow him to achieve at the highest level: the NHL.

Hockey had always been a big part of Jacob's life, and that was largely due to his mom, Darlene. While other boys at school competed and talked of playing baseball for the LA Dodgers or dreams of scholarships in football to nearby USC or UCLA, and of course the basketball Lakers were always in every conversation, Jacob and his family stood alone in their love of hockey.

Jacob's mom was a true Canadian. Born in the city of Leduc in Alberta Province, Darlene Newton was always a die-hard hockey fan, to this day stating that she can only watch "good hockey". That same mindset encouraged Jacob to adopt one of the most popular NHL teams of the '90s, the Detroit Red Wings, as his favorite team. Following Jacob's birth in 1988 near his father's hometown in Arizona, the family moved to Leduc where his sister Sarah was born, with the full intention of staying in Canada. But upon learning of an illness to Jacob's grandmother, the family moved to California to be close to her in her final years, and there they would remain.

And on a desolate street in San Jacinto, California, Darlene inspired her three sons and two daughters to play street hockey, using only sticks, a puck or ball, and makeshift goals. After three family members moved into their household, the team grew, and soon local neighborhood kids came to join them in what would be a year-round display and passion for the sport. Eventually, roller blades replaced tennis shoes and set the stage for what would eventually take them to the ice rinks in larger communities closer to Los Angeles.

So, Jacob certainly did not follow a normal path which took him to the Showcase in the British Columbia on that late Friday afternoon and he wasn't exactly sure what to expect. After registering and meeting the coaches, the boys were assigned to teams and provided with sharp colorful jerseys. Noting that he was the youngest entrant, the organizers decided to pair Jacob with his older brothers on the same team to provide some semblance of familiarity. The move proved fortuitous.

With their knowledge and experience in playing together, Jacob's team, which included a goalie and two other entrants, found immediate success on the ice. Jacob felt no pressure, as if back home and playing on the street. He skated with ease and joy as the team continually won their games, often dominating the opposition. Between games, coaches and event organizers frequently approached and commended him on his performance, offering encouragement to continue his fine play.

That evening as the group assembled for dinner, the organizers formally announced the All-Stars who would compete for a final event on Sunday. To his surprise, Jacob was named an All-Star. He and his two brothers would compete in the Showcase All-Star game. Jacob, the youngest entrant and competing with teens and young men up to age 19, had arrived! For the first time in his life, he realized that he was more than just a street hockey player from the unknown San Jacinto.

Russell's mom interrupted his daydreaming with an announcement.

"Boys, it's getting late and we're getting close to Sacramento. How do you feel about getting some rooms and one more night in a motel?'

"YES!"

"Can we get one with a pool?"

His concentration and focus now turned to the decision at hand, Jacob joined the group in discussion and options for the evening, their last night on this glorious road trip.

In later years throughout his hockey career, Jacob would often travel by bus on lengthy trips to other towns and cities to compete in conference and tournament play. It was not uncommon for players to complain of the travel and uncomfortable conditions on their tired bodies. Jacob never complained. Instead, he was warmed by the memories of what would be three road trips to the Showcase in British Columbia. They set the stage for what would be a lifetime love for road trips, special time and bonding with family and friends.

Returning to San Jacinto, life soon eased back into a routine to which Jacob had grown very accustomed, in an area that he was most familiar with. The city of San Jacinto lies in a scenic setting in the San Jacinto desert valley, surrounded by wine country and located between San Jacinto Peak and below the San Bernadino Mountain range.

Just east beyond the San Jacinto Peak lies the city of Palm Springs, known for its modern architecture, hot springs, spas, and luxurious accommodations which attract wealthy travelers from around the world. On the other side, west of the San Bernadino mountains lies one of the largest and most dynamic metropolitan areas on earth, Los Angeles.

In between these two iconic locations, the desert valley features two nondescript cities, San Jacinto and Hemet, which offer quite a different perception. Both towns were recognized by one regional writer as two of the worst cities to live in California, using an index measuring crime, activities, city parks, and other quality of life indicators. But Jacob and his family and friends didn't concern themselves with such rankings. Their primary focus was simply hockey, even on hot summer days when temperatures routinely hovered above 110 degrees.

Jacob, along with his two brothers and two sisters lived in a three-bedroom one-story home on the corner of Fig Street and Oleander Drive. While Fig Street did earn him constant reminders of the name resemblance to the tasty Fig Newtons, Oleander Drive had the benefit as a cul-de-sac which limited interruptions in their daily street hockey duals.

Soon after the birth of Sarah, who was one year younger than Jacob, the family took on even more members with the adoption of three more children following the death of Jacob's Uncle Daryl. This decision would be met later with much anguish and regret, but at the time of Uncle Daryl's passing, Jacob's parents found it in everyone's best interest to raise their nephews John and Chris and niece Robin with their own children.

Growing up, Jacob soon lost any memories of John, who was eight years older and abruptly taken from the house when Jacob was just seven years old. Those memories would return later and shape Jacob in profound ways that would impact his entire being. His cousin Chris was seven years older than Jacob and soon a part of the street hockey group. Even cousin Robin, three years older and more interested in figure skating, became a regular and competitive player in their street hockey games.

Outside of hockey, life in the household resumed its normal routine. Jacob's mom rose early every morning to drive to work at the United Airlines reservation office in Los Angeles. The two-hour drive, assuming normal traffic, kept her away from home for over twelve hours every day, sometimes returning home as late as 10 p.m. As the main breadwinner of the family, she took her job responsibilities of managing flight reservations from calling customers very seriously. On the day she received her bi-weekly paycheck, the family celebrated as if winning the lottery. They splurged on groceries, dining, purchasing small items, feeling normal for a period until having to minimize again. Although the driving distance kept her away for so long and often made life more difficult, the UA flying perks would go on to serve Jacob and the family quite handsomely. Especially when his youth hockey career required flights to cities which the family would not otherwise be able to afford.

His father's daily routine was polar opposite. Jeffrey Newton was a quiet man who had some prior experience in painting and construction but couldn't seem to hold onto a job. He would sometimes help friends and neighbors do their taxes, but typically did so pro bono, asking for nothing but maybe getting some small favors in return.

Two things he did take seriously. One was a habit which Jacob would go on to acquire was his daily workout routine. His father awoke early every morning to do yoga and other fitness workouts. Many days he would follow this with bike rides of up to 100 miles, before returning to indulge in his second love: watching TV with alcohol.

His father would sit in front of the TV with a large can of Foster's beer. Fox News host Bill O'Reilly's program was among his favorites. Jacob and his siblings often joined him after dinner to watch the daily game shows, especially his favorite, *Jeopardy*. Jacob marveled at how Dad was able to answer almost every question, at least 80% accurately. Some days at 90%. They tried to encourage him to go on the show, but he was more content to watch at home with his beverages. Before the night was done, he typically consumed six of the large Foster's cans and a bottle of wine. Somehow, he then managed to get up early the next morning to conduct his daily workout routine.

Jacob and his brothers took full advantage of their father's diversions. Some days they would simply stay home from school to play street hockey and could pretty much do as they pleased around the house. However, this also enabled other problems, some of which Jacob had come to remove from his memory, and such inactivity did not sit well with their mother.

It was not unusual to hear the arguments late at night after mom had returned home from work. Privacy was minimal in the 1,200-square-foot home shared by nine people. Because the house only had three bedrooms, Jacob and the other three boys shared an open room that had been converted from the former garage. There were no beds; they slept on sleeping bags or mattresses. The younger girls Sarah and Robin shared one bedroom, while his oldest sister Bethanie enjoyed the privilege of her own room.

With such cramped living conditions, the arguments heard from his parents' bedroom were unavoidable.

"Why can't you get a job and help out? We can't go on like this. And enough of the drinking!"

"You have no idea what I'm doing to keep this family together! I'm here with the kids every day and not shirking my responsibilities!"

As obvious as the problems were, the arguments were in fact minimal. Much more common was the sound of sobbing from their parents' room whenever dad was out of the house. Mom had largely come to avoid the arguments and accept their fate in silence.

Jacob lay awake in his sleeping bag after overhearing a heated exchange late one evening and reflected on his family situation. Despite the growing tension and an unexplained unease which sometimes crept in from his past, he loved his parents and the closeness of the family. Even during the most difficult times, they were always there for one another.

He felt some bitterness toward his father for not doing more to help out Mom but also couldn't deny the many times when he supported the children, especially the boys' hockey aspirations. When they were little, he often served as goalie when a team was short-handed. Jacob laughed to himself when recalling the road trip where his father took the boys and two friends to an open tournament one March, halfway across the country in St. Louis.

Jacob was only seven years old when they packed the old station wagon, embracing the adventure. And an adventure it was, albeit not in the hockey rink. Driving through a blizzard in Colorado, their equipment was blown off the outdoor racks. The group of six scrambled to retrieve all their equipment on the roadside against the biting wind and cold. On the way back, their father stopped at a roadside shop to purchase fireworks.

"We'll put on a show for the neighbors for the Fourth."

However, those plans never materialized. The car broke down in the Arizona desert with no people or town in sight. Jeffrey pleaded with the boys to stay put while he set off to find help.

Hours passed and boredom set in as the boys sat outside the car with nothing to do. Almost in unison they came up with an idea. The fireworks! With nothing but the cactus in sight, they moved the trove of fireworks to a nearby hill and proceeded to enjoy a most spectacular fireworks display.

When their father finally returned with help, nothing was said as the car was repaired and they were soon back on the road. Rather than show anger, Jeffrey seemed to smile knowing that the boys must have enjoyed quite a spectacle.

His dad also routinely drove the boys to skating rinks in the Los Angeles area once they began competing on the ice, since there were no such facilities around San Jacinto. He made sure they were properly equipped, even if not with the state-of-the-art equipment that their peers who arrived in expensive family cars enjoyed. Jeffrey would hustle to secure the required gear for his boys, sometimes a donation or sponsorship from the local sporting goods store as payback for his tax help. And of course, as the youngest, Jacob always had the hand-me-downs from his older brothers. Once on the ice, it never mattered. From day one, even with inferior equipment, Jacob routinely outskated the richer and older kids from LA and the surrounding suburbs.

His nostalgic thoughts now interrupted by silence as the argument from his parents' bedroom wound down. Looking around the room, Jacob expected the others were also awake in their own attempts to tune out the noise though nothing was said. His imagination turned to the one thing that always brought comfort. He fell asleep with dreams of gliding on ice like a bird in flight with the Red Wings emblem adorning the front of his bright red jersey. A clean slap shot as he watches the puck find the net to the screams of adoring fans.

** ** **

Jacob and Russell continued going to the British Columbia Showcase for two more years, with Mikey now old enough to join them on the ice. Although the travel party diminished in size each year, the road trips proved equally enjoyable. They would vary the stops in nature to hike and explore new scenic areas, but one thing that didn't change was the annual visit to the Seattle Hooters. With age came some added confidence, and Jacob made a point of impressing the waitresses even further with his singing voice at the karaoke bar.

Another area where he continued to grow and excel was in hockey, coupled with a growing physique. Jacob was always tall for his age, and now with puberty came muscle development that still had plenty of room to expand on his broad frame.

Scouts and the event organizers took notice. "If you're serious about a hockey career, playing in the Juniors is the way to go."

"We can set you up with a place to stay and everything will be taken care of."

The most persistent scout was a gentleman representing an expansion team that would be playing in the city of Beaverton, a suburb of Portland, Oregon.

Sharing the opportunity back home with his family, Jacob couldn't hide his excitement and enthusiasm. Adding further incentive in making this decision was the fact that Russell and Mikey were also provided offers to play for the new team. Jacob's parents expressed some concern over their youngest son leaving home for the first time but were clearly open to allowing him to pursue his hockey dreams, just as they did for Jacob's older brothers.

The three hockey families met up to discuss the opportunity, encouraging the boys to look out for and support one another, and made the joint decision to sign the paperwork. Jacob, Russell, and Mikey had little idea of what was in store, but joined in celebration of their hockey careers getting started with a new team in Beaverton, Oregon: the River City Jaguars.

## Chapter Two

# The Shy Boy Awakens

### 2004 - 2005 season

**River City Jaguars – Beaverton, Oregon**

The River City Jaguars were to play their inaugural season in the North Pacific Junior Hockey League, sanctioned by USA hockey. Jacob was assigned jersey number five after his favorite player Nicklas Lidstrom, the popular Swedish defenseman for his beloved Detroit Red Wings. That number would remain with him throughout his amateur and professional careers, with only a few exceptions when that number or later the number 55 were not available. Playing in the Tier III Junior League offered a chance to compete against players from teams as far north as Fairbanks, Alaska and as far east as Billings, Montana. Jacob was thrilled to team up with Russell and Mikey to join their new teammates and quickly established himself as a leader on the ice. Further enhancing the experience, their friend Jonathan Medina from a small town near San Jacinto also joined the team, and Jonathan had his own car which brought the added benefit of transportation for the boys to get around.

*Jacob, Russell, and Mikey*

Just like back home, life centered around hockey. And their tight circle grew even further with a group of skaters from the higher-level Portland Junior Winter Hawks sharing the same ice rink for practices and games.

Even off the ice, the players quickly established themselves as a close-knit group, taking classes together at the nearby Beaverton High School and hanging out after practice. Jacob was joined by a teammate at the home of a local family in a middle-class neighborhood. Families were offered $250/month per player and expected to provide food and suitable arrangements with sleeping accommodation.

Jacob found the arrangements modest but comfortable, and life was quite normal with their reserved family on the quiet street of their suburban home. But the arrangements and atmosphere were about to take a drastic turn.

While back home in San Jacinto during Christmas break, Jacob received a call informing him that he would be relocated to a new home upon his return. It seems the couple at the home where he had been staying were filing for divorce, so a move was required for Jacob and his roommate Woody.

Returning to Beaverton that January, the team placed Jacob in a hotel for several weeks before suitable arrangements could be made. Russell was the first to inform him of the news.

"Hey Brother, welcome to the party house!"

Russell, Mikey, and another player named Reed were living in a home owned by a friendly outgoing couple and their young daughter, and they were opening their home to allow Jacob and Woody to join them when no other accommodations were found. The family would now be earning $1,250 per month to house and feed five teenage athletes in their middle-class home.

The change of atmosphere in Jacob's new home could not be more glaring. Reserved and quiet was replaced with noise and laughter. Every morning, the father watched the news with his morning drink before heading out to work. In some ways, this actually felt more normal to Jacob, with thoughts of his own father drinking beer in front of the TV.

The drinking didn't stop there. After practice and dinner, the father routinely joined the boys and visiting teammates in the finished basement, furnished with a pool table, card table, and other amenities for partying and entertainment. Beer and alcohol were readily available to the underage teens, though Jacob refrained from alcohol, wanting to focus on his conditioning for practices and games. Unfortunately, sleep was generally limited due to the fact that Jacob's bed was a couch in the basement, and the group often stayed up late into the evening or early morning.

The general lack of sleep didn't seem to affect Jacob's performance on the ice, but did have an impact in the classroom. Jacob always performed well in school, and his family was pleased to see the 3.6 GPA that Jacob had earned for his first semester at the new school. But things were growing more challenging between the grueling hockey schedule and an advanced Chemistry class.

An exhausted Jacob returned with the team from a weekend of games to start the new year in Helena, Montana. He felt overwhelmed with the class assignments, particularly for Chemistry. The next morning, after the parents had left for work, Jacob decided to relieve himself from attending class for the day. He called the school and mimicking the father's deep voice, informed them that Jacob Newton would not be in class that day due to an illness. He then proceeded to fall fast asleep on the couch.

The mother was the first to return home and found Jacob sleeping in the living room. Visibly upset, she shook him awake and asked for an explanation why he wasn't in school. Jacob didn't miss another school day for the remainder of the year.

Back at school, Jacob wasn't sure where to turn for help. The only person he knew in the class was fellow hockey player Michael Sauer who was skating for the Junior Portland Winter Hawks team. Unfortunately, Michael was also having difficulty with the subject. The two tried to work together but it soon became clear that their Chemistry skills were not up to par with their hockey skills. Michael would go on to enjoy a career with not only the NHL New York Rangers but also helping others through his faith and ministry. Unfortunately, he and Jacob were not a lot of help for one another in the classroom and Jacob decided to drop out of the Chemistry class.

While certain subjects brought challenges, the school did offer other perks. Like with most teen boys, Jacob found another distraction at the school ... the pretty young ladies. With his blond hair, friendly demeanor, and athletic stature, Jacob was used to attracting a fair amount of attention from the girls in his classrooms. However, due to his shyness he was never able to hold onto any meaningful dialogue or conversation. His teammate Zach Johnson did not have the same problem. Zach's confidence and outgoing personality were like magnets, and he always seemed to be surrounded by the prettiest girls in the school. One girl in particular caught Jacob's attention.

"Hey Zach, what do you know about that blonde Ashley?"

"Dude, I know for a fact that she's interested in you. I'll introduce you.'

"No, no. Maybe we can just all hang out together."

The following weekend was a Saturday home game, and the Jaguars had Friday off. With the Beaverton Beavers basketball team playing crosstown rival Southridge High on the road, Zach arranged for Jonathan to drive Reed, Jacob, and himself to the game.

"Ashley and her friends will be there. They're expecting us."

The boys showed up at Southridge High's Skyhawk gym, and almost immediately Jacob spotted Ashley sitting with some friends and a group of students in the lower section of seats on the visitors' side. His heart began racing with nervous energy. *How do I start a conversation with a girl who's so pretty and surrounded by all her friends?*

Zach had no such concerns. He confidently led the group of athletes up the bleacher steps before settling within proximity to the girls and other students, making sure that all in attendance were aware of their arrival. While Zach moved around throughout the game, Jacob spent most of the time in his bleacher seat chatting and joking with Reed and Jonathan.

"Hey Dude, she's been looking at you. Better get going before Zach steps in."

Jacob did manage to look up at various times during the game and was quite sure that Ashley returned the smile. That was the extent of their communication during the game. However, Zach surprised him and the group as the clock wound down to close the game.

"Hey Jonathan, since we need to be up early and they're not going out after the game, I told Rachel that we'd drive her and Ashley home."

Jacob could barely believe what was happening. And almost before he realized his predicament, he and Ashley were squeezing in the back seat with Zach and Rachel while Reed and Jonathan sat up front.

Jacob found the small talk with Ashley made all the more awkward by the fact that Zach and Rachel almost immediately fell into an embrace amidst much giggling and laughter. While looking outside from his window seat, Jacob suddenly felt a smack on the back of his head before being shoved almost directly into Ashley's face. Without even thinking, he placed his left hand inside her open coat and their lips touched. Softly at first before gentle exploring as Jacob soon experienced his first real kiss.

His mind and body raced with excitement. He slowly moved his hand up from her waist before resting on the magical feeling of her covered breast. He froze in wonder of how she would react. But the kiss continued so Jacob allowed himself to fall under the enchanting spell of her feminine charms.

When they finally arrived at Ashley's house to drop the girls off, Jacob was experiencing such a natural high that he found himself at a loss for words. He got out of the car and took Ashley's hand to escort her out of the back seat. The two smiled at one another and Jacob wasn't sure what to do or say. So, he simply reached out to hold her close for one final kiss.

Arriving home and retreating to the couch, Jacob was relieved to find the basement empty as the others were all retiring for an early night before Saturday's morning game. Lying down with eyes wide open, he could smell her scent, hear her voice, feel her warmth, and taste her breath. For one of the few nights that Jacob could remember, he fell into a deep sleep immersed in a heavenly dream that had nothing to do with hockey.

** ** **

The Jaguars' season was winding down. The team showed much growth and promise throughout the season and managed to stay competitive, with impressive wins against the more seasoned and experienced teams in the league.  Jacob continued enjoying the bus trips all across the Pacific Northwest, and his own game and confidence grew.  As the team's leading defenseman, he took great pride in the Jags' budding reputation as one of the stingiest defenses in the league.

However, it soon became apparent that their youth and general inexperience would be too much to overcome. With each heartbreaking loss came increased realization that a spot in the playoffs and chance of winning the Cascade Cup in their inaugural season would fall short.  Along with this realization and winding down of a challenging season came an increase in activity at the party house.

Following practices, more and more teammates joined them in the basement, and the level of drinking and partying only grew as the season wound to a close.  The outgoing group had much in common, the players representing states from all across the Pacific Northwest.  Adding color to the mix was a player of Japanese descent whose name was so confusing to pronounce that they simply referred to him by his hometown in Pennsylvania.  "Pittsburgh" enthusiastically introduced his teammates to the joys of saki, which he always brought along with him. Even Jacob, who had for so long refrained from drinking in an attempt to maximize his personal performance, finally relented.

His teammates coaxed him with a dare and challenge to drink an entire bottle of Boone's Farm Strawberry Hill Wine, the cheap, sweet-tasting wine beverage being a favorite among the players.  Enjoying the attention that came with pleasing those around him, Jacob accepted the challenge to a chorus of cheers and laughter.

Taking his first sip, the familiar taste of strawberry was not so bad and he felt the challenge would be easily met. So, with encouragement to take larger sips, he brought more laughter with exaggerated gulps from the open bottle. The group settled and resumed their normal banter, toasting Jacob from time to time and mixing in a bottle of his first malt liquor to help wash down the fruity taste.

The wine bottle was quickly emptying and Jacob found himself in a most euphoric state, blurting out random comments that kept the entire group laughing. He gamely went along with them before looking around to see the room suddenly spinning around him. In an attempt to regain his bearings, he stood up but quickly fell back into the soft couch, rolling over and falling into a drunken stupor.

When he finally opened his eyes to the hysterical sound of his teammate's laughter, he was surprised to see them all staring at him with looks of amusement. He sat up in an attempt to shake off the cobwebs, and the first thing he noticed were the rainbow-colored toenails on his bare feet. Confused, he then observed his arms covered with crude characters made from magic markers. Someone then stuck a mirror in front of him and he was almost unrecognizable; his face covered with smiley faces and bold lettering.

"Welcome to the club, Jacob! You're now officially initiated into the Jaguars' Den!"

Laughing, Jonathan handed him a wet cloth, saying that it was going to take some time to get off, and his teammates all shared how funny Jacob was entertaining them during his first drunken escapade. His head pounding and heavy, Jacob managed to laugh along with them. The team was together, having a good time, and Jacob was openly accepted into the group. He wasn't sure why acceptance was so important to him at the time. But that, along with hockey, was all that really mattered.

** ** **

The legacy of the River City Jaguars' inaugural season did not end with their final game. Shortly after returning to San Jacinto for the summer, Jacob received an urgent phone call from Zach.

"Dude, my parents will pay your entire trip on the cruise. All you need to do is make it to Galveston Bay by next weekend. It'll be epic!"

Jacob scrambled to generate the funds needed to make the flight and convince his parents of this opportunity of a lifetime. A nine-day Caribbean cruise on the Carnival Cruise Line. Stops at Grand Cayman Island, Jamaica, and Cozumel. The challenge grew with mom's UA perks no longer available due to a job change, but his big brother came through. Josh, who often helped out with spending money for Jacob, provided the funds needed to make the flight. He'd even have some left over for spending. Jacob couldn't believe his good fortune.

Arriving in Galveston, Jacob met with the family and learned more details. The group was made up of Zach's parents, his younger sister Courtney and a friend, two of Zach's friends from Oregon, and four River City teammates (including Zach and Jacob). Before entering the luxurious cruise ship, the boys ran off to make a final purchase for the cruise: twelve bottles of hard liquor. Jacob only drank one more time following the Boone's Farm initiation in Beaverton but joined in their anticipation and excitement.

Once on the cruise ship, things got even better. Five rooms side by side, each looking out at magnificent ocean views. The group settled into their respective rooms to unpack and further explore. With the ship setting sail, the six boys all met in Zach's room to make their first toast on the voyage. Feeling on top of the world, they eagerly toured the expansive ship, enjoying all the sights and sounds when someone spotted the karaoke bar. Seemed as good a place as any to continue.

With confidence buoyed by the alcohol, Jacob grew further intoxicated with an urge to sing. Sometimes alone, sometimes with Zach or the others, he felt like a star and took subtle note of the approving nods and cheers around them. When the group finally decided to go back and make plans for the evening, Jacob reluctantly joined them. But once back in the room and each person showing an interest in different activities, Jacob decided to go solo back to the karaoke bar.

Invigorated by a delicious meal and yet more toasts in Zach's room, Jacob's confidence soared to further heights. He rhythmically moved with the words and beat to each song and soon had the growing evening crowd requesting more. When someone asked if he could do "Livin' La Vida Loca" by Ricky Martin, he eagerly jumped to the stage amidst more applause.

With the aid of lyrics on the screen and feeling relaxed from the drinks, Jacob belted out the lines and had some of the crowd off their seats dancing with him. He soaked in the applause and went back to his seat, thanking those around him when a distinguished-looking gentleman with the Carnival logo on his blazer approached him.

"Son, we'd like for you to perform this song on the last night of the cruise in the Entertainment Hall. It won't be karaoke, so you'll need to memorize all the lines. We just need your name and some details."

Jacob quickly sobered as he provided the required details. He was honored, surprised, and at the same time somewhat nervous about singing in front of a large crowd without the aid of lyrics. He did take comfort in noting that the liquor was a great relaxer and would help get him through the evening.

Jacob couldn't wait to tell his friends the next morning. They delighted in the chance to be a part of something so cool and searched out the Hall to get a look and feel for the venue. After finally locating and arranging to see the Hall, Jacob froze. The expansive elegant room was way more than he had ever imagined. High vaulted ceiling, massive stage, various levels of seating with comfortable chairs and tables for dining. Was he really going to do this? And with no words to aid him? Once again, Jacob took comfort that the liquor would calm his nerves but felt an immediate need to get some practice and memorize the song.

Several days into the cruise, the ship made its second stop at Montego Bay on the tropical Island of Jamaica. Upon disembarking, eager passengers rushed to the open market to partake in the colorful display of exotic fruits, clothing, accessories, and souvenirs being hawked by the Jamaican merchants. After spending some time with the family to get a feel for the surroundings, Zach motioned for his friends to break away and see more of Jamaica. His father, trying on a straw hat as they walked away, cautioned: "Now stay out of trouble and make sure to get back in good time before departure."

The group exited the tourist area and soon found themselves in a more desolate area of town, where Zach once again worked his magic. Easily mixing in and making conversation with the locals, he met a dealer in a nearby alley where he made his first purchase on the island: Jamaican weed.

Jacob, who had only recently experienced his first alcoholic beverage, was not overly interested in partaking in yet another new experience. But Zach's Oregon buddies seemed quite knowledgeable in their cannabis and after sampling, informed Zach that he got ripped off. Unable to spot the seller who quickly departed upon their purchase, Zach was determined to find a more respectable supplier who would sell them some "real" Jamaican grass.

He sought other locals, discreetly voicing his displeasure with their prior purchase and demanding a sample of something that would meet their needs. A confident well-spoken young man was identified, and he convinced them that he could help and they would not be disappointed.

"No need to worry Mon, I'll take care of everything. Just come with me and you'll be rewarded with the best that our Island has to offer. Jamaican Pearl!"

The words rolled off his lips as poetry and the bright eyes and broad smile on his rich mocha-colored face took away some of the apprehension they were feeling, so they agreed to follow him.

He sought out an old cab that the group squeezed into, continually reassuring them with his warm smile and friendly manner. After a short drive, they got out at a street corner dominated by an old Burger King. While the boys purchased an early lunch, their new friend spoke to two other Jamaicans seated at a nearby table.

Finishing their burgers, the Jamaicans motioned for them to follow and took a walk. Descending deeper into the old part of town and farther from the busy port, Jacob surmised that this was not a part of Montego Bay that the cruise coordinators would want you to see. He was a bit comforted that their group of six did make a somewhat formidable appearance. Belying their confident outward appearance, the silence and collective apprehension grew with the walk.

They finally approached an abandoned warehouse and were led up a steep flight of concrete steps that revealed broken glass and dilapidated rooms visible through window openings. When they reached the top, Jacob breathed a sigh of relief as he was met with a most unexpected sight ... a crudely-decorated rooftop bar.

"Make yourselves comfortable Mon and enjoy our spectacular view."

Relieved to settle on bar stools to the steel drum beat of reggae piped through oversized speakers, they eagerly accepted Red Stripe beers and observed distant views of Montego Bay through the jagged openings.

After some time, one of the Jamaicans returned with two rolled joints and a bag of weed for their purchase. Now much more relaxed and enjoying the company in a most unique rooftop setting, the group passed around a joint and quickly agreed that this was top-quality Jamaican weed.

True to his word, the Jamaican had produced the finest Jamaican Pearl. And well aware that they were on the cruise ship, he offered some words of advice.

"Now listen Mon, there is only one way to safely get this back on the ship with you. Make sure to hide it in your butt cheeks, and not loose in your underwear. If you do that, they will catch you."

Jacob was riding high. Experiencing his first taste of marijuana, he found the comment, along with everything around him, extremely funny and couldn't stop laughing. He was ready to continue the partying in this exotic tropical paradise.

The group laughed the entire way while retracing their steps back to the Burger King and port area. With more activities available as they closed in on the tourist area, they broke up into groups partaking in the variety of options. Jacob was drawn to the limbo contest going on in Margaritaville.

Two pretty girls clad in bikinis seductively moved the limbo rope lower and lower as Jacob remained alive in the contest, adeptly bending his knees and torso to the cheers of the patrons. His body limber from years of training coupled with the relaxed sensation, Jacob easily won the contest. The girls provocatively lowered the rope even further as another woman lit the rope in flames. The patrons gasped. Sensing his cue, Jacob rushed to take on the challenge but was quickly stopped amidst much laughter as three experienced limbo dancers approached to perform this death-defying act.

Walking back into the crowd, a sudden realization hit him. The ship! Checking his pockets, he had no required ID to get back on board. Panic set in as he sprinted back to the dock in search of his friends and the family. With people boarding, he yelled out in search of Zach and wondered what to do.

Just before calling home to contact his family, Jacob spotted Zach's mom. She appeared in her own sense of panic in an attempt to collect Zach and his friends but reassured him that everything was fine. She was holding onto all the IDs.

Unfortunately, it didn't go as smoothly for all the teen boys. Only one of the two Oregon friends smuggling the pot on board took the Jamaican's advice. Viewing boarders to depart Jamaica, agents were randomly patting down travelers who they targeted as individuals most likely to smuggle pot. The one friend who stuffed the pot in his butt cheeks passed inspection. The other friend who placed the bag in the front of his boxers was caught. With a tug of his shorts, they immediately heard the rustle of plastic.

He was detained in Montego Bay, where he was held in the local jail awaiting his outcome.

Back on the ship, Zach's parents worked feverishly to secure the young man's release, and the boys were relieved to learn while in open sea the next day that he would be rejoining them at the next port of call. The sobering events did not slow their appetite for adventure. The ship's playground offered numerous activities, and they all delighted in the temptations. With scores of attractive young ladies on the ship, Zach was in his element, and they all searched for romantic possibilities.

One morning while working to memorize his lines for the final evening, Jacob was politely asked by a young lady what he was working on. Explaining his upcoming appearance and intrigued by her South African accent, the two found themselves lost in conversation learning about their respective backgrounds. Jacob went back to his nearby room to pour a couple of drinks and upon his return was brusquely stopped by several ship security officers.

"We've been observing you and there is no underage drinking allowed on this ship! This is a warning but if we spot or suspect you of drinking again, you will be confined to your room for the duration of the cruise."

Jacob wasn't sure what was worse. The fact that he was caught or the realization that he was now going to have to perform on the final night without the aid of alcohol. Disappointed in the sudden departure of the attractive South African teen, Jacob vowed to be on his best behavior and learn the song's lyrics.

The night finally arrived. Jacob spent the entire day going over the lyrics practicing the song and now was ushered behind stage with other performers while the audience wined and dined in anticipation of the evening entertainment. While most of his fellow performers were to perform in groups, he stood alone as an organizer handed him an outfit and provided some details. He would be performing solo but accompanied on stage by a group of go-go dancers to further liven up the show.

Changing in front of a mirror, Jacob could feel himself getting into character as he viewed himself in the leather pants and buttoned-down shirt under a stylish blue jacket. Still, some apprehension remained. *Come on, man. Relax! This is no different than skating on ice in front of a big crowd.* But it was different. He took a deep breath and stepped out in wait to hear his name, stating aloud: "It's SHOWTIME!"

Jacob went over the first few verses in his head and tried to remain calm, remembering the organizer's parting words as he left to change: "Just be yourself and have fun!"

When his moment finally arrived, Jacob was surrounded by the colorful dancers as they waited for the rousing introduction to end before walking on center stage, the girls bouncing up and down all around him. His confidence growing, Jacob could spot his friends and the family in their reserved seats near the front center stage, all standing and screaming in anticipation of the performance.

The clear sound of horns came alive through the high-tech sound system, and instinctively Jacob broke into rhythmic movement to open the song. Once through the opening line, things slowed down and he soon found himself back in the karaoke bar, his voice growing stronger, spurred on by the electric energy received from the crowd.

He completed the first verse and nailed the refrain, ready for the second verse when the unexpected happened.

Come on

She's livin' la vida loca....

---

Suddenly his mind went blank and he forgot the words. The crowd now standing and the dancers gyrating wildly around him, he decided to forego the words and join them in dance. The applause grew even louder before the music caught up for the second refrain, so he picked right back up where he left off.

When the song ended, the entire audience remained standing in applause mixed with laughter as they delighted in the playful performance on their final night of the voyage. Escorted by the dancers, Jacob smoothly strode off stage waving to the appreciative crowd. His heart was racing with excitement. He realized right then and there that he thoroughly loved the attention ... and was meant for the bright lights.

# Chapter Three
# The Hockey Guy

2005 - 2006 season

## Los Angeles Junior Kings – Los Angles, California

With his mindset back to his beloved hockey, Jacob was determined to expand his game and move up the hockey ladder. He spent considerable time that summer honing his skills with the help of his brothers Josh and Andy. The older brothers capitalized on their own experience in the Junior Circuit to open a hockey clinic in nearby Riverside, California: Newton's Hockey. They could both see the clear potential in their little brother and pushed him to achieve his dream of playing at the highest level for the nearby Anaheim Ducks or Los Angeles Kings.

As the summer wound down, Jacob and Mikey seized an opportunity to move to Kansas City to compete in the competitive 18-and-under league at the AAA level. Arrangements were made and the boys packed their bags to leave home again and compete for the first time in the Midwest, where they would play for the Russell Stover Stars.

Upon their arrival, Jacob and Mikey headed straight to the hockey rink. Due to the last-minute arrangements, they were told to practice with the team where they would meet the coach, sign all the required documents, and learn of the living arrangements.

Almost from the moment they entered the rink and took to the ice, the two felt a disconnect with the coaches and skaters around them. Following the closeness and camaraderie they experienced the prior year with the River City Jaguars, something was amiss in this new environment. The practice was void of emotion, yelling, laughter, chatter, and the two couldn't help but feel like outsiders among their fellow skaters.

Nothing was said between them as they trudged into the locker room following practice, but their shared expression spoke volumes. They quickly agreed upon a mutual understanding of what they would say before being called into the coach's office.

Jacob was somewhat apprehensive as they entered the crude space, the coach relaxed and seated behind his desk sorting papers for them to sign. The two sat down across from him and following some introductory words from the coach, allowed a moment of silence before Jacob broke the news.

"I'm sorry Sir, but we've decided to go back to California."

Not knowing what else to do or say, he simply let the words hang in the air, observing the coach's own reaction as the words sunk in. Coach was visibly upset. Face turning red, he demanded an explanation.

Jacob did most of the talking, and the two remained steadfast in their decision. They just didn't feel comfortable away from home in the current environment.

When it became clear that they were not going to change their minds, the coach abruptly called in one of his assistant coaches and asked him to take the boys back to an airport hotel where they would arrange for flights back to California.

Back home, time was running out to find a suitable team to compete with for the upcoming season. Russell had already made his decision to also move east, playing for the Peoria Mustangs, a Tier III hockey team playing in the Central States Hockey League. Jacob was not willing to make that move, with Tier III lower than the AAA level they were offered in Kansas City.

Jonathan contacted Jacob to have him consider coming back to Beaverton for one more season with the Jaguars if unable to find another team. Jacob gave it some thought, but was soon haunted by a feeling of what might have been had he taken Jonathan up on the offer when disaster struck.

Reed called from his hospital bed with the horrible news. Jonathan was in a terrible car accident. Reed was the only passenger who survived, Jonathan and a local girl were killed in the crash. Jacob was stunned. He could only ask who the girl was, somewhat comforted upon learning that it was not Ashley, the attractive blonde who shared his first kiss. Jonathan, their trusted friend who was always there to drive them whenever and wherever the boys needed to go, who always offered encouragement with his words and actions, was gone from their lives forever. Jacob had no doubt that had he returned to Beaverton, he would have been with them in that car crash.

Just when it seemed that things could not get any worse, Jacob was struck with another setback. Acne. It started modestly enough, and his mother recommended a cream which he hoped would clear his face up in time for the upcoming school year. But rather than improve, the condition grew worse. As the school year approached, Jacob's face turned a crimson red. Angry pimples multiplied to create a mass of swelling that masked his well-defined facial features.

Jacob was horrified. How can I return to my old high school for senior year looking like this? He wanted to hide and not be seen by anyone, dreading the prospect of feeling humiliated on the first day of school. They arranged to visit a dermatologist, where they explored solutions and learned that he was having an adverse reaction to the cream he was using. Switching to alternative medications, nothing was providing quick results, and it was not until his Aunt Michelle intervened that he felt some relief. She recommended a product from her Arbonne collection, and Jacob finally started to see some improvement with the start of the school year. The redness slowly vanished along with reduced swelling, and life gradually eased back into some sense of normalcy.

Even during the worst bouts with acne, the ice rink remained the one happy place where Jacob felt a sense of joy and freedom from all his worries. Skating freely on the ice with the sole purpose of either defending or scoring goals provided the purest sense of purpose. Freedom felt with the speed and smoothness of gliding on ice replaced the awkward stares, and his confidence continued to soar with the accolades heard from all around him. Another opportunity arose.

"We'd like for you to try out for the Junior Kings! We provide top-level hockey that will allow you to stay home right here in California."

Jacob and Mikey were provided with an opportunity to play for the Los Angeles Jr. Kings, a AAA team performing under the shadow of the NHL's own Los Angeles Kings, with games played at the Toyota Sports Performance Center in El Segundo, California. Further enhancing the opportunity, Jacob would play under the coaching of former King and long-time NHL player Nelson Emerson, whose twelve-year career included stints with eight different NHL teams.

The opportunity did not come without sacrifice. The 100-mile drive from San Jacinto to El Segundo, a coastal suburb just south of the busy LAX International Airport outside of Los Angeles, was daunting even without the notorious LA traffic jams. Further, transportation costs for select tournaments would have to be undertaken by the players. But the two families readily agreed to share in transportation and other responsibilities for their two eager teens. They would rotate in driving the boys to hockey practice after school, and to the airport for weekend road trips when not playing at the Toyota Center. Jacob and Mikey's dreams remained alive when it was learned that they had both made the team.

For the boys, life took on a grueling routine centered around school and hockey. For four days each week after school, Jacob's father Jeffrey would drive him the 30 miles to Perris, where Mikey's dad took over and drove the boys to and from El Segundo for hockey practice. Jeffrey would then pick Jacob up on the return, often arriving home well after midnight.

The grind of travel did not come without its enjoyable and memorable stretches. With Mikey riding shotgun, Jacob was able to stretch in the back seat and indulge in their favorite chew, Copenhagen smokeless tobacco. The boy's addiction grew to the point that Mikey's father finally relented in buying them both spittoons, thereby minimizing the disgusting litter of sprayed tobacco missing open cups in the cramped car. Jacob also appreciated that the spittoon removed any chance of mistakenly gulping from a rancid-tasting, tobacco-filled water bottle. Unfortunately, the spittoons did nothing to hide the car's strong odor, their sweat-soaked hockey gear creating an unmistakable smell of hockey.

Creeping along the congested highways to and from practice, Jacob often got lost in the lyrics and rousing music blasting from the speakers. The sounds from Rise Against most popular among their listening.

*"...I give it all, now there's a reason why I sing...."* Their screaming voices in harmony with the vibrant music, the drive was shortened considerably.

As the season progressed, Mikey grew disenchanted with his limited playing time and arranged to join Russel in Peoria, affording increased ice time with the Peoria Mustangs. This meant that Jacob's father or mother was now required to make the 200-mile round trip in heavy traffic for four days every week and stick around for entire practice sessions. Just as they did throughout his hockey career, the family continued supporting Jacob. On the weekends when they were not playing home games at El Segundo, they drove him to away games across the entire state of California. Even his younger sister Sarah often joined Mom and Dad to watch and cheer him on when playing at home or on the road. She became his biggest fan.

As promised, the Junior Kings provided competitive hockey that Jacob readily embraced. Their hockey season offered plentiful games and road trips all across California against stiff competition. Games were played in both the SCAHA (Southern California Amateur Hockey Association) and CAHA (California Amateur Hockey Association) Leagues. Jacob stood out as a leading defenseman and took great pride in the team's stout defense. Once again, he proudly represented jersey number five and was named Assistant Captain on the team. Further, with the help from the personal coaching received from his brothers during the summer, his game expanded into a goal-scoring threat in addition to his defensive prowess.

A reputation that would follow him throughout his amateur, and later, professional career.

At the top of the standings in their respective leagues, the Junior Kings now set their sights on winning the 18U National Championships. Before advancing to the Finals, they first needed to win the Pacific District Championship held in Fairbanks, Alaska.

Arriving in frigid Fairbanks, the team was in high spirits. After checking into the hotel, Jacob and a group of his teammates met up in the lobby in search of something to do on the eve of their first game. Despite the early afternoon hour, they were in awe of the cold and darkness viewed outside when they came upon a realization. Nobody brought chewing tobacco! Someone recalled a gas station and store down the road that surely must sell it. So, the group decided to venture outside and make the purchase to satisfy their nicotine addictions.

For the first part of the walk, the bitter cold actually felt somewhat liberating to the energetic young athletes. However, with each bend in the road revealing yet more open space with no establishments in sight, the chill quickly set in.

"Damn! What do you suppose the temperature is?"

"I thought I heard someone say minus forty."

They were relieved when a van stopped to pick them up, the driver probably wondering why anyone would be out walking on such a cold day. Arriving at the General Store, the players eagerly loaded up on their coveted tobacco and warmed up enough to begin the three-mile trek back to the hotel. There was no van to drive them back or pick them up, but they all took comfort in the flavored chew to relieve their minds and bodies against the biting cold.

Back on the ice, perhaps invigorated by the walk, the team found success! The Los Angeles Junior Kings captured the Pacific District Championship. As champions of their district, they now had a chance to compete against the nation's top teams at a tournament the following week in Rochester, New York for the National 18U title.

Arriving in Rochester, Jacob took note of the highly-regarded teams against which they would be competing. Perhaps most notable among the eight finalists was the Shattuck St. Mary Sabres. The elite boarding school spread across 35 pristine acres in Faribault, Minnesota, was well known within the national hockey community as a hockey factory. Considered a favorite coming into the tournament, the Sabres had produced numerous outstanding NHL players along with many other celebrities, including legendary actor Marlon Brando. Among their many notable hockey graduates was the highly touted Sidney Crosby, who had just been selected first overall by the Pittsburgh Penguins in the most recent NHL draft. As luck would have it, the Junior Kings were to face off against St. Mary in the opening round of the tournament.

Jacob could feel the beating of his heart reverberating above the ice as both teams lined up for the opening face-off. Sporting their iconic maroon, white, and black jerseys and cheered on by an impressive contingent of fans, their opponent moved and skated with the confidence of seasoned champions. Jacob and his teammates knew they were in for their most severe test of the season.

Facing an early onslaught of pressure and shots on goal by the Sabre center and wings, Jacob could sense their frustration mounting as the Kings defense continually foiled the relentless pounding. He could see exasperation on the faces of both players and coaches with each shift change. Coupled with this frustration was renewed confidence in the Junior Kings, and the entire team erupted into celebration when they scored the game's first goal.

As the periods and minutes crept along, the Kings' defense continued to stymie the Sabres offense, and every Kings player skated even harder with victory in their grasp. When the horn finally sounded to end the game, the exhausted players rushed the center ice in celebration as if they had just won the championship. The Junior Kings had advanced to the semifinals with a most impressive upset.

The following day, the physically and emotionally drained team put up a gallant effort but fell just short to the eventual champion Junior Bruins.

Before leaving Rochester, they quickly got over that disappointment on the final day to win the consolation game and take third place in the tournament. Although not crowned as champions, the players and coaches viewed the season as one of great accomplishments and success, with the upset victory over St. Mary providing a crowning achievement for the season.

The ending of the hockey season enabled Jacob to finally relax and settle back in to wrap up his senior year. Despite the heavy hockey schedule which limited his social and school activities, Jacob managed to maintain a 3.5 GPA throughout the school year. Unable to participate in any extra-curricular activities, he often felt like an outsider with only one close friend outside of his hockey circle. He and long-time friend Ray Ramirez, who moved on from street hockey to excel in baseball, enjoyed time together while getting out of the sixth period study session. The young drama teacher, noting Ray's woodworking skills, got the two to help out in creating background scenes for the school plays. Under Ray's guidance, Jacob enjoyed learning new skills while creating colorful scenes out of wood, and the friendly teacher could not be more pleased with their work.

Unfortunately, the teacher's time at the school would be short-lived. Jacob was surprised to learn years later from Ray that the drama teacher had been sent to prison for having sex with a student, and while in prison he took his own life. The two had not seen any evidence of his illicit behavior, recalling more the enjoyment they experienced in creating scenes for the plays.

Another thing unbeknownst to Jacob at the time was the attention and recognition that he was attracting from class members, particularly the ladies. It seemed that his time away and success on the ice was creating an aura of mystique, and he became known around the entire school as simply, "the hockey guy".

Awards and recognitions were voted on by the senior class to commemorate fellow students for their year-long accomplishments. And Jacob, who at times felt invisible due to time away with his hockey brothers, was voted as the senior class member "most likely to become famous".  Even his younger sister Sarah, a cheerleader at the same school, complained that she couldn't have any meaningful conversations with friends, stating: "All the cheerleaders and all my friends have a crush on you."

Jacob had no idea.  He almost didn't go to his senior prom, only asking the quiet and long-time friend Kaylie to go at the last minute because he didn't really know any other girls.  He wouldn't have had it any other way, as he and Kaylie had a wonderful evening doubling with Ray and his date, but throughout the dance Jacob just assumed that nobody at the school even knew who he was.

On the day that Jacob sat in the crowded auditorium to receive his diploma, he reflected that he would have never guessed the year would turn out the way it did.  A year that began with so much trauma and turmoil.  He recalled the rash decision and sudden disappointment in leaving Kansas City with Mikey, the tragic loss of his close friend Jonathan, the humiliating bout with acne, and the grueling five-hour round trips to practice for the Junior Kings.  His parents told him at the start of the year, "Either get a job or pursue your hockey career.  But if you choose hockey, we will support you only as long as you do well in school."  The choice was simple and now validated.

Jacob walked up the stage to accept his diploma.  He stood tall and proud, smiling at those around him; his dream of playing at hockey's highest level remained alive.

# Chapter Four
# A Haze Over Texas

2006 - 2007 season

## Texas Tornado – Frisco, Texas

The city of Frisco, Texas was going through big changes with the new millennium. Founded as a railway town in 1902 with completion of the St. Louis to San Francisco railroad, the area became a major center for grain and cotton production, serving as a shipping hub for farmers. However, with the rapid technology and population growth of the metropolitan Dallas-Fort Worth area in the 1990s, spillover into the suburbs made Frisco the fastest-growing city in the United States during that period.

Along with this growth came a passion for sports from the growing base. One decade before the Dallas Cowboys officially moved their football headquarters to the city, Frisco's Texas Tornado enjoyed unprecedented success on the ice. They closed the 2005-2006 season with their third consecutive Robertson Cup, defeating the St. Louis Bandits 4-3 in overtime. Thus, making the Tornado the first team in fifteen years to win three consecutive championships in the North American Hockey League (NAHL).

The team played their home games in front of rabid fans in their six-thousand-seat Dr. Pepper Arena, enjoying the facility's numerous amenities and spacious locker room, and basking in celebrity-like status from their adoring fan base. This was the situation that Jacob arrived to for the upcoming season. A step above AAA hockey and one step closer to his NHL dream.

Jacob was joined by fellow Californian and Junior Kings teammate, Troy Puente. The two were recruited heavily during their successful season at AAA and arrived separately at their new destination. As with his first season in Beaverton, Jacob was assigned to a host family. And like those of the first season, the living arrangements would not last. His host family, no doubt eager to experience the joys of hosting an aspiring young member on the popular team for the first time, were not quite ready for the expected freedom that the party culture Tornado players were accustomed to. Although Jacob was polite and respectful to the family members for the minimal time he was around, they asked to be excused from the responsibility. He was then assigned to join fellow rookie Troy in a home more accustomed to the players' active lifestyles. To further enhance the new living arrangement, Troy provided transportation with his silver Ford Ranger pickup truck.

As one of eight rookies on the team, Jacob enjoyed the benefit of having graduated from high school with his late September birthday making him up to a full year younger than his classmates. Relieved of the need to attend school, he was allowed more freedom than he had ever experienced. During the week, he and Troy could sleep in, stop for coffee with some teammates, and head to the gym for a light workout before practice. The weekends took on a different routine.

At home or on the road, time spent away from the ice was a party. The Tornado capitalized on their legendary status of both playing and partying hard and took great pride in this reputation. Jacob and the other rookies also soon learned the expected norms and protocols of the team hierarchy. And it carried another chilling reputation.

Every Monday after practice the team gathered in the expansive locker room to conduct a Kangaroo Court. Seats were arranged to have the team facing two chosen veteran players: the Judge and his Sergeant of Arms.

Completing the look, the Judge wore a robe while seated on his elevated chair and the Sergeant of Arms stood next to him holding a modified goalie stick. The goalie stick served a menacing purpose. Holes were drilled into the wide base used to help the goalie in stopping shots on goal, and the top end of the stick was crudely sharpened to a rounded point, replacing the handle.

Not sure what to expect for the first court hearing of the season, the rookies were told to sit in the front row amidst much laughter and chiding from the veteran players. Aware of the hazing rituals well known among many teams in Junior hockey culture, the players good-naturedly went along and hoped for the best.

The first offenses were innocent enough and meant to ensure that rookies were aware of team protocols. Minimal fines for being late to practice, failing to bring enough donuts on your stated day, among other harmless offenses. Individual players were called up and asked to pay toward a fund that would go on to provide entertainment for an end-of-year party.

The Judge brought to everyone's attention a more serious crime that must be addressed.

"Gentlemen, we have a serious offense that carries the most severe punishment. Cock blocking!"

Amidst laughter behind them, one of the unsuspecting rookies was called before the Judge to make his case against this most serious offense. It seems that he committed the unthinkable crime of attracting the attention of a young lady at a recent party, and away from a veteran player who was expecting to hook up with her. Asked to explain his actions, the accused made light of the situation in an attempt to diffuse his discomfort, but it was obvious how the Judge would rule.

The ruling was made and the teammate who lost the lady was asked to come up and choose the appropriate punishment, which he would dish out. The Sergeant of Arms handed him the goalie stick among much dramatics and the Judge asked: "Which punishment will it be?" The veteran players all laughed as the accuser pondered the decision and motioned for his victim to take his position.

The rookie was led to a chair across the room and told to drop his shorts and briefs, bend over holding the chair, and accept his punishment. Positioning the stick, the accuser stood back ten paces before getting a running start and laid into the accused with a loud "WHACK!"

The veteran players all howled in laughter while the rookies went along smiling in discomfort. Jacob felt a sudden trigger that left him feeling nauseous. One of the rookies quietly asked what the other option was. The Judge overheard and replied, "Best that you never take that punishment. Just don't cock block."

The accuser and Judge acknowledged their new teammate with hardy backslaps for taking the punishment so well and having learned his lesson while the entire team joined in lively conversation. The coaches sat huddled behind the partially closed door of their adjoining office. They voiced encouragement that the boys were growing closer and coming together for the upcoming season, unaware or without care of the scars and triggers placed on Jacob and others.

The hazing was not confined to Kangaroo Courts. The next week, the Tornado were invited to a tournament in Minnesota to kick off the season. The players packed for the long sixteen-hour bus ride. About halfway through the trip, with most players sleeping or relaxing to bide the time, an announcement was abruptly made for all players to meet at the back of the bus. The rookies, going along with the veteran players' laughter, suspected that they were in for something unwelcome.

"Gentlemen, welcome to your cross-country bus trip initiation. We have just a few simple tests that will build teamwork and bonding. To get started, strip off your clothes, and everyone is required to get inside the bathroom. We will give you instructions once you're all inside."

Incredulously, Jacob and his seven fellow rookies all looked at one another in wonder of how they could all squeeze inside the tiny bus bathroom, and in such a humiliating fashion.

"Come on Gentlemen, time's a-wasting."

Accepting their fate, the players grudgingly removed their clothes and one by one entered the cramped bathroom, trying to joke and make light of the situation. Enabling everyone to fit required creativity and dexterity, standing on the toilet seat, bending over the sink, all moving in strategic positions so as not to face one another, minimizing their discomfort as much as possible, with the veterans finding amusement in the awkward verbal banter heard from inside the open door. When all eight rookies finally squeezed inside, the Judge closed the door and told them to await further instructions.

Moments later, the door flung open and two packs of playing cards were thrown inside the room, the cards scattering everywhere. The rookies were told to pick up the cards and rearrange them in proper order, sorted by suit and from Ace to King. Fifty-two cards from two separate decks needed to be returned to their proper order.

The team roared in laughter outside the door as the rookie players frantically worked to pick up and sort out the cards. They struggled to minimize the bumping and touching that was impossible to avoid, while working to coordinate their efforts and put an end to the humiliation. Jacob was first to try calming everyone down, asking for an inventory of the cards being held and a system for two people to collect and sort appropriately. Jacob and Troy took the lead in holding and sorting from the two decks. Before long, the group was so focused on the task that they barely thought of their predicament.

When they finally completed the task, seeming much sooner than the players outside were anticipating, they handed out the cards and awaited the next task.

"Not bad. Not bad. Okay, I'm sure you all want to get out of there. Here's what we'll do. We're going to throw in all your clothes, and whoever changes first can come out. But you have to wear your own clothes. No wearing others' clothing or you'll be sent back in."

Again, the door was opened, and their clothes were thrown in, strewn all across the room or landing on top of the standing players taking up most of the space available to them.

Chaos ensued, causing panic as bodies bent and contorted in a frantic attempt to find and put on their own clothing. Jacob, the largest among his fellow rookies, could barely breathe. Once again, he experienced a nauseous feeling but tried to bring order to the room. He took a deep breath.

"Guys! The only way we can do this is to work together. One by one, hold up an item, give it to the proper person and allow them to put it on."

Against backlash from players who just wanted to get dressed and the hell out of there, the group eventually slowed down and allowed the methodical procedure to dress and depart the room, thereby making more room for others to follow.

It was dark when the players were settled back in their seats, nodding off with exhaustion and thoughts of the craziness that had just occurred. While the mood was mostly light-hearted with even some sense of accomplishment for what they were able to do, there was also lots of thinking that Jacob tried to understand.

His first thought: Where were the coaches? Sure, they were taking up the front seats but they had to be aware of something very uncomfortable going on in back of the bus. Team bonding is one thing, but this was not only humiliating but also potentially dangerous. It took all his focus to bring everyone together and complete the required tasks without any physical or mental breakdown. And of course, the exposure of private parts that were a constant distraction or hindrance to completing their tasks was an image that Jacob wished to burn from his memory. And for reasons that he couldn't understand, a trigger for deep-seated discomfort that always brought on this nauseous feeling.

On the other hand, it did somehow seem to bring the team closer. Jacob could sense the rookies slowly being accepted more and more into the tight-knit fraternity among the veteran players. It was clear that the players inflicting the humiliating tasks were at one time victims themselves and simply saw this as a rite of passage for the rookies to endure before being fully accepted. Still, Jacob could not help but note that some of the veterans took this role of inflicting humiliation much more enthusiastically than others. He empathized that perhaps they suffered the most and embraced their opportunity for payback.

Jacob gazed out the window at the occasional lights highlighting open farm country. He looked forward to the chance to get back and compete with his brother on ice. And he vowed that if and when his time came, he would be the person to remove the need for humiliation as a part of future hazing on rookie players.

** ** **

The Tornado season got off to a hot start, picking right up from their recent success and positioning themselves for an unprecedented fourth straight championship. Coupled with excellent play on the ice was their continued reputation for partying. Life took on a predictable pattern of practice on Monday through Thursday and games on Friday and Saturday. When on the road the team often left on Thursday evening for the longer bus trips. Team members met virtually every night at a host house after practice, and several notorious party houses became favorites for the postgame rituals. Host families at these homes became part of the culture, purchasing alcohol for the underage players and participating in the festivities.

Jacob quickly adapted to the party culture. He became more and more popular among his teammates with his stellar play on the ice and as the guy to make everyone laugh at parties. His appetite whet from the Jamaica experience, he began smoking every day of the week in addition to drinking. Thursday was his one and only day of sobriety, in preparation for the weekend games.

The Kangaroo Courts grew tamer with increased acceptance of the rookie teammates. During Court, more time was now spent sharing adventurous stories of sexual encounters than meting out punishments, and the rookies looked forward to the highly anticipated rookie party which would unofficially complete their initiation period. A house was selected to host the party, and the team along with their building fan base of willing young ladies arrived for a big night following another win on the home ice.

Jacob and all fellow rookies were required to wear thongs, but this was hardly the worst punishment for good-natured young athletes looking to attract the many admiring female fans in attendance. The next Kangaroo

Court was sure to include some juicy tales. Everyone was mingling and in good spirits when the Judge raised a glass in toast to the team's rookie class.

"Here's to our new Tornadoes, who have helped us get off to another exciting season. And now for your final test of loyalty, we invite you to the goldfish challenge. And remember, if we cannot hear the crunch of the goldfish, you have to eat another."

Amidst much laughter and anticipation for the final test, the Sergeant of Arms brought out a large box filled with goldfish swimming in tiny plastic bags.

One by one, the rookies were handed a plastic bag holding a goldfish in water. They were required to remove the rubber band and grab a slippery goldfish swimming to escape their fate. Once that challenge was met, they needed to drop the fish in their mouth and bite down before swallowing. Everyone silenced to hear the crunch, before erupting in cheers for the player. When Jacob's turn came, he felt such need to delight the crowd that he would not settle for just one, but five. With the mix of alcohol and pot numbing his senses, Jacob easily met the challenge to loud approval.

Not to be outdone and in an attempt to capture legendary status, Troy stepped up and asked how many goldfish remained. Twenty-five! "You all ready to watch a new Tornado record? I'll eat all twenty-five!"

Jacob laughed along with everyone at the audacity of his friend as Troy began the process of crunching and eating twenty-five goldfish.

The initiation complete, the music cranked up as Jacob glanced around the room to observe the many young ladies who had arrived. Most clearly dressed to attract attention, they mingled easily with the players, perhaps in hopes of meeting their future husband who would go on to lucrative NHL career. Jacob grabbed a drink and sought out among the admirers not a potential wife, but a story to be shared at the next Kangaroo Court.

With the season winding down, Jacob was thrilled to learn that his family would arrive to watch a home game against one of their top competitors in the South Conference, the Santa Fe Roadrunners. He met his mom, brothers Josh and Andy, and sister Sarah at Dallas Fort Worth International Airport, excited to have them meet his teammates and witness Tornado hockey in front of their rabid fans at the Dr. Pepper Arena.

Jacob's excitement and anticipation for the game was even higher than normal, and he sought out his family during pregame warm-ups. Jacob's earned reputation as a solid defender with a growing ability to score goals had made him a fan favorite and he was excited for his family to be a part of the experience. He could see that his brothers were geared up to cheer him on, and he wanted to make sure that he would give them all something to be proud of.

As anticipated, with the two teams vying for first place in the competitive South, the game was tense and extremely physical from the opening face-off. Just when it appeared that one of the team's leading players was about to break away with a clean shot on goal, a Roadrunner defender reached out with his stick to trip him and stop the shot. The Tornado player crashed violently into the boards as players from both sides rushed to the scene. The referees desperately scrambled to ward off the inevitable. They were too late. Jacob's teammate took off his gloves to confront the defender who tripped him, and before the two could go at it, Jacob noticed another Roadrunner aggressively going after the Tornado star from behind, stick and gloves flying off. Instinctively, Jacob rushed to stop him and the two squared off as other fights broke out all around them. Despite multiple fights, the crowd placed all their attention on Jacob and his combatant. Unbeknown to Jacob, he was squared off in hand-to-hand combat with a six-foot-six behemoth who had a reputation for dirty play and penalties for fighting.

In the stands, Sarah wasn't sure what to do. Her mother on one side rushed out to leave the stands, unable to watch what was transpiring. On the other side, Josh and Andy were banging the boards and cheering wildly for their little brother along with six thousand screaming fans who were all on their feet.

Back on the ice, Jacob aggressively held on to his opponent with all his strength, stopping his punches while inflicting jabs of his own. The refs moved cautiously around them not wishing to get too close to this melee, more focused on stopping the other fights. Up until then, Jacob had never been in a fight and for reasons that he couldn't explain had found himself in great discomfort whenever the infrequent fight occurred. He prided himself as more a physical technician than an undisciplined fighter. But now, fed by a rush of adrenaline, the two were locked in an intense standoff as others moved on from their broken-up fights and all the players crowded around them.

The referees simply skated around them and allowed the combatants to drain off energy before finally stepping in to break them up. The crowd cheered wildly as the refs scratched their heads trying to sort out the upcoming penalty minutes. Jacob was surrounded by teammates appreciative of his willingness to singlehandedly take on the most feared player in the NAHL. Nobody showed more appreciation than the teammate who was probably wondering what would have happened had he been blindsided by the massive and fast-charging Roadrunner.

When things finally settled and Jacob entered the penalty box with several others to a roar of applause from the appreciative crowd, he looked up to see his brothers leading the cheers. Sarah was seated next to them with a look of concern hidden behind an uneasy smile. His mother was nowhere to be seen.

The Texas Tornado closed the season in the highly competitive South Conference with a 38-18 record and now prepared for what many believe to be the most intense battle in sports: playoff hockey. Vying for a fourth consecutive Roberson Cup, Tornado players knew they were the villain with a mark on their backs, especially in the visiting arenas. They were ready to take on the challenge.

They got through the first highly competitive series and were now ready to take on their biggest challenge of the season in the upcoming semifinals. A rematch against the team they beat last season for the Championship, their archrival St. Louis Bandits.

The Bandits were sweeping all the postseason awards, let by League MVP Patrick "Big Rig" Maroon, who would go on to win three Stanley Cups in a distinguished NHL career. They also had the league's top defenseman Jeff Dimnen, and an outstanding goalie in Rookie of the Year Pat Nagle. Adding further intrigue to the matchup, Jacob's old buddy Russell was skating for the Bandits. But perhaps what they had going for them more than anything was revenge. The Bandits were still stinging from their overtime loss to the Tornado to close out the 2005-2006 season. The fans were ready, the teams were ready, and Jacob was ready for a series that was sure to attract college and professional scouts from across the country.

Having home ice advantage, the Bandits got off to a 3–2 lead in the best of seven series, meaning the Tornado had to win Game Six on their home ice to force a Game Seven. Filling the arena during warmups, the Tornado fans were even more boisterous than normal. But Jacob and his teammates noticed another change on the ice. Where was Patrick Maroon? It was hard to miss the six-foot three, 230 pound forward but he was nowhere to be seen. Perhaps the hard hits he's been taking in the series were taking a toll. Maybe they were saving him for Game Seven.

Jacob chose not to get his hopes up. With or without Maroon, the Bandits were a formidable team. Following the playing of the anthems, Jacob took his spot on the ice and saw the massive Maroon glide to his position. The Bandits were going for every possible angle and the game was on.

For Jacob and his teammates, spurred by their fans, the game was most definitely on. Jacob, skating with the joy and ease of rollerblading on a desolate San Jacinto street, was stopping shots and finding openings to score two goals, leaving the crowd in a frenzy. With the game tied and clock winding down, Jacob once again found himself on open ice with the puck as the St. Louis defenders scrambled to defend their goal. Skating at full speed, he deftly flipped the puck to a charging teammate on his left, where Nielsson Arcibal took the assist to score the winning goal. They were going to St. Louis for a deciding Game Seven.

The team was in high spirits for the ten-hour bus trip to St. Louis. The hazing from their first bus trip now far removed from their collective mindset, the hockey brothers joined in camaraderie and talk of how to stop

Maroon and make the plays necessary to get to the Finals. Only one player did not join them. Looking for every edge, the team decided to fly their Italian goalie Thomas Tragust to St. Louis, resting him as much as possible for the big game.

Game Seven was a classic. Hard-hitting and intense, both teams skated with everything they had to get through this most physical series and to the Championship. The Tornado defenders did everything they could to stop Maroon, but even with bodies constantly around him he still managed to score two goals. Despite that, the Tornado applied their own pressure, and both teams skated off the ice in exhaustion for a much-needed break as the horn sounded to end the third period in a tie. They were going into overtime.

The overtime session took on the same mentality. Fighting, scratching, clawing, doing everything possible knowing that the next goal was not only game deciding but series deciding. Finally, spurred on by the crowd which had to be almost as exhausted as the players, Maroon slipped past a defender and scored the winning goal. His third goal, a hat trick for the League MVP, won the series.

The entire team was devastated on the long bus ride back to Frisco. But for aspiring hockey players the agony of defeat is quickly replaced by the excitement for what lies ahead. For Jacob, the options were growing.

The Texas coaches clearly wanted him back.

"You can be a team leader and get us back to the Robertson Cup."

Colleges were reaching out. There were requirements to get in of which his family was not yet aware, but the calls were coming. Then came a call from the NHL Los Angeles Kings. Jacob, along with three other teammates from his season with the Junior Kings, was invited to the Kings development camp. A chance to compete with top prospects, including players selected by the Kings in the most recent NHL draft. And finally, a spot on the Lincoln Stars. The United States Hockey League (USHL) had just completed their draft, and Jacob was selected by the Stars in the seventh round. USHL was the highest level of Junior Hockey (Tier 1), on par with D1 college level and the final step before professional hockey.

Others were telling Jacob that he should have been selected higher, but it was still an honor. All he needed were opportunities to prove himself.

Jacob readied himself for the summer. There were decisions to be made and it was going to be a busy period in preparation for the upcoming season.

## Chapter Five

# The Ice Box

2007 - 2009 seasons

## Lincoln Stars – Lincoln, Nebraska

From the moment that Jacob arrived at Lincoln Airport to collect his overflowing luggage of clothing and hockey gear, he could sense a vibrant energy in the air. Government workers and business travelers blended in with incoming college students and welcome signs for the State Capital and home of the University of Nebraska Cornhuskers. It came as a pleasant surprise to Jacob after observing nothing but open farmland on their approach to the city.

The spirited atmosphere confirmed at least one of the main selling points that Coach Jim McGroarty had impressed upon him with a video used to promote Lincoln as his next hockey destination.

"You see this unique experience we provide for our players? You will be a part of this. Introduced as a starter for the Stars on opening night."

Jacob had heard about the Star's theatrical introductions at their sold-out Ice Box Arena, but watching videos of the actual introductions, complete with fire and inspirational music to voracious cheers brought chills to his entire body. Still, it was not until the personal advice from LA Kings head coach Marc Crawford following the development camp that his decision was sealed.

Jacob performed well at the camp. Holding his own against more seasoned players and even the NHL Kings incoming rookie class. Coach Crawford took the time to talk with Jacob, having observed his play with the Junior Kings and showing interest in his development. Upon learning that Jacob was considering going back to Texas to take on a leadership role for the Tornado, he convinced him otherwise.

"Playing in the USHL will provide a better opportunity to get drafted into the NHL. It's the top-tier Junior Hockey and on par with the top colleges which get the most attention from NHL scouts."

So, Jacob eagerly embraced the hockey experience in the vibrant college town, both on and off the ice. On the ice, just turned nineteen-year-old Jacob quickly adapted to the higher level of play. Filling out to a well-defined 205 pounds on his six-foot three frame, he provided a unique combination of physical strength and technical skills to frustrate opposing attackers and also create scoring opportunities.

Throughout the preseason, Jacob and fellow Tornado teammate Lyon Messier, son of the legendary Mark Messier, blended in well with the veteran team. The Stars carried a well-deserved reputation as a tough physical team, led by the intimidating Brandon Bollig, the team's designated enforcer who would go on to win a Stanley Cup with the NHL Chicago Blackhawks. Surrounded by such physical and skilled players, Jacob was able to play to his strengths, focusing on his technical skills which kept him away from the occasional fight and also limited time in the penalty box.

Just as promised, Jacob was introduced as a starter on opening night. And there was no other show in the entire USHL that could match the spectacle put on by the Lincoln Stars. The entire experience was electrifying, and it began right from the moment one entered The Ice Box Arena.

From the exterior, the Arena resembled an old barn, which was no accident. The building was originally designed to hold livestock and general fair events in an open area that once served as the Nebraska State Fairgrounds. In 1995, the building was redesigned for hockey, where it became one of the most unique venues in the sport, and one in which every opposing team dreaded to play. Every game was standing room only crowds in the 4,300-seat arena, and the noise captured and reverberating inside the barn-like wooden structure was deafening.

For opening night, the spectacle was even more pronounced. Fans eagerly embraced the start of a new season, and even their opponent stood in awe to view the light show and introductions. Following the playing of the national anthems, Jacob took his spot on the red line with four others, lined up on both sides of the goalie perched in his crease. The Arena went dark as strobe lights delighted the crowd with the blaring music of AC/DC's "Thunderstruck".

The song's introduction got the crowd on their feet, and the Arena erupted when the word "thunder" came across the massive speakers. Over and over, with the anticipated refrain of thunder, lights merged with an explosion of THUNDER that shook the entire building. Looking around in the dark, Jacob could only see his teammates standing next to him when the thunder struck, and he could see that they were equally jacked, ready to explode onto center ice.

The song wound down and the music transitioned to the rhythmic drum beat of Marilyn Manson's "The Beautiful People." The Arena now dark, a spotlight shone on Jacob as the PA announcer's deep voice brought a hush to the crowd as they awaited to erupt with the much-anticipated intros.

"And now, ladies and gentlemen, introducing YOUR Lincoln Staaaaaaaars!"

Roar from the crowd.

"Starting at Defenseman and making his debut with the Stars, from San Jacinto, California, welcome.... JAAAAAAAKE Nuuuuuuuuuu-ton!

His heart racing and stick swinging side to side, Jacob sprinted to center ice accompanied by the spotlight to a roaring ovation. He could barely feel the ice below him, as if experiencing an out-of-body moment with his skates soaring above the ice.

Spurred on by the crowd and their high level of play, the Stars opened the season with an impressive victory. Celebrating in the locker room after the game, the players knew it was going to be a party night. And once again Jacob became the life of the party and center of attention.

Just like in Frisco, host families enabled the party lifestyle. Most players continued living with families and there was no shortage of homes willing to host get-togethers or parties for the team. During the week, coaches often made phone calls to ensure that the players weren't breaking curfew. But the weekends when games were played offered much more freedom. Especially after a sweep of victories over the Friday and Saturday games.

"Outstanding team victories! You've got the green light to enjoy your Saturday night. Just don't lose this privilege by getting into trouble and have me reading about you on Monday in the Lincoln Journal Star."

With that opening, the show was on, and nobody took advantage of the party lifestyle more than Jacob. In his ongoing desire to please others, Jacob became the life of the party. First to get drunk, dancing on a table with an open bottle in hand. Whatever drew laughter and attention, Jacob was there to provide. Further, the team's popularity coupled with their proximity to the college campus provided an embarrassment of riches for players to enjoy. When playing at home, the weekend hockey parties became a popular attraction for sororities and attractive coeds. Fueled by alcohol and drugs, the young participants basked in a casual lifestyle that encouraged hookups with no commitments. Whether or not that was always the lady's expectation was unclear, but that was the overt mindset of the players.

Just like in Frisco, the team held weekly Kangaroo Court that allowed team legends to emerge through the storytelling portion of the hearings. Players laughed at the outlandish escapades shared by their teammates, and Jacob's place in Stars' lore grew rapidly. There was one notable difference in the Courts between the two teams. Humiliating punishments were nonexistent. The Stars' Court hearings focused more on the mundane offenses of a rookie's failure to properly complete expected tasks. Like with most teams, rookies were expected to load and unload luggage on bus trips, tidy up the locker room, provide donuts or snacks before team meetings, among other menial tasks. Other than the occasional offense which only required a nominal payment that went towards a party fund, the sessions were more geared toward team bonding and entertainment. Jacob wasn't sure if the difference was due to age, with most Stars players being in the older bracket of the Junior 16 – 20 age eligibility, or simply team culture. But whatever the reason, he was relieved and appreciative of the removal of hazing which was so prevalent during his prior season with the Tornado.

Given his growing reputation for breaking the rules, it was only a matter of time before Jacob was caught for breaking curfew. Entering the rink for a practice session during the week, he noticed that coach was not his normal jovial self and uneasily felt his glare directed at him. When the team assembled on the ice for practice, the coach had them all gather around him on center ice for an announcement.

"Gentlemen, it seems that despite all my warnings, one of you has let his teammates down by breaking curfew. As a result, practice today will be dedicated to a series of overspeed drills. Oh, and one more thing, there will be no breaks for water. Jake Newton, while your teammates suffer you are to watch from the stationary bike. You are allowed a bottle of water."

Groans heard all around him, Jacob stood stunned before heading to the stationary bike for what would be a more tortuous hour than what his teammates had to endure. Seated on the bike and allowed to pedal at his own pace, Jacob was forced to watch the grueling workout from his front row seat unfold right before his eyes.

Players were split into two groups and placed in opposite corners. At the first whistle, multiple players from each group skated full speed around cones to reach the opposite end of the rink. The movement was nonstop, and the coaches berated anyone for not skating at full speed. Little time for rest before the next whistle. From time to time, a very slight reprieve while coaches deftly skated to reposition the cones to create different challenges for the skaters. When not skating, each group of players increasingly bent over to catch their breath while gasping for air.

Jacob dared not sip from the water bottle visible to all on the cup holder of his stationary bike. He regularly increased his speed for prolonged stretches as if to ease the burden of his teammates, but it was no use. He kept looking at the clock for an end to the agonizing hour, and the final minutes seemed to last an eternity.

He was met with silence when joining his teammates in the locker room. Most players slouched on chairs with heads down or leaning against their locker. Only one player spoke out. Brandon Bollig, the team's designated enforcer was visibly and understandably upset, and he let his feelings be known.

"Damn you, Newton! This is all because of you! You and your fuckin' attitude. You owe the entire team an apology right now!

Expecting more anger to be displayed, the others simply remained in their positions. Most were looking down and nothing was said. Perhaps it was Jacob's growing popularity with his teammates or the realization that it could have been any one of a handful to get the call that would have exposed them to breaking curfew. Jacob was feeling terrible for what he caused but did not want to so easily give in to the demands of the veteran Bollig with an outright apology.

"Look, I feel terrible and I promise I will find a way to make this up to you guys."

Visibly not satisfied, the bearded and imposing Bollig merely walked away swearing under his breath loud enough for everyone to hear.

As the season wore on, Jacob held true to his word with stellar play and by the end of the season, he was playing his best hockey. He finished as the team's eighth leading scorer and second among Defenders. The team won their first playoff series before losing to the Omaha Lancers in five games in their best-of-five series. Despite the loss, Jacob did everything possible to lead the team to the Finals, racking up seven points (goals plus assists) in the highly competitive semifinal series.

Jacob left Lincoln for San Jacinto that spring feeling good about the season and excited for the next path on the journey. After some rest, his brothers were quick to get him back into training as he sorted out the letters and offerings for the upcoming season. Only then did Jacob take seriously the NCAA Clearinghouse rules and regulations.

Jacob was always interested in the experience of playing college hockey as a steppingstone to the NHL and was continually receiving letters of interest. Now more and more interest was shown with his final year of Junior eligibility approaching. Included among the offers was a scholarship with full ride to the University of Alaska-Fairbanks. All he had to do was sign. An official visit was not even required due to the lengthy distance to Alaska. However, before accepting a scholarship to compete academically, he needed to register with an NCAA identification number to prove his eligibility for participation in collegiate sports.

Time was running out. Having focused so much time on hockey the past few years, Jacob had fallen behind in the paperwork. While meeting the academic requirements for GPA and courses taken, he needed to take the standardized ACT test to meet the NCAA standards.

So, in addition to his hockey conditioning that summer, Jacob hastily studied and registered to take the ACT at his old high school. Summer was winding down, but Jacob was ecstatic to learn that he had met the minimum requirements on the ACT exam to accept the scholarship. There was only one problem. The coach who offered him the scholarship was fired during the summer. The new coach called to introduce himself and bluntly laid out the situation.

"Son, the offer has been made, and you are welcome to join us for the upcoming season on a full ride. But I must be honest, I did not recruit you and I'm bringing in some of my own recruits to join me. There is a place for you on the team, but like all others you will need to earn your playing time."

The comments were enough to diffuse the enticement of accepting the offer, especially knowing that other offers were made from colleges who clearly wanted him. With the upcoming season rapidly approaching, Jacob chose to return to Lincoln for his final season in Juniors. Now that he had all his college clearinghouse credentials established, he'd have his choice of the best colleges next season, maybe even realize his dream of playing for Boston College. Of course, that was Plan B. This final season also provided an opportunity to prove himself and get drafted directly into the NHL.

Returning to Lincoln, Jacob was now considered one of the leaders and veterans on the team. Although star players like Brian Bollig and leading scorer Jacob Gregoire had moved on, some exciting talent was arriving to complement Jacob on defense and the team's second leading scorer from the prior season, Ryan Kretzer. It didn't take long for the team to show it was going to be a special season.

The annual USHL Fall Classic to kick off the season was held in Sioux City, Iowa. Scouts representing every NHL team filled the stands to watch a showcase featuring all twelve teams in the League competing nonstop throughout the weekend. This was an opportunity not only for the Stars, but for Jacob to cement a place in the 2010 NHL draft.

When the team arrived by bus to enter the arena, a brisk wind blew in a noticeable stench from a nearby meatpacking facility. Thus, the city became known among the players as Sewer City, but their play on the ice was anything but garbage. Winning all three games in convincing style to open the season, Coach McGroarty could not hide his joy, and Jacob was convinced that he had made the correct decision to return to Lincoln.

The Stars soon received more welcome news. Garrett Vermeersch was acquired from the Cedar Rapid RoughRiders. It soon became clear that he, Kretzer, and another newcomer Kirt Hill were going to provide a formidable scoring trio for the upcoming season. That group, along with Jacob leading the defense and also scoring, was primed to bring many thrills to The Ice Box for the upcoming season.

For Jacob, the arrival of the free-spirited Garrett sporting his long wavy hair held another bonus. The two became inseparable, kindred spirits with a love of hockey, more hockey, partying, and seeking adventure. Garrett joined Jacob as the life of the parties, and when not partying on the weekends, they spent copious amounts of time hanging out and drinking, smoking, talking hockey, and getting into trouble.

One evening, soaking in the vibrant University of Nebraska campus area with Garrett and a high schooler named Garrett Peterson, the three decided to continue hanging out past what they viewed an unnecessary curfew. So, living in close proximity, they went to their respective homes and informed their families that they were staying out a bit longer, thinking the notice was cover enough. They were mistaken.

The next day prior to practice, Jacob sat in a chair in The Ice Box lounge when he saw Coach McGroarty enter from down the hall and felt his glare. Coach said nothing, but stared at him with a look of anger as he walked right past him. Jacob looked around to see if there was someone behind him, and figured that maybe Coach was simply having a bad day.

Entering the locker room, he did not see either of the Garretts. Someone informed him that they were in Coach's office and a panic immediately overcame him. A few minutes later, Coach came out and locked his stare directly on Jacob.

"Newton! Get in my office right now!"

Entering the office, Coach stormed back to his seat as Jacob noticed the two Garretts both seated with dejected looks on their drawn faces.

"Newts, I have no idea what to do with you. Do I release you? Trade you? Just what does it take to get through to you? Put on your helmets you three. Grab a chair and bottle of water and come with me."

The four stepped outside the office where the entire team waited in anticipation.

"Gentleman, leave your skates here. Practice today is outside, courtesy of your three teammates."

The entire team was led outside of the arena and to an open field on the old Fairgrounds property. The air was hot and thick from Nebraska's Indian summer heat as the players tried to figure what was going on.

Finally, upon reaching the center of an open field, Coach instructed the three to place their seats in a triangle and sit looking out. He then broke the team into groups and informed them they would be running wind sprints, starting and stopping at the sound of his whistle.

"Now, you three, keep those helmets on and you are to take a sip of water at the completion of each sprint that your teammates run. To the rest of you, there will be no water until we're done with the workout."

Once again, just like the prior year on the stationary bike, Jacob was subjected to the torturous dilemma of watching his teammates suffer because of his actions.  Adding insult to injury, he had now also subjected two of his friends to the same ordeal.

The heat bore down with not a speck of shade in sight.  Hearing the huffing and puffing, Jacob could  only imagine the discomfort that his teammates were feeling as sweat poured down his face inside the plastic helmet.  With every blow of the whistle, the three were forced to take a sip of water, knowing that their teammates were in even more need of hydration, which they were denied.

Just when it seemed that the highly conditioned athletes had reached their breaking point, Coach blew the whistle multiple times to signal the workout was over.

"All right, that's it.  Go inside and take your showers."

He then approached the three and directed in his brusque voice, "You three stay right where you are until someone comes to get you."

It was not until the field was clear that they finally spoke.  Locked in their positions and staring blankly in opposite directions, the two Garretts were convinced that they were all going to get cut from the team.  Jacob expressed more confidence, having faced a similar experience from the prior season and understanding their collective impact towards the team's success.  Still, they contemplated the unknown for close to an hour before someone finally came out to tell them they could go inside and shower.

When they got inside, the locker room was empty.  The three hastily showered and changed to go home for the evening, with no intent to meet with the others or venture out.  Nothing was ever said about the incident, from neither coach nor the players.  But Jacob and his teammates made certain not to break curfew again, even with an okay from their hosts.

The team's opening success carried on throughout the season.  Crowds at The Ice Box loved the spirited play and grew even more raucous, spurred on by increasingly creative and spectacular light shows.  Jacob's favorite was the Halloween Night spectacle, complete with haunting music and black and orange lights.  Off the ice, perhaps inspired even further by the team's success, Jacob continued his role as the life of the party.  And now joined by Garrett, as the two had become inseparable.

The season was winding down. The team was in a celebratory mood in the locker room following another decisive Friday win on their home ice, when Ryan Kretzer approached Jacob at his locker.

"Best be on your game tonight, Bro. My lady is here and she's got her hot girlfriend with her. I've been talking you up."

Jacob knew that Ryan's girlfriend was arriving for the weekend from St. Louis, but wasn't aware of any other friends. He went along but mostly shook it off. There were always plenty of ladies to pick from at the parties. Arriving at the house for the postgame fun, Jacob was immediately drawn to the newcomers. Standing next to Ryan and his girlfriend was a statuesque brunette, politely holding a drink and searching out the group in a shy but friendly manner.

Jacob readily approached them as if charging the net for a shot on goal.

"Hey, all the beautiful people!"

"Jake! I'd like you to meet Carson, and this is her friend, Annie."

Jacob spent the rest of the evening transfixed on the attractive Annie. She was a bit on the quiet side, at least compared to the rowdy partygoers around them, but seemed to enjoy his humor and laughed along with the others. With a game to be played on Saturday and the party drawing to a close, Jacob was pleased when they accepted his invitation for a nightcap at his house.

Once there, Jacob could sense almost immediately that Annie was not about to accept any overtures to stay for the evening. He could see that she not only had grace, but class and principles. It was actually a welcome change from the norm. Walking them out of the house late into the evening, Jacob was most sincere in telling Annie that he hoped to see her again.

The Stars' 2007-2008 season concluded with a sparkling record of 37 – 17. Ryan and Garrett finished second and third on the team in scoring, and Jacob finished tied for fourth, tallying 38 points while playing stellar defense. Using technical skills honed from hours of practice going back to San Jacinto, he was able to continually stifle opponents while racking up only 22 penalty minutes.

The Stars received considerable postseason recognition for the out-standing play, and Jacob was selected as an All-Star. A chance to compete against the League's best at the All-Star game in Sioux Falls, South Dakota. Once again, NHL scouts filled the stands and Jacob was on top of his game, showing off his skills in the action-packed contest. He looked forward to going home to California and spending time with family and friends in wait of the upcoming NHL draft to be held on June 26-27. But before going home, another exciting opportunity arose. Ryan invited him to spend a week in St. Louis to celebrate the just-completed season.

"You can stay with my family. We'll have a blast. Oh, and I told Annie you might be coming."

That sealed the deal. Their group, joined by Ryan's high school team-mate and Tornado nemesis Pat Maroon, who just completed a successful campaign in Canada's competitive Ontario Hockey League (OHL), was in high spirits as they went out every night in celebration. It was a wonderful way to conclude Jacob's final season in the Juniors, and cemented his feelings towards Annie. Jacob now had two things to look forward to, the NHL draft and a potential future with Annie.

Back in San Jacinto, Jacob and his brothers eagerly awaited the 2009 NHL draft. The draft was a two-day affair held in Montreal as part of the Canadien's centennial celebrations. On a Friday night, the family sat in front of the living room TV glued to ESPN, taking note of amateur players drafted from North American Junior Leagues and colleges, and the wide array of European leagues. Although North American players went in the first two picks, European players dominated the first round. Jacob went to bed that night in anticipation of the second day of the draft when a bevy of USHL players were sure to be selected.

Because the second day was not televised, Jacob kept close eye on the internet throughout the day. With his phone at hand, he also policed the home landline to make sure nobody used it for any reason. The picks slowly came across on his computer screen, and his anxiety rose with the conclusion of each round. Although dominated by players selected from the European and Canadian leagues, more and more USHL players were now being selected. Players that Jacob competed against and in many cases, clearly outperformed. He continually looked at his phone, willing for it to ring. The call never came.

As the seventh and final round unfolded, he retreated to his parents' room for some privacy and laid face down on the bed, sobbing with the reality that his name would not be called.

Unbeknown to Jacob at the time, NHL scouts spent as much time researching players off-the-ice behavior as they do their on-ice performance. Jacob had developed a reputation of a partier who had been almost kicked off the Lincoln Stars on two separate occasions. In his quest to please others for reasons he did not yet understand, he was reducing the odds of achieving his lifelong dream. His physical makeup and hockey skills were NHL ready, but the maturity aspect needed to succeed at hockey's highest level was considered by some NHL scouts to be at risk.

In the brutal hockey world, an aspiring athlete cannot afford to stay down for too long. Jacob was back at the gym early the next morning to work out before heading to the rink for ice time. A pile of scholarship offers sat on the dining table for his consideration, and one in particular was intriguing. There was work to be done.

# Chapter Six

# Hockey, Boston Style



## Northeastern Huskies – Boston, Massachusetts

Few cities in the United States, if any, can boast of a passion and love for hockey that rivals that of Boston. The historic city has been a hotbed for hockey since the late nineteenth century. The Boston Bruins became the first U.S. based team to join the NHL in 1924, winning their first of many Stanley Cups in 1929. Those early Bruins teams were made up of Canadian tradesmen who brought their hockey skills and love for the game to the bustling port city. And the love did not stop there.

Boston's history as a major trading port during colonial times coupled with the recognition of educational institutions contributing to the economy created a wealth of colleges throughout the region. Harvard University was founded in 1636 just years after the first settlers arrived, and was followed by dozens more, all sharing in the passion for learning and another love of Bostonians: sports. With the popularity of hockey growing across the region, the Boston universities created their own culture as a hotbed of competitive hockey which was easily assimilated into the passionate Boston sports culture.

Jacob had dreamed of skating for Boston College since he was nine years old, competing in the local Squirt hockey league. As an incentive for the young skaters, the boys were invited to attend a college hockey game hosted by the Boston College Eagles. Fortunately for Jacob, his mother's UA perks enabled the family to pay for his trip, and he was wide-eyed from the moment he stepped into Conte Forum inside the picturesque campus. Maroon and gold filled the arena. Glittering horns blared from the band ensemble to the beat of cymbals and drums that echoed across the ice. Raucous fans cheered on their Eagles who skated with physical precision. Jacob fell in love with the entire atmosphere. He left the Forum vowing to one day come back and skate for the Boston College Eagles.

An opportunity to impress the famous Boston College coach Jerry York actually arose the prior season skating for the Lincoln Stars. York would go on to be the winningest coach in NCAA history, and knowing that he was in the stands to watch a Stars game against the Indiana Ice, Jacob was well aware that he was singled out among a handful of athletes that York was interested in. Unfortunately for Jacob, he allowed the pressure to get to him and had his worst performance of the season in a sloppy loss. He figured his dream of skating for Boston College was gone forever. So, when Northeastern University offered a scholarship covering 85% of total expenses to attend class and play hockey, Jacob jumped at the opportunity. It may not have been Boston College, but it was Boston hockey played at a major Division 1 university. Making the move even more enticing was that he was joined by Stars teammate and close friend Garrett Vermeersch, who was also offered a scholarship. The two eagerly arrived in Boston well before the start of the school year to get an early start on acclimating to college life and skating for the Northeastern Huskies.

Jacob and Garrett joined other incoming freshmen for summer classes in preparation for the upcoming academic school year. He was assigned to share a dorm room with teammate Justin Daniels, a twin whose brother would be rooming with Garrett. Unpacking his clothes in the cramped room, Jacob reconciled that it was no different from sharing a room with two brothers in the converted garage. In other facets, the transition from full-time hockey to college life on the East Coast did not come without challenges.

It had been years since he attended school, and the twenty-one-year-old freshman was not quite sure what to expect regarding the collegiate academic requirements. After meeting with a counselor, it was highly recommended that the hockey player from California forego his business degree aspirations for now and settle for something more agreeable with his busy schedule: Communications.

Further challenging the academic requirements, the incoming freshmen and a handful of available players met every morning at six a.m. for workouts before attending class. After class, Jacob and Garrett enjoyed exploring the vibrant city, which had plenty of attractions to keep them busy. They quickly mastered "The T" transportation system, getting around easily without the need for a car. As with other new experiences, mastering the rail system did come with some comical mishaps.

One day, after sitting in Garrett's room following class and smoking pot, the two decided to take the train and go to a movie theater near downtown. Without any further thought, they purchased tickets for the Green Line and joined other passengers on the crowded train.

The two stood in conversation for some time before noting the outdoor landmarks were not what they expected. With each stop appearing to take them further from their intended destination, they got up to depart at the next stop which had many passengers exiting.

Jacob and Garrett drifted into the Harvard University campus. Historic brick buildings blended with tree-lined malls in the picturesque setting. The area was alive with students and professors walking all around them, deep in conversations that sounded foreign to the hockey recruits attired in shorts and tank tops. It suddenly struck Jacob that the language and appearance of the two hockey jocks could not be more starkly in contrast to those viewed all around them, and he suddenly broke into uncontrollable laughter. He laughed so hard that he held his stomach before falling to the ground, settling alongside a street gutter.

Garrett started to laugh along with him but then didn't know what to do when he observed that Jacob appeared unconscious. He was laughing so hard that he briefly blacked out. It took some time before Jacob regained his senses and Garrett helped him up from the curb. Nobody bothered to stop or assist them, probably more alarmed or maybe even threatened than concerned for the two outsiders. Jacob and Garrett walked back to the train station, now even more amused by their predicament.

The following week, one of the coaches gave Jacob an idea that sounded like a great opportunity to earn extra spending money. Unlike many of the players who came from money to attend the elite University, the coach knew Jacob could use some money so sought to help him out.

"It's easy money. Vendors can easily make $200 a night. Up to $500 on good days."

So, Jacob filled out an application to work as a vendor at the nearby historic Fenway Park. The Boston Red Sox were winding down another playoff drive, and their rabid fans were sure to bring in some welcome income for the remaining games leading up to the hockey season.

Walking to the park in the late afternoon, Jacob noted cloudy skies and a cool breeze approaching from the north for the late-season game. When he entered a large dingy room inside the bowels of the stadium for vendors to meet, he was handed a bright yellow jumpsuit and told to await his assignment. All around him, names were being called and vendors of all ages, shapes, and sizes approached a front table and were given their choice of items to sell. Apparently, vending is a time- vs. merit-based system, and Jacob watched the more experienced vendors grab the beer and hot dogs, which went quickly. The room soon dwindled and Jacob wondered why the gruff head vendor even called out his name in his thick Boston accent. He was the last vendor.

"Jake NU-ten. Looks like you get the Italian Ice."

For nine innings, with nighttime bringing an even colder breeze above the Green Monster and center field walls, Jacob was confined to selling the one product that was made for hot summer days. Walking up and down the same three sections over and over, he grew excited when someone finally called him over, only to have them ask: "Where's the beer vendor?" Hot chocolate was another popular choice for the evening game.

Jacob tried everything. He pulled out his best Boston accent. Toyed with a number of unsuccessful jingles, including: "Let's make nice, Try some Ice." But nothing worked.

When he reported back to close the evening, he watched others enthusiastically claim their earnings to celebrate another successful night from the sold-out crowd. Jacob was last to be called up and handed a meager seven dollars for his evening's work. That was his first and last day vending at Fenway.

The closing of summer brought the entire team together in preparation for the school year and upcoming season. Recruits from all across Canada and the United States sat down to hear Head Coach Greg Cronin lay out his expectations for the team. Jacob was interested in hearing what the coach had to say. The coach cut an intimidating presence. He was often visible to the players through the renovated hockey facility's glass enclosure in rigorous workouts that would rival any of his players. He carried that same level of intensity to the locker room, and Jacob was most appreciative of one of the team rules.

"There will be no foolish hazing that takes place on my team! I will not tolerate such behavior and anyone responsible will have to deal personally with me."

Jacob certainly welcomed this culture and it was obvious that nobody on the team had any desire to deal with this coach personally. The message, however, didn't stop the team's reputation and propensity to party. Following the team's opening exhibition victory at home and before an upcoming road trip to Colorado for their season-opener, the team got together for the annual "Freshmen Initiation" party.

The party was held at an off-campus house which was reflective of any number of frat or party houses across the American college landscape. The older wood frame structure was complete with a keg of beer on the oversized porch under a Northeastern banner, used and mismatched furniture throughout, and strewn with half-empty beer cans and whiskey bottles in every room. But perhaps what stood out most was a prominent hockey skate perched as the centerpiece in the middle of the living room.

Jacob and Garret arrived in good spirits, joining their fellow freshmen skaters in their indoctrination to party life with their new teammates. Attractive coeds mingling and laughing with the players, the drinks and music flowed freely. After taking count that all the freshmen had arrived, the veterans called them all together and led them into an empty bedroom where they were given an assignment.

"Here is a bottle for each of you and some other refreshments for you to enjoy. You can't come out until you drink a half liter from your bottle. Oh, and one more thing. When you come out you must be naked and tell a joke. If we laugh, you can put your clothes back on and join the party. Your initiation is complete. BUT, if nobody laughs, you need to go back and come up with another joke. Have fun!"

The freshmen players were expecting some sort of ritual to take place, but sat momentarily stunned by the audacity of what they were to do. Jacob was the first to take a swig from his bottle and get the party started.

He reasoned that it wasn't like they didn't see each other naked every day in the showers. And why not give the lovely ladies outside a show and have some fun?

Every so often a player filled and raised a shot glass with a toast to a made-up joke, which they all drank to amidst much laughter and colorful critique. They made sure to hydrate with plenty of water to help get through the task. With every shot the group grew bolder as any remaining inhibition was replaced with swagger and confidence.

With the bottle half finished, Jacob got up and declared himself ready.

"I'm going for the kill, boys!"

He disrobed and proudly stepped out, raising both arms while holding the bottle in his left hand and shouted out, "You all ready for a joke?"

The music was turned down as everyone approached applauding his entrance, the ladies in particular paying close attention. Some covering their faces with open hands as if they didn't know how else to react.

Jacob awaited his opening and spoke out.

"What do you call hemorrhoids on a gay guy?"

Silence from the crowd.

"Speed bumps!"

The crowd broke into laughter. More for the comical shamelessness that they just witnessed than the distasteful joke itself. But it worked.

"Looks like you're in, Jake. Get dressed and join the party."

But Jacob wasn't through. Going back inside to the room full of freshmen now awaiting their turn, he only put on his boxers before walking out to join the laughing, boisterous crowd. He then learned the use of the hockey skate in the living room. One of his teammates led him to the skate and handed him a plastic cup.

"Nice job, Jake! This calls for a drink."

Observing the skate filled with a mixture of whatever others decided to pour inside, Jacob lowered and filled the cup with a purplish liquid from inside the skate.

He raised the cup, clad only in boxers, and proclaimed: "GO Huskies," before gulping down the entire contents. The party-goers cheered wildly. Having already established himself as a leader on the ice as the team's top defenseman, Jacob was now fully entrenched as the undisputed leader and life of this new party.

There was one notable difference in Jacob that was immediately recognized by Garrett and established with his new teammates. He was in love. After leaving St. Louis where he spent time with Annie the prior summer, Jacob continued corresponding and the two entered a committed long-distance relationship. They discussed their futures; Annie was looking at transferring from Washington University in St. Louis to the Art Institute in Boston the next year to be with Jacob. But those plans were for the future. Jacob excitedly awaited Annie's first visit to Boston.

Adding further anticipation to Annie's arrival, Jacob's mother and sister were visiting the same weekend. An opportunity for them all to meet for the first time and enjoy hockey games to be played on the scenic campus. Jacob could not wait for them all to enjoy a perfect New England autumn weekend together centered around the city's beloved sport.

To Jacob's delight, his mother and sister Sarah hit it off with Annie as if they were long-time friends. The artistic Annie surprised them all with wrapped gifts that she eagerly waited for them to open. Sarah opened her package first, and shrieked in joy as she raised a perfectly fit jersey for all to see. A long-sleeved black jersey trimmed neatly in red and white. The name "Northeastern" wrapped around the Husky logo in front, and the name "Newton" was proudly printed on the back. Their game attire was now set for the weekend.

The Huskies got off to a decent start in the highly-competitive Hockey East conference. They bussed the short distance to Boston College with a record of 3 – 3. Arriving at the Conte Forum for the first time since visiting as a boy, Jacob was rudely reminded of the team's imposing reputation and high level of play. The Huskies skated off with a humbling 5 – 1 loss.

Despite the loss, the team regained their footing and came away with some impressive wins to close out the 2009 calendar year. Jacob took note of the increased visibility of scouts in attendance at every game, and ended the year with another score that would be his highlight. Before going back to California for Christmas, he stopped to see Annie in St. Louis. He had a surprise for her that he couldn't wait to share.

After proposing to Annie with the engagement ring, he felt almost immediate regret for not finding a more romantic setting to pop the question. She feigned surprise and happily accepted his proposal. But he also couldn't help but sense that the $300 ring, which was all he could afford at the time, must have been seen as quite a disappointment within the well-heeled family. Although they were all friendly enough to Jacob, he suspected that a hockey jock with one year of college only to play hockey was not exactly what they were hoping and expecting for their daughter. Jacob left St. Louis with a vow that he would one day return as the successful professional athlete of whom her entire family would be proud.

Returning to Boston following the Christmas break, Jacob continued his mission to make that dream a reality. Northeastern was invited to the four-team Leyland Bank Classic in New Hampshire, where they won the tournament, defeating both Dartmouth and UMass Lowell. Once again,

Jacob was recognized for his play and named as the Tournament's top Defenseman.

Jacob was playing excellent hockey with the team riding a five-game winning streak when the nation's eighth-ranked Boston College, led by their star player Chris Kreider, arrived on the Northeastern campus for a mid-February rematch. The historic Matthews arena, once known as the Boston Arena, and the oldest ice arena in the USA, was packed for the Friday night matchup against their crosstown rival. After getting off to a quick start with a first period goal, the Huskies faced relentless pressure from the vaunted Eagles offense. Hanging on to a 3-2 lead in the final period and facing continual power plays, the Huskies defense, led by Jacob, fellow Defenseman David Strathman, and Goalie Chris Rawlings continually thwarted the Eagles' relentless pressure. Jacob made sure the 230-pound Kreider was never able to have the open space needed to get off a clean shot. Kreider was visibly frustrated. When the horn finally sounded, the crowd erupted as the team celebrated on center ice. But undoubtedly the best moment for Jacob arrived during the postgame handshakes.

Boston College's decorated coach Jerry York sought out Jacob and approached closely for a private conversation.

"Jake, that was one amazing game that you just played out there. You are one hell of a player and I wish I had you on my team!"

Jacob, remembering his poor performance in Indiana where he failed to impress the coach and secure a scholarship from Boston College, was speechless. He simply smiled, thanked the coach, and skated off the ice as if he'd just been handed the Stanley Cup.

Northeastern went into the final week of the season with an excellent opportunity to make the NCAA playoffs. All that was needed was just one win in the home and away series to be played against another crosstown rival, the Boston University Terriers. Two teams being evenly matched left Jacob confident in at least one win, especially with their home crowd already selling out Saturday's night game to close out the season. One obstacle Jacob was not familiar with was the Huskies reputation of always starting seasons strong before fading down the stretch. Jacob was soon to learn what may have contributed to the reputation.

Coach Cronin, in an attempt to build character and toughen up his players, had an unconventional idea for the final week of practice before the big games. He brought in some local professional boxers, and set up sparring rounds for each of the players. One by one, the hockey players entered a boxing ring to face off against a professional boxer who was only allowed use of his left hand. Even at half speed and limited to their off hand, the highly trained boxers deftly moved and frustrated the players with lightning-quick jabs while easily avoiding counterpunches. Although fitted with head gear to protect them, the hockey players were no match for the professional boxers and clearly out of their element.

As Jacob sat to await his turn, he grew increasingly incensed with the exercise. *Why are we subjecting ourselves to this punishment when we should be preparing on ice and resting our bodies as much as possible for the upcoming games?* When his turn finally arrived as the last player to spar, he observed the boxer step away to take a water break and was in no rush to re-enter the ring.

Coach looked up at the empty ring and yelled over for Jacob to enter the ring.

"Newton, what are you doing? Get in that ring right now and fight."

"He's taking a break, Coach. He's probably tired."

Before even finishing the statement, Jacob noticed a change in the boxer's demeanor that he hadn't seen before. The fighter took a final gulp of water as Jacob swallowed his words, observing over two hundred pounds of thick muscle on brown skin sweating rage enter the ring to take care of business. Jacob knew it was too late to take back the misplaced comment.

Dancing around the ring, Jacob felt a flurry of left jabs strike his body with a combination of speed and force unlike anything he had ever felt before. He tried to sneak in a few punches but was more intent on blocking the incoming onslaught. With all his focus on stopping the left hand, the boxer's right suddenly caught him square in the jaw, sending his mouthpiece flying in the air.

Jacob barely kept his balance but was momentarily stunned. He had never been hit so hard and immediately understood the concept of seeing stars. Everything stopped. Even his opponent now looked on as if not sure what to do.

Irate, Jacob tore his head gear off and threw it down to the mat. He climbed through the ropes out of the ring and continued walking right out of the gym. Perhaps there was a method to what he viewed as Coach's madness, but this did not seem the way to prep for their biggest weekend of the season.

Friday arrived and the Huskies found themselves in a nailbiter inside the packed Agganis Arena. Jacob was on top of his game, scoring two goals in a game that saw three separate ties before Northeastern came up just short, losing 5-4. They still had one last shot to get a win and secure a spot in the NCAA tournament, their final game to be played before a sellout crowd in the friendly confines of Matthews Arena.

Saturday's game picked right up where Friday's game left off. The two teams again squared off in a showdown. Midway through the first period, Jacob intercepted a pass and found Garrett streaking to his left. Placing a clean pass to his close friend, Garrett deftly collared the assist and scored to put the Huskies up 2-1.

Early in the final period and down by one, Jacob once again found himself controlling the puck with the power play unit while Terrier players scrambled to defend their goal. This time a perfect assist to Wade MacLeod for a game-tying score. The arena shook as the Huskies now only needed one goal to get the win and secure a spot in the tournament.

Unfortunately, they fell short once again. An unassisted goal stunned the crowd as Boston University put an end to the Huskies' season. It was Boston University who would be advancing to the Hockey East Quarter-finals.

The physical and emotional stress associated with the long season finally caught up to Jacob. No sooner had the season ended when he came down with a virus and lost all energy. Confined to his bed in the tiny dorm room, he lost thirteen pounds and struggled with what to do regarding all the letters of interest that had been coming his way throughout the season. Because he was not drafted into the NHL the prior season and the upcoming draft was still months away, Jacob was free to sign a professional contract. Now at least he had some time to sort them out.

The first serious letter which attracted his attention was an envelope stamped with the NHL Washington Capitals logo. Tearing it open, Jacob had to look twice to make sure he was reading correctly. They were interested in signing him to a contract worth $650,000 per year over three years if he made the team. Coupled with that, $60,000 per year with their American Hockey League (AHL) affiliate if he was sent down to prep for NHL play. That AHL contract was significantly more than the average pay received by the league's players. Several days later another letter, this one from his hometown Anaheim Ducks, the offer even better at $800,000 per year for three years and $67,500 with their AHL affiliate. More letters and calls were coming in. All in financial and legalese language that the hockey-focused Jacob could not clearly understand. It was time to get some help.

Jacob reached out to Garrett, who had introduced him to a sports agent earlier in the year who was looking for prospective clients to sign with his agency. Garrett arranged to have the agent fly to Boston to meet with them.

Wade Arnott looked every bit the role of a professional sports agent. He met the two at Boston Logan Airport attired in a sharp business suit. The young professional, not much older than his prospective clients, showed confidence in a relatable manner that assured them that he could get their careers off to the right start. Jacob could see shades of Tom Cruise in "Jerry Maguire".

The three sat down at a lively pizza restaurant in the busy downtown district to discuss business. Wade was a part of Newport Sports Management; a premier representation and management agency dedicated to professional hockey athletes. Among their impressive array of clients was Nicklas Lidstrom, the legendary Red Wing defenseman after whom Jacob modeled his game and even his number 5. Upon learning that fact, the deal was pretty much sealed. Jacob was strongly considering Wade Arnott from Newport Sports to represent him in all future contract negotiations.

However, there were still matters to take care of. Jacob was slowly regaining weight and strength, enabling him to spend time in the gym and back on ice. He was not quite 100 percent when he got the call to meet with Coach Cronin for the end-of-year meeting.

The meeting did not go exactly as planned. Jacob had just concluded a successful season, making the Hockey East all-rookie team and was now receiving interest from NHL teams. But rather than review the season or share his gratitude, Coach seemed more intent on lecturing Jacob that he was not ready for the Washington Capitals. Apparently, Coach only knew of the interest received from Washington, and the one-sided conversation directed at Jacob was focused on the need to stay in college, because he would now be getting a full ride and he was not yet ready for the one NHL team that had shown interest.

Jacob sat back and couldn't help but drift into a belief that Coach was merely trying to get him back for one more season, with little thought of Jacob's own interests. In reality, the message was likely the correct one. One more year of college hockey could put him in a position to succeed and prep for the NHL draft, where his options would be strengthened with additional guarantees. But the animated delivery that was borderline screaming from the intimidating coach did not connect with Jacob in a way he could fully recognize the message.

Jacob continued listening without speaking and silently made up his mind. His college and amateur career had come to an end. He would go with Wade and Newport Sports Management to sign his first professional contract.

# Chapter Seven

# Life as a Duck

Spring & Summer, 2010

## Anaheim Ducks, Anaheim, California

It was not long after the year-end meeting that Jacob returned to California and found himself living in a posh apartment right across from the Honda Civic Center. There was no need to finish the Spring Semester at Northeastern, things were moving fast. Although not on the active roster, twenty-one-year-old Jacob was enjoying the lifestyle of a professional athlete as a recognized member of the NHL Anaheim Ducks, receiving NHL pay on his prorated salary that would count as year one. Jacob eagerly accepted the money, not concerned or even aware that the partial year pay would count as one full season towards the three-year contract.

After signing with Newport Sports, Wade placed all focus on the Ducks' offer and getting money now. Not only was Anaheim close to Jacob's hometown, but it was the largest initial offering of the three on the table. He managed to raise the offer from $800,000 to $925,000 per year if he made the team, along with a guaranteed signing bonus of $270,000 over three years. Upon signing the contract and knowing of Jacob's hometown in nearby San Jacinto, a proud Ducks' front office official asked Jacob, "Who is your favorite NHL team?"

Not wanting to disappoint the grinning official with truth of the Detroit Red Wings as his favorite team, Jacob gave him the answer he eagerly anticipated.

"The Anaheim Ducks, Sir!"

Jacob was invited to participate in all team activities, even in team meetings after several days of individual skate time before joining the team practices.  He kept his head down and tried to conceal the awe he felt skating alongside NHL stars he had followed since a little boy.  Lining up with fellow defensemen, he noticed a player with the number 27 on a practice jersey glide up next to him.  Scott Niedermayer.  Five-time all-star and one-time winner of the league's top defenseman.  Just a few weeks earlier, he was skating with college students when not getting hammered in the boxing ring.  Now he was skating alongside the world's best, easily assimilated into orchestrated drills and professional preparation for the playoff drive.

Following practice, Jacob simply walked across the street to a furnished apartment that was paid for by the team during his introductory phase. Jacob had more money than he had ever known and wasn't exactly sure how to manage it.  When he received his first check for $61,000, he refused the offer to work with a financial advisor, thinking it would simply be the first of many.  He wanted to return favors to his brothers who had always been there for him in the past.  So, he purchased some marijuana and invited Josh and Andrew to join him for the weekend.  Fancy restaurants, impulse purchases, all expenses on him.

Just fourteen games remained in the regular season when the Chicago Blackhawks arrived for a crucial game at the Honda Civic Center.  Jacob soaked up the atmosphere in the team lounge before the game, taking delight in the wide-eyed youngsters who approached him for autographs. Singling him out among the older and more formally attired team employees, the young fans figured he must be a player of some sort.  Settling in their sky box seats, they were treated to a raucous affair highlighted by a flurry of fights.  The crowd loved it.  Those seated around him showed concern.

Duck defenseman James Wisniewski was in the middle of every fight, serving a total of twelve penalty minutes for the game. In the second period, his hit on Blackhawks defenseman Brent Seabrook knocked him right out of the game. While the crowd roared, Jacob heard mumblings of suspension all around him. To Jacob, this could be the break to get on the active roster.

The team was concluding its homestand with upcoming games against the New York Islanders and Colorado Avalanche when news of an eight-game suspension for Wisniewski was announced. Jacob kept up with his diligent work and was riding an emotional high when after practice one of the coaches called him over to have a chat while riding on a stationary bike.

"Son, you're doing a great job and we want you to keep up with everything that you're doing. Just remember, you're here for the experience and not to play. That opportunity comes next year."

The words following the last statement were never heard. Jacob thanked the coach for his words of encouragement and walked right out of the Honda Center. He slammed the half-full power drink down to the ground and continued walking to his apartment.

He got over the disappointment quickly. With the home stand coming to a close, Jacob learned that he was to accompany the team on their upcoming road trip across Canada with stops in Calgary, Vancouver, and Edmonton.

"Make sure to bring your passport. You'll be flying with the team."

Unfortunately, Jacob had no passport. When asked for his driver license to expedite the process to get the passport, the assistant was stunned to learn he had no license. Jacob had been so focused on hockey since his first year of Juniors that he bypassed all the normal protocols and rituals of his fellow teens. Using their vast connections of networking, the team was able to secure his passport just in time for the upcoming road trip.

If Jacob thought he was living in style with the team's stay in Anaheim, he was in for yet another treat of experiencing life on the road as an NHL athlete. Long bus trips replaced by well-coordinated chartered flights.

Five-star hotels in all three Canadian cities, lucrative per diems enabling lavish meals and spending. Hotel lobbies and arena clubhouses filled with TV and print media looking to get stories. Fans everywhere looking to get an autograph or even just a glimpse of their favorite players.

Jacob slowly began to feel more and more a part of the team, like he belonged. Although keeping a low profile with a focus on gaining experience of life as a pro off the ice, he could sense increased recognition and acceptance from the players. He was often accompanied by fellow developmental player Nick Bonino, who like Jacob left Boston after his team's season ended. The two were already familiar with one another. Nick skated for Boston University and was involved in their fierce battles during the last weekend of the season. While on the road, they roomed together and Jacob shared in Nick's joy when he was added to the active roster for the final game of the road trip. Nick made his NHL debut on March 26 in Edmonton, and would go on to a long and distinguished NHL career. On the flights, Jacob took the back seat, seated next to Swiss goalie Jonas Hiller who spent most of the time reading or listening to music on his headphones. By the time the team returned to Los Angeles, Jacob identified without hesitation as an NHL Anaheim Duck.

The season ended in disappointment. Despite wrapping up the season with a record of 39 – 32 – 11 (the last figure representing 11 additional losses in overtime), the Ducks failed to make the playoffs. For Jacob, things were just getting started. He vowed to be ready for the following season and arranged to train during the offseason with the team's strength and conditioning coach. After a few sessions, Jacob's conditioning was boosted to an even higher level when he began working out with respected team veteran George Parros. Parros was a Princeton grad who had just recently been chosen as the fourth-smartest athlete in sports by the Sporting News. Jacob, who had always been an avid workout junkie, eagerly participated with George in the innovative and strenuous workouts to further prepare for the upcoming season.

Outside of the rink, things were also moving fast. He moved to an even bigger apartment not far away and close to Angel Stadium. Every night, a juicy steak dinner at the nearby Catch restaurant. Jacob got his driver license and purchased his first car from a friend, a sparkling new Mazda CX-7.

Following completion of her college season, Annie joined him from St. Louis. The two celebrated with a scenic drive along the Highway 1 coastline to San Francisco. Endless views across the spectacular Pacific symbolized the hope they were feeling for their future. Jacob even noticed a change in tone from her family on Annie's frequent phone calls back home. Her parents made a point of expressing how much they were looking forward to spending time with the two on an upcoming trip.

The NHL draft was held on June 25–26 at the nearby Staples Center in Los Angeles. With their 12th pick, the Ducks selected Cam Fowler, a young defenseman who was projected by most experts to go much earlier in the draft. Jacob knew this meant another defenseman to compete against for the upcoming season, but he was feeling confident about his place and position on the team. Long-time Duck Scott Niedermayer was retiring after a celebrated 18-year NHL career, and he was hearing nothing but positive feedback among the front office personnel concerning his place on the team.

"Keep up the great work. Remember, you were brought here to replace Scott as our power play defenseman."

Jacob eagerly awaited the upcoming Development Camp for all incoming draftees and select invited players. This was his chance to compete with others on the ice and show that he truly belonged.

The Anaheim Ducks Development Camp and Summer League were held that summer in the Canadian city of Penticton, British Columbia. Jacob's parents and sister Sarah eagerly joined him and Annie to enjoy the scenic city on the edge of Okanagan Lake. A chance to tour and sightsee when not watching Jacob and the young Ducks compete against other draftees and invitees from the NHL Edmonton Oilers, San Jose Sharks, and Calgary Flames.

The camp got off to an inauspicious start for Jacob. Before the team's first intrasquad scrimmage, all players were required to undergo an EKG test to measure their heart conditions, a standard test to ensure no heart abnormalities. Following his test, Jacob was told to meet with the team doctors. They needed to discuss the results and perform further tests.

They scheduled a follow-up test which required him to perform activities to get his heart rate up above 170 beats per minute. The doctors showed concern when he was unable to get his heartbeat that high, despite the strenuous activities they were putting him through. They had him wear a heart monitor so they could check his heart activity throughout the night.

The next day, the doctors were shocked to learn that his heart had slowed down to 24 beats per minute during the night. His heartbeat virtually almost stopped. More tests were needed to determine if there were underlying health conditions that were causing problems. The doctors conducted further tests while looking for signs of dizziness, fatigue, or trouble breathing. Throughout the testing, the heartbeat remained below 170 and no symptoms occurred. They finally surmised that Jacob was simply the owner of an amazingly athletic heart. He was free to rejoin the team and skate in the Tournament.

This actually made sense to Jacob. Throughout the summer, he had been conditioning with George Parros who was arguably the most conditioned athlete on the Ducks' roster. Among the workouts they put themselves through was a series of 330-yard sprints which they challenged themselves to run under 60 seconds. Each sprint followed by a brisk 110-yard walk to complete the track lap before bounding into the next sprint. Lap after lap they ran, vigorously challenging one another. Jacob lost track of the laps and for the first time in his entire career he finally experienced the unpleasant moment of throwing up during a workout. Up until then, he had been the lone skater to never lose his lunch during the infamous and grueling hockey workouts. Although this was a first and only time in his career, Jacob placed more blame on his rapid intake of cranberry juice just prior to the workout. Whatever the cause, he now had some explanation for why (until then) he was always able to push himself further in conditioning than his peers.

Back on the ice, Jacob played in all three summer league games and once again established himself as a team leader and top defenseman for the young Ducks. If that wasn't enough to raise his confidence level, his brother Josh heard news upon their return to Anaheim that raised it even further. Josh, who was often seen at the Ducks' facilities along with his brother Andy, had spoken to the team's Strength and Conditioning Coach about Jacob. The coach inferred that Jacob was highly thought of in the organization, and even viewed by him personally at a level above the highly touted young defenseman Luca Sbisa. Sbisa, the Italian-born Swiss, was a former first-round pick who had been acquired the previous season from the Philadelphia Flyers. To be even considered in the same conversation with Sbisa was an honor, and to be ranked above a former first-round pick was something that buoyed Jacob's confidence even further.

Jacob and Annie were in high spirits when Jacob's older sister Beth came to visit with her daughter Madelyn and help the couple unpack things in the new apartment. While the three sorted items, Beth delighted in Jacob being so close to their home in San Jacinto and anticipation of the family watching him play next season for the Ducks. It was only when the three took a break from unpacking that the mood in the room changed. And only momentarily. Beth casually mentioned in conversation the abuse that Jacob suffered as a child. Jacob sat unsure, noting the confused look on Annie's face. Rather than question Beth the two allowed the conversation to continue and soon got on to other, more mundane topics before they continued their work.

Later that evening when the two were alone, Annie asked Jacob what Beth was referring to when she brought up the past abuse. Jacob honestly answered that he wasn't sure. Thoughts and wonder crept into his mind. Recollection of triggers that sometimes brought about uncomfortable feelings. A subtle element of uncertainty crept into the mindset of Jacob as he and Annie settled into their Anaheim apartment in preparation for the upcoming season.

# Part 2

# Chapter Eight

# "I Will Destroy You!"

## 2010 - 2011 season

### Team 1: Anaheim Ducks, Anaheim, California

Jacob stood frozen on the ice in front of 16,000 screaming fans at the SAP Center in San Jose, California. The game had barely started when his world was suddenly turned upside down. His tunnel vision pointed to an escape. An opened door alongside the bench revealing his teammates screaming toward the ice with raised sticks. The raucous noise spilling from the arena crowd slowly faded into the singular sound of a hollow, haunting voice: "If you do or say anything, I will destroy you!"

He tried to remove the fear and bring himself to the reality of chaos that was littered all around him. Several fights were going on with players and referees scrambling in all directions. Standing at six-foot-three with 215 pounds of lean muscle fine-tuned by the most rigorous offseason training, Jacob stood out as the team's likely enforcer. The player expected to confront any opponent who dared get too physical with the team's star players. Similarly, his presence also presented the player most likely to be challenged by an opposing bully trying to gain a reputation and name for himself. But he stood alone, helpless to participate in the mayhem so eagerly embraced by the players around him.

The fact that he was even on the ice proudly donning his visiting Anaheim Ducks jersey came as an unexpected surprise to him. Jacob came into training camp with the utmost confidence, but quickly grew confused and somewhat disenchanted by the events surrounding him. During practice sessions, he was grouped with players shooting shots on goal in lieu of the group working on power plays. It was the power play that was his specialty and ticket to the NHL. That's what they told him he was here for. Further confounding him, he hadn't appeared in either of the first two exhibition games. But he survived both cuts and was told to pack for an upcoming road trip to San Jose and Vancouver. He enjoyed a pregame steak at their five-star hotel in San Jose but it was only when Coach Randy Carlyle approached him during pregame warmups that the nerves set in. "Get yourself ready, Jake, you're playing tonight." And that's where he now found himself. Standing alone on an island of ice surrounded by brawls and a packed house of their fierce rival Sharks' fans.

Jacob took a deep breath in an attempt to regain his senses, gently moving in the direction of the bench while trying to drown out the haunting words that overtook him. For reasons that he couldn't explain, he always felt some sort of trigger whenever hockey fights occurred, but never to the level he had just experienced. He even managed to win over the home crowd and his two brothers when confronting the behemoth while skating for the Texas Tornado. But that was done instinctively, without time to think. What just happened here was much different. Here he was in a once-in-a-lifetime opportunity, playing against the best in the world in front of more fans than he ever played for before. He had just experienced his entire being paralyzed and in fear as if observing the scene from another dimension. Somehow, he had escaped the mayhem. Nobody took a shot at him and he was certainly in no position to enter the fray. Did anyone notice? How would this be viewed by his teammates and team officials?

Jacob gathered himself to join his team while the referees sorted out the penalties to be served.  He regained his focus while on the bench.  There was a job to do and opportunities for him with a game that was sure to feature plenty of power plays.  The same energy force that took his mind out of the game was now replaced with tunnel vision to focus and compete on the ice.

Sure enough, power play opportunities arose.  More fights continued to occur in a preseason game unexpectedly played with playoff-level intensity.  The triggers that Jacob felt with the opening fight continued to a lesser degree while on the ice, but so did his intensity to succeed.  The Ducks were up 1-0 when Jacob was summoned to join the power play group following yet another Shark penalty.

With just five minutes and 29 seconds into the game, Jacob took a pass from team captain and holder of numerous Ducks records, Ryan Getzlaf.  The pass enabled Jacob to get a close shot on goal, slipping the puck past the Sharks' outstanding goalie Antii Niemi.  The horn blared.  Getzlaf and other veterans embraced Jacob in celebration for a preseason game that had become quite personal for the Duck veterans against their intense rival.

The Ducks were unable to hold onto their 2-0 lead.  Rugged play and fights continued.  It was clear that the game was becoming increasingly personal between the two rivals and Shark players clearly did not want to disappoint their fans.  As more and more fights took place, Jacob fought to control himself against the triggers that he was continually battling.  He managed to stay clear of the fights and focus more on the opportunities presenting themselves in a game that was played with such great intensity.

Early in the 3$^{rd}$ period the game was deadlocked in a 3 – 3 tie.  Jacob once again found himself on the power play unit with a chance to take the lead.  The game's intensity continued and San Jose sent out their best.  Their top penalty killing line was on the ice hoping to stifle a Ducks' power play and swing momentum back to the home team.  The fans were cheering them on and Jacob was riding the emotion.

The Ducks kept the pressure on but the Sharks battled and their two-minute penalty was about to expire.  The fans roared their appreciation in anticipation of getting back to full strength when Jacob and Ryan Getzlaf combined for two crisp passes that found Corey Perry for his third goal of the game. The four-time all-star scored the hat trick and the Ducks took the lead in a game they would go on to win, 5-4. Jacob received accolades from his teammates all the way to the bench and was riding an emotional high that would not leave him for days.

In the visiting locker room following the game, Jacob took questions from reporters, describing how it felt as a local kid to score his first goal and points as an Anaheim Duck. Jacob was all smiles, explaining how great it felt, and how it meant even more to occur in a hard-fought win. It may have been a preseason game, but the intensity was real and the appreciation and satisfaction of getting a win on the road in San Jose was clear from the reaction of veteran players and coaches in the locker room.

It was not until he sat on the plane late that night that he allowed the reality of the moment to sink in. Most around him were now fast asleep as he tuned in to the humming and occasional airplane sounds before partially opening the shade from his window seat. For Jacob, sleep was not an option. He was too excited in replaying the power play goal and assist that led to a Ducks win. Every second of both plays replayed in his mind. Over and over. Every movement. The position of his defender and anticipation of plays, the noise from the crowd. The deafening quiet from the crowd following each game-winning play was no less satisfying than hearing a roar from your home crowd.

Then another reality. *I'm going to make the team!* Only four preseason games remained before the opening of the 2010-2011 season. In Jacob's first game, a difficult test on the road going up against their fierce rival San Jose Sharks, Jake Newton tallied two points. A goal and assist against the Sharks top-line players. Cam Fowler, the Ducks' first-round pick against whom Jacob was competing for a spot on the roster, had played in all three preseason games and had yet to score a single point. Fowler was almost guaranteed a spot given his lofty draft status, but surely there was a place for Jacob to claim a much-deserved spot on the opening day roster. This game, coupled with the acceptance he'd been receiving throughout the offseason from both veteran players and team officials, had to seal the deal.

Jacob closed his eyes but sleep didn't come. The emotional triggers he felt during every fight, especially the first, cast an unsettling feeling. But he managed to get through them and put himself in a position to achieve his lifelong dream. An Anaheim Duck. The hockey guy from San Jacinto skating in front of appreciative fans at the packed Honda Civic Center. His high school class naming him the person most likely to become famous. All the hard work and practice was now going to pay off. The first thing he would do is take care of Mom and Dad for all their time and sacrifice in helping him achieve his dream.

A beeping sound and mild tilt indicated the plane's slow descent into Vancouver. Jacob shut the window shade. He doubted that he would get much sleep upon their early morning arrival at the luxury hotel before another game to be played that same night. It didn't matter. He was feeling on top of the world.

Jacob arose early that Saturday morning eagerly awaiting an opportunity to get back on the ice and continue building upon the momentum from his NHL debut. Arriving by team bus late afternoon at the downtown Rogers Arena, he enjoyed the attention from the scattering of fans eager to get a sight or autograph from one of the visiting players. The team arrived hours before face-off, allowing time to dress and warm up on the ice as arena workers prepped the venue in anticipation of the evening crowd.

Following warmups, Jacob was provided with unwelcome news in the visiting locker room. He and several other players were told that they wouldn't be playing in the game.

"You can get dressed and join others in our designated press box seating."

Thoughts began running through his head. *Was I traded? Are they sending me down? Did they see enough from last night's game for me to secure a spot on the final roster?* He tried to calm his nerves as he and several other hopefuls dressed and joined team officials from the travel party in the visiting team's press box.

Watching the game unfold from their posh seats, Jacob could see that the team was not playing with the same intensity that they showed the prior night in San Jose. Back-to-back games and an early morning arrival in Vancouver surely had something to do with the team's lackluster play, but Jacob felt something awry from the moment he heard word in the locker room that he would not be playing.

The Ducks were down and showing little sign of life when Jacob received a text from the team's General Manager during intermission. Jacob walked down the hall where he was welcomed into a spacious room and warmly greeted by the team's GM, Bob Murray.

Jacob's heart raced as he sat down across from the GM to learn the status of his place on the team.

Right from the start, Jacob could see where the verdict was going. Murray was cordial throughout and said all the right words. Words to the effect of, we really like you and you've done everything that we've asked of you. But the reality was he was being sent down to Anaheim's American Hockey League (AHL) affiliate in Syracuse to get more seasoning and playing time.  He was told that he'd get plenty of playing experience against top competition, and the coaches would work with him to learn the Duck's brand of hockey to prepare him for the NHL.  As the words wound down, Jacob clearly heard the one statement that would come back to haunt him.

"With your size and strength, we'd like to see you play with more, uh ... physical presence."

The fights!  He was certain that despite everything he did to help secure the win, the team took note of his reluctance to join the fights that continually occurred all around him.  The reality was, he was frozen, unable to even move following triggers that came with each altercation. Jacob could only imagine how that must have appeared to anyone observing him. Was this the factor that led to him not making the team?

Jacob tried to mask his disappointment.  He held a strong belief following last night's game that he had made the team.  Further, he wasn't even provided an opportunity to show what he could contribute on a night when the Ducks clearly were not at their best.  But he chose to forego an uncomfortable explanation for not fighting and swallowed his pride while thanking Murray for the opportunity and having belief in him. He stood up to leave and promised that he would do everything asked of him to make it back to the Ducks. The return flight to LA would be much longer than the arrival to Vancouver.

Life as a professional athlete does not provide much time to tend to personal matters. Shortly after arriving back in Anaheim, Jacob needed to get to Syracuse for the start of their season. A disappointed Annie had more time but needed to manage arrangements in moving things from their newly decorated apartment to a new life in Syracuse. Just when they were on the cusp of living their dream in Southern California on a rookie $925,000 NHL contract, the couple was now forced to move over 2,500 miles away and find a new place to live on Jacob's $67,500 AHL contract.

There was no time to feel sorry for themselves. The AHL money was still quite good and Jacob was certain he'd make it back to Anaheim. He learned that teammate Timo Pielmeier was making the long drive alone to Syracuse. The German-born goaltender was among the cuts and he happily welcomed Jacob to join him on the long trip. The two spent the drive reflecting on their respective journeys and shared dreams of making it back to the NHL.

## Team 2: Syracuse Crunch, Syracuse, New York

Jacob comfortably settled into his new home in Syracuse. He found a nice one-bedroom apartment close to downtown and the War Memorial Arena made famous as the arena used for the beloved hockey movie starring Paul Newman, *Slap Shot*. He was quite certain Annie would approve and enjoy the apartment. The area offered plenty of life and added vibrancy from their proximity to Syracuse University. Jacob was also familiar with a number of players from the Ducks who had been sent down with him and was soon in for a pleasant surprise when another familiar face was added to the team. Shortly after the start of the season, the Anaheim Ducks made a trade with the Philadelphia Flyers and acquired Patrick Maroon.

Before he would go on to enjoy a lengthy NHL career that continues to the time of this writing, the Ducks sent Maroon to Syracuse. The two hockey buddies with a long history of competing and partying were reunited with an opportunity to play together for the first time.

Outside of the social activities and friendships, life in the AHL was certainly a big change from what Jacob had grown accustomed to for the past six months in the NHL. Gone were the first-class flights and five-star hotels and restaurants, star-studded attention, and comfortable accommodations in major cities. The bus rides were also back, mixed in with flights to the further destinations. But it was still professional hockey with its own culture of rabid fans and media attention. The bus rides did create team chemistry with plenty of hours of lively card games and good-natured ribbing at the expense of all when not fighting to get sleep. It may not have been the NHL, but it was a far cry from toiling in the Juniors, although Jacob retained fond memories of the simple hockey in those smaller towns with their appreciative fans.

Jacob soon learned a few other realities that made life on the ice much more challenging than off. The coaches sat down with him and explained that for the Ducks he needed to change his style of play to be more physical. With his size and strength coupled with his stick handling skills, they felt that he could develop into an intimidating presence who would stifle opponents with physical contact while creating more scoring opportunities for the wings. Jacob grudgingly went along with the coaching, but this played directly against his personal strengths while also raising the potential to introduce yet more triggers. Jacob had always been a tactician with an uncanny ability to both stifle attackers and score goals. Changing to a more physical style would reduce his scoring and initiate more fights, which is exactly what was causing the triggers which impacted his play.

Struggling to fit into the new style now asked of him, Jacob couldn't help but reflect on what could have been had he signed the competitive offer sheet with the Washington Capitals. In their recruitment, the Capitals pointed to Jacob's style of play as being conducive to what they were looking for. Further, Capitals Coach Bruce Bourdeau was well-established as a player's coach and Jacob had heard nothing but praise for him.  His players loved playing for him.  In his haste to sign Jacob to the Ducks' offer and assuming a desire to play for his home team, Wade Arnott never really explored the Capitals offer, but Jacob couldn't really blame Wade as it was his own decision to sign the contract.  A lesson learned not to simply go for the money or leave all decisions to his agent.

Another reality was the more individualized style of play in the AHL. The league was made up of high-level professional skaters who generally fell into one of two categories.  Roughly half of the league was made up of grizzled veterans who had bounced around between the NHL and AHL or top-level European leagues for years.  Many of these players were looking at their last real opportunity to prove themselves and get that NHL contract before their playing days were over.  The other half were relative newcomers like Jacob who just missed out on their dreams and now had to prove themselves to get called back up.  This mix of players was not conducive for team hockey.

For Jacob, the combination of trying to play a different style of hockey while also teaming with skaters more intent on padding their stats than winning games was unlike anything he had experienced.  His own play suffered while the team's performance was uneven to begin the season.  A rare win buoyed by a strong individual performance was too often followed with a blowout loss where it appeared the team never even practiced together.  The team headed into the new year with a very uninspiring record of 12-18 with 4 OT losses, rapidly sinking out of playoff contention.

Off the ice was a different story.  Annie had now joined him and was easily making friends with the other players' wives and girlfriends.  The players enjoyed meeting up after games, especially on the weekends, and Jacob once again became the center and ringleader of all activity.  If someone wanted to go out or get together, Jacob was the person they called or texted.

The tight-knit group often met at one of the many bars located around the Syracuse campus and their presence was quite visible and well established among the Syracuse community of bar patrons.  Just as he had done in the past, Jacob was always looking to please others and unable to say no to any party. Although not as wild as in his Junior and College days, he remained the life of the party. With or without Annie, who often accompanied him. While some of the veterans, especially those serious about getting called up to the NHL, took the time to rest their bodies and minimize the after-game activities, Jacob took the opposite approach, often chastising those teammates for not going out and having some fun.

If his extroverted and partying reputation was not known to Jacob at the time, it became crystal clear after a team function. The team organized an evening for Crunch season ticket holders with a number of players on hand to sign autographs and mingle with the fans. The owner's wife made a point of working the room, greeting fans and thanking them for their support to the team. As she approached Jacob who was signing autographs and joking with a small crowd, she welcomed them with an unusual introduction for the young skater.

"Good evening! I see you've met the team troublemaker."

Jacob laughed along with the group. But he couldn't help but shake an unsettling feeling of just how he was being perceived by the team's front office. If the owner's wife is saying this so casually, what else was being said behind closed doors? And could it be viewed in some ways as a positive, or was it purely negative? The comment did not change Jacob's actions in the present environment, but would cause wonder as the season wore on.

The team spent New Year's Day with a road game against the Rochester Americans. On the first day of 2011, Jacob's season spiraled even further. In a concerted effort to please the coaches with more physical play, he had a vicious collision with Rochester's left wing A.J. Jenks, who landed awkwardly on his leg. Jacob lay on the ice in agony, initially unable to get up. After a few moments and with help from several teammates, he got up and managed to skate off the ice. But the leg was unstable and Jacob feared the worst.

Back in Syracuse, Jacob received the bad news. A torn MCL. A straight sleeve was placed over his leg for two weeks to give the knee time to heal. Following that would be weeks of strenuous rehab. Jacob braced for an intense period to heal his first major injury. The workout junkie eagerly accepted the challenge.

The first hurdle to clear in increasing the leg's mobility was dealing with the constant pain. The team's Strength and Conditioning Coach, Mark Powell, set a goal for Jacob to get the knee to bend at 90 degrees. Every added stretch brought excruciating pain. Jacob knew it would be a lengthy process but was determined to get back on the ice as soon as possible.

Another hurdle was an inability to work on cardio. Unable to use his legs, the active Jacob was starving for something to get the heart pounding. He noticed extra weight quickly adding due to his voracious appetite and inability to skate off the calories. Powell had a solution that became an instant hit and would go on to become a favorite workout for Jacob. Rope training. Bent forward in a stationary position, he grabbed the end of two heavy ropes with both hands and began the rhythmic movement; 20 seconds of intense movement followed by a 10-second rest. Over and over the long, thick ropes snaking across the gym floor. It felt good to feel the heart pumping and Jacob soon noticed muscles growing even larger on his chest and arms.

The time off the ice also afforded Jacob more time to spend with Annie as the two entered a new phase of their relationship. Shortly into the season, Annie met with a therapist in an attempt to get her fast-paced life back into order. Lots had changed for her over the past year and she found the talks with her therapist extremely helpful. She convinced Jacob to join her at the next appointment.

Jacob initially joined in as a favor to Annie but soon found himself at the center of the sessions. During one of their early sessions, Annie brought up the conversation with Beth at the Anaheim apartment where she mentioned the abuse suffered by Jacob as a child. Both sets of eyes turned to Jacob. He now had no choice but to focus all energy in confronting the demon of his past. He closed his eyes.

*Faded images of John, his older cousin who abruptly left their lives. He appears large and intimidating. A towering presence that controls him at all times. Fear is introduced. Forced into a room. Trembling. Eyes shut tight as if a shield to fight off the demon.  A hallway suddenly appears.  Now a voice echoes against the narrowing walls.  The hallway appears endless.  Is this from nightmares that continually awaken him or reality? Jacob is confused.  He opens his eyes, unsure if able to continue.  The therapist reassures him; he is safe and is doing wonderfully.  It's safe to go back.  We're all here together and we're here for you.*

Jacob takes a deep breath.  His mind turns blank as he returns to the scene that continually haunts him.  He again drifts into his past.  *The room turns heavy. A bathroom. His mind confused and spinning, he knows this is not right.  The little boy turns to run out of the bathroom in fear.  The hallway ahead appears narrow and long, transforming into an endless tunnel.  All bodily movement is slowed as if fighting paralysis, he moves in vain to separate from the imposing shadow that is closing behind him.  Tears rolling down his cheeks, he yells out the lone defense available to a helpless child: "I'm going to tell."*

*The breath behind him lands in a terrifying tone.  "If you say or do anything, I will beat you up.  I will destroy you."*

Silence entered the dimly lit room.  Annie took his hand. Jacob instantly made the connection with the voices that he constantly heard whenever triggered with an uncomfortable physical confrontation.  The hockey fights.  The hazing.  Their therapist noted the connection and closed her notebook, joining Annie and Jacob at their seat.

"This has been a long, intense session.  We've made wonderful progress and thank you Jacob for showing such strength and courage.  Let's take a pause to reflect and we can pick up next time."

Continual visits brought back more memories.  Painful fragmented reminders of abuse suffered at the hands of his elder cousin John.  The eight years of separation a lifetime to a little boy just entering childhood between the ages of five and seven years old.  Much clearer in Jacob's mind was the fear.  The frightening image and words of an abuser who controlled and tormented the helpless child.  Jacob came to learn that it was only when his sister Beth suspected something wrong upon arriving home early one morning when she noticed the bathroom door was locked.  She broke in and viewed a most disturbing sight of her older cousin abusing little Jacob. The abuser stood in fear and Jacob was saved from his tormentor. Following much hushed discussion and movement within the household, John was abruptly sent away and any mention of him or the abuse simply erased from any family discussion. The abuse mercifully stopped but the scars remained. Resurfaced with triggers brought on by any incident which raised fear or intense uncertainty.

Each visit to the therapist also brought out further explanations of his actions, many of which had grown destructive. The incessant partying and always going out of his way to please others. Symbolic of the one tool he learned as a child. The art of not upsetting his abuser in the hope of stopping or at least delaying any further suffering. This nature of pleasing others was so strong that it continued to this day and became a part of his very nature.

Jacob now also understood why John had suddenly been removed from their home. The fearful image and memories had long been removed from his thoughts but never from his conscious. Jacob was still suffering from the abuse. Clearly not in the same way as a child. But now in more complex ways which impacted his everyday life and ability to make decisions. He was now able to look at his life and understand his actions in a more open manner, but remained in search of the tools to help him reach the goals that he strived for. Both on and off the ice.

Along with this realization came improvement in his physical health. Jacob now had enough range of motion to get back on the ice and begin conditioning. It felt good to be skating again and burning calories with rigorous individual skating drills that quickly erased the 20 pounds he put on during his hockey hiatus. He was also back to spending more social time with the boys and woke up one morning with a soreness that made it difficult to even get out of bed. The drinking and dancing from a late night got the better of him and set him back for at least a week just as he was about to participate in team drills.

The season was winding down when Jacob finally returned to the lineup on March 4th. The Crunch was languishing with a record of 20-33-7.

They were clearly out of the playoffs and could have easily folded just to get through the season. Jacob felt revitalized and began playing his best hockey, helping to spur the team on to a winning streak. He continued playing the uncomfortable and more aggressive style of play pushed by the coaches but did his best to play physically and enable scoring opportunities for the forwards.

As the team continued winning so did the call-ups. Nick Bonino received a call to report to the Anaheim Ducks on April 7. Two days later Patrick Maroon got the call. Jacob congratulated his hockey brothers who told him that he would be next, but the call never came. The combination of the injury and a playing style that didn't produce the required comfort level or desired results was too much to overcome. It was also not lost on Jacob that the very players he was earlier chastising for not going out after games were now getting call-ups.

The Crunch won 15 of their final 20 games upon Jacob's return, finishing the season with a more respectable record of 35-38-7. Jacob finished the season with the lowest point total of his career, but remained hopeful that the front office and coaches took note of his willingness to change for the team and contribution to their late-season success.

It had been a challenging season that began with such hope. But the injury opened a door to spend more time with Annie. Their couple therapy also brought them closer and at least temporarily awakened Jacob from demons that were holding him back. The sessions had opened doors but he realized that he now had more questions than answers. There remained much work to do. He was committed to the process and a more complete understanding, but for now was ready for a break.

First there were matters to take care of. Although Jacob was hopeful for a permanent return to Anaheim the following season, there were no guarantees. They opted to move out of their lease in Syracuse, place the furniture in storage, and return to California for the summer. Annie's father agreed to fly to Syracuse and drive her back to St. Louis. Jacob would join her there after a stop that had been penciled on his calendar for some time. His former Northeastern teammates invited him back to Boston for their end-of-year party and Jacob looked forward to a reunion with his fellow Huskies.

The Huskies season had followed a similar path to their prior season. They played .500 hockey in the challenging Hockey East conference, and again faced off against Boston College in the final weekend in hopes of reaching the Tournament. This time the Huskies tied on the final game to make the tournament. They then went on to defeat Boston University in their best-of-three series, before losing a close game to eventual champion Boston College to close the season.

Jacob appeared back at the party house, the familiar hockey boot once again the centerpiece of activity. It was good to be back with his old teammates who had all been closely following his season between the NHL and AHL. Filing through the handshakes and embraces, Jacob came upon an unexpected figure who was grinning from ear to ear. Coach Cronin. The two sat down, talking and laughing throughout the evening. Reliving the entire 2009-2010 season. The impressive individual workouts with the intimidating coach making sure he was visible to his players through the glass windows. The emotional victory over Boston College. The ups and downs of the prior season. Finally, Jacob had to ask.

"Coach, you are without a doubt the most knowledgeable coach that I've ever played for. But what the hell were you thinking when you had us go up against those professional boxers for the final week of the season?"

Cronin laughed his gruff laugh and explained that he was just trying to build character and toughness. But also took note.

"That was one hell of a punch you took. I still don't know how you managed to stay on your feet."

Jacob left Boston with nothing but good feelings for his former teammates and Coach Cronin. Sitting in the window seat, he now set his sights on rejoining Annie in St. Louis and looked forward to a surprise he had in store for her. He arranged to meet with a long-time friend when returning to California to purchase a more suitable ring to replace the $300 engagement ring he presented to her last Christmas. There was a wedding to plan for and he was going to make sure that it was special.

Joining Annie in St. Louis, they spent a few days with her parents before easing into the 27-hour drive to Los Angeles. They would take their time and enjoy the ride, make it a vacation. Unfortunately, the air conditioning unit broke down on the way, requiring a stop for repairs. The mini-vacation was cut short.

Back in Anaheim, Jacob moved fast. He met with the friend and purchased a $6,000 ring for Annie. He and Annie then found a wonderful apartment in Newport Beach, where plans were being finalized for a wedding that would open doors to a new life.

The outdoor wedding and reception met all of the couple's expectations, and more. Jacob splurged, covering all expenses to make sure that Annie would have a day to remember. At 22 years of age and with his entire hockey career ahead of him, money was not a factor. The wedding was held at the Newport Beach Marriott Resort & Spa. The newlyweds shared their vows on an open lawn before a backdrop of the Pacific Ocean's sparkling waters, visible to all 75 guests through openings between tall and graceful palm trees.

A beaming Jacob was surrounded by his family and closest friends since childhood as the sun slowly disappeared beyond the Pacific. The San Jacinto street hockey team was reunited with Mikey, Russell, and others from the old neighborhood in attendance. The entire crew that made the memorable road trips to British Columbia, including Mrs. Anderson, which got his hockey career on track was all together. He chose his long-time friend and biggest fan, Spanky, as his best man. Spanky had also been part of the street hockey games and came to visit Jacob at every stop on his hockey journey. During his visits, Spanky earned quite a reputation as a partier who brought much color and enjoyment to Jacob and his hockey teammates. And of course, his hockey brother Garrett Vermeersch came from Boston to join Jacob on his special day.

Perhaps the event's only mishap occurred during the photo shoot, leaving a lasting imprint for posterity on the family's remembrance. On the morning of the wedding, Jacob's father ventured out early for one of his daily bike rides. While on the ride, he got stung by a bee on the side of his face, causing great pain and discomfort. By the time he raced home to dress up for the big day he noticed that the left side of his face was swollen to the size of a golf ball. He tried everything to minimize the swelling and cover the redness, but nothing worked. In fact, by the time he got to the wedding, the swelling had actually grown and even dropped to where it was now drooping down to his chin.

Jacob and the others could only laugh once they got over the shock of seeing his dad's disfiguration and learning how it occurred. Jeffrey Newton had to be talked into posing for the family photos, and did his best to hide the side of his face that was in such discomfort.

Jacob smiled at Annie before turning his gaze to the Pacific Ocean. The family was together and the possibilities were endless.

# Chapter Nine

# A Downward Spiral

2011 - 2012 season

## Team 1: Syracuse Crunch, Syracuse, New York

Jacob knew the cut was coming well before the official announcements were even made.  Gone was the comfort level he felt from the prior season while training and participating in virtually all of the Ducks' off-season and even end-of-season activities.  It was nothing specific or any words that were spoken, but the overall feeling generated from coaches and front office personnel.  Further, Wade Arnott was not returning his phone calls.  The agent who was so visible 18 months ago when interest was shown from competing NHL teams was now nowhere to be found.  Because the time spent with the Ducks at the end of the 2009-2010 season counted as one full year towards the contract, Jacob was now on the last year of his three-year deal with Anaheim.  He needed direction and answers.  While Jacob fell deeper into the background, the Ducks were actively promoting several veteran newcomers and their most recent draft class, including number one pick, Rickard Rakell.  They had high hopes for the young offense-minded Swede.

As in the prior season, Jacob did get into one preseason game and performed well.  In their opening game at home against the Phoenix Coyotes before a crowd of 12,544, Jacob tallied an assist on a power play goal midway through the third period to pull the Ducks to within one goal. His performance brought a ray of hope that perhaps there was a chance. But that was his last game as a Duck.

Beyond the uncertain feeling, there was a factor much more direct that let Jacob and a number of his teammates know that the cuts were coming. They had already been told to drive their cars and personal belongings to Syracuse before flying back to Anaheim for the start of training camp. Over two days of straight driving with stops only for eating, breaks to fill up the tank, and short naps. When Jacob shared this with Duck's veteran Teemu Selanne, the veteran nicknamed "the Finnish Flash" couldn't believe the audacity of asking the young hopefuls to put their bodies through such strain before the start of a rigorous training camp.

"Newts, I'm entering my nineteenth year in the league and I thought I'd seen everything but never this. One day you're going to write a book about your career and share this bullshit."

Along with news of the final cut came devastating news to the Ducks organization, as well as the entire world of hockey. On September 7, a Russian flight carrying players and coaching staff of the Lokomotiv Yaroslavl professional ice hockey team crashed during take-off near Yaroslavl Oblast, Russia. All but one of the 45 people on board were killed. Included among the dead was former Duck, Ruslan Salei, who was a regular participant with Jacob during their informal offseason conditioning workouts in California. Jacob had fond memories of his workout buddy from Belarus, and in fact everyone who had come in contact with him had nothing but kind words to say. As difficult as the drive was back to Syracuse, it was made even longer upon hearing of the tragic news during the drive.

The certainty of being sent down did afford Annie time to prepare for the upcoming season back in Syracuse. She arranged to get the stored furniture moved into a new apartment and began decorating in preparation for a new season. Most of the Crunch players from the prior season were coming back and she enjoyed the friendships forged with the tight-knit community of hockey families. They all had much in common, and spending so much time together eased some of the challenges and uncertainty that they all faced, along with the sadness in learning of Ruslan's death.

After the cuts were finalized, Jacob joined Annie back in Syracuse with the reality of opening the season in the AHL. Despite the cut, he tried to remain positive. His base salary for the final season of his three-year deal was $67,500 for the Crunch, but he was determined to prove himself and get called up to the Ducks with their $925,000 annual salary on the table. And that was just the start. Once proven, salaries for established NHL players grow exponentially.

The Anaheim Ducks opened their 2011-2112 season overseas with games in Finland and Sweden. This pushed the Crunch schedule back and they had the weekend off while the AHL season got underway. With the War Memorial Arena available, the organization brought in Darius Rucker to perform on a Saturday night. The city was abuzz and the Crunch players were treated to front row seats and a backstage pass to meet up with the country legend made famous with his band, Hootie and the Blowfish.

Jacob and Annie arrived early at the Arena and it was good to be back with the guys without the stress of preparing for a game or performing to survive cuts. Everyone was in good spirits as they mingled with the eclectic combination of professional athletes and musicians. They were indeed all entertainers and the entire entourage seemed to be enjoying themselves and having fun. The drinks were going down easily and the hors d'oeuvres were delicious.

By the time that Jacob and Annie settled in their VIP seats along with the other Crunch players and their guests, Jacob was feeling no pain. It had been a long and stressful preseason and he was ready to let loose and enjoy the evening. The music blended perfectly with the mood. The crowd was on their feet almost from the start, and when Rucker performed the popular "Only Want to Be With You", Jacob looked at Annie and mouthed the words. They both laughed while the entire Crunch section sang along with Rucker.

As the song wound down, Jacob could sense from the vibrations that he had been getting a number of rapid calls on his mobile phone. Someone was really trying to get in touch with him. Against his better judgement, he took the phone out to view who was calling. It was David McNabb, the Ducks Senior VP of Hockey Operations and the person who signed Jacob to his NHL contract. He tried to forget about the call, recognizing that it would be impossible to talk under these conditions and besides that, he was in no condition to talk with the high-ranking executive. But the calls continued and finally a text. McNabb asked Jacob to call him ASAP.

Jacob figured it could only be one of two things. An injury on the team requiring his immediate call-up or a trade. He hoped for the best but feared the worst. One thing was certain. He had to call McNabb. Jacob sobered quicky and his mood changed entirely as he told Annie he needed to step out to make a phone call. Annie's concern now matched Jacob's and nearby teammates looked on quizzically as he rushed out to exit the loud Arena.

Searching for a dead zone in the concourse, Jacob tried his best to straighten up as he pressed the numbers. His heart was pounding.

Between his anxiety, alcohol-induced state, and the rumble of noise audible in the distance, Jacob could only filter in a few words from their conversation. They were impactful. He was traded to the Colorado Avalanche. The GM of the Avalanche would be calling him any minute, and the Ducks wished him luck. Jacob closed the call and leaned against a concrete beam in his dark corner of the concourse. He was numb. How would Annie take this? The couple had just settled into their new apartment and were trying to move on from not only the cut, but also devastating news that Annie had suffered a miscarriage. Their original excitement upon learning of Annie's pregnancy paled in comparison to the dejection they felt with the loss that followed. They were just now getting back on track and feeling hopeful with the upcoming season in Syracuse. Jacob's phone beeped with a buzz. A phone call was coming from the 303.

Again, recollection of the conversation was hazy and brief. Jacob couldn't help but feel that he didn't make the best first impression in his introduction to the Avalanche. They were happy to have him. He would be reporting to the team's AHL affiliate in Cleveland. They would arrange for all travel. Welcome to the Avalanche organization.

By the time Jacob returned to his seat the concert was winding down. He shared the news with Annie and she immediately broke into tears. Word spread quicky across the VIP seating and his teammates all voiced their displeasure. The evening that began with such joy and anticipation had turned somber. Jacob tried to think positively. Even though he always hated the Avalanche growing up due to their rivalry with the Red Wings, they must have seen something to at least want him in their organization. And his brothers, both fans of the team, would be thrilled. He took Annie's hand in an attempt to comfort her and tried to look hopeful. But it was no use. His eyes could not mask the disappointment and concern for added challenges that the newlyweds were about to face.

## Team 2:  Lake Erie Monsters, Cleveland, Ohio

There was little time to adjust to the new surroundings. Jacob flew into Cleveland where the Monsters had already begun their season. The team arranged for him to stay at a nearby hotel in Berea, affording some time to acclimate and find suitable living arrangements while Annie stayed back to settle things with their Syracuse apartment before joining him.

The Monsters played their home games in a downtown Arena known at the time as Quicken Loans Arena, shared with the National Basketball Association's (NBA) Cleveland Cavaliers. Across from the Arena and downstream from the winding Cuyahoga River stood an apartment complex in a mixed use industrial and entertainment district known as the Flats. From the many establishment patios, the end of boating season's few pleasure boats could be seen navigating around massive ocean freighters along the mouth of the river's entrance into Lake Erie. Jacob chose the area to rent with the hope that Annie would find its proximity to the Arena and restaurants both exciting and comfortable to begin a new life.

With little time to practice or get to know his new teammates, Jacob made a brief appearance for his Monster debut on October 14 before the team embarked on a five-game road trip. Following a loss at Toronto, the team travelled to Syracuse for two games where Annie eagerly awaited him.

Jacob experienced mixed feelings upon his return to the ice at the familiar War Memorial Arena. From the moment he entered the Arena, he received friendly recognition from workers prepping the ice and stands for the Friday evening game. During pregame warmups, former teammates skated up to warmly embrace and ask how things were going with his new team. Once the game began, the focus changed. Jacob wasn't sure if his energy was fueled more to help the Monsters secure their first win of the season or to prove to the Anaheim organization that they made a mistake in trading him.

The game started with a bang. Jacob had barely settled into his seat on the bench searching for Annie in the stands when he watched the familiar tandem of a Nick Bonino goal assisted by Patrick Maroon just 21 seconds into the game. His instinctive reaction was almost to celebrate for his teammates before regaining his mindset to now help in stopping that duo from scoring.

Jacob's time on the ice came and he quickly helped turn the game to the Monsters' favor. Skating with his customary intensity in the comfortable surroundings of the War Memorial Arena, he helped to stifle a number of Crunch attacks while creating scoring opportunities for the team's forwards. Early in the third period, his assist put the Monsters out in front of the highly contested game, 3-2.

It didn't last. The Crunch scored late in the third period to send the game into overtime, before scoring early in overtime to send the Monsters to their sixth consecutive defeat to open the season. The following night the Monsters returned the favor, securing a 3-2 overtime win to finally get into the win column. His teammates celebrated and the coaches congratulated Jacob for his leadership and play in helping to secure the tough road win.

Jacob didn't have much time to spend with Annie or his former teammates while in Syracuse. Following the Saturday evening affair, the team was headed back to Toronto where they were scheduled to play their third game in three nights. He only had a few minutes to say his goodbyes outside the locker room as team officials rushed the equipment managers and players to embark on the idling bus out back. They were hustling to make the late-night flight back to Canada. Jacob gave Annie a final hug, telling her that she would enjoy the apartment in Cleveland and thanked her for all her work and patience throughout another hasty transition. He knew it wasn't easy for her and noted how alone she appeared when he stared out the grainy window to watch her disappear from view as the bus departed the Arena.

The following night in Toronto saw the Monsters secure their second consecutive overtime win, but it came at a cost. Jacob hurt his shoulder and had to leave the game. Just as he began growing comfortable with his new team he would be sidelined for a period to allow the shoulder to heal.

Annie finally joined hm the following week and sat with Jacob in the stands to watch the visiting Syracuse Crunch crush the Monsters by a 7-0 score. It was hard to ignore the celebrating going on among their established friends as the Monsters put on a disappointing show for the home fans.

By the time that Jacob was able to return to the ice, he found his playing time spotty and his play uneven. Unable to stay on the ice for regular shifts, he was unable to establish an identity with his new teammates and find his groove on the ice. Plus, the shoulder never healed completely and it seemed that nagging injuries kept creeping in. He did manage to find some success, but they were few and far between. One player he found chemistry with was the team's wing player, Greg Mauldin. On a cold night in Milwaukee, Jacob scored the game winning goal in overtime on a perfect assist from Mauldin to seal the victory. Jacob had no way of knowing that the friendship forged with Mauldin would have a profound impact on his life and career later on down the road.

Fortunately for Annie, she was hired at Lululemon in an upscale neighborhood on the east side of Cleveland. The time away not only provided some extra income but also enabled Annie to make friends and escape from the constant hockey grind.

Due to the irregular playing time, it came as no surprise when Jacob was informed that he was being sent down to the Avalanche's Central Hockey League affiliate in Allen, Texas. The team tried to put a positive spin on the demotion, stating that increased playing time would enable him to get past the nagging injuries and get his game and confidence back on track. But the timing of the demotion did Jacob no favors. He was sent down on the day of the trade deadline. Had his agent known the demotion was coming, they could have requested a trade with the knowledge that several AHL teams had expressed an interest in his services. Given what he had experienced to date, Jacob was not convinced that his fit with the Colorado organization was in his best interest. But the demotion forced his hand. He had no choice but to go down and do his best to get back to the AHL, and ultimately the NHL. Expecting the time in Allen to be short, they agreed for Annie to stay back in Cleveland while Jacob would room with other players who were being called back and forth between the two teams. Jacob packed his bags and hockey gear for the third time since driving the car from Anaheim to Syracuse before the start of training camp.

## Team 3: Allen Americans, Allen, Texas

In a season marred by waves of disappointment, Jacob's arrival in Allen created a sense of reprieve almost like returning home. The thriving Dallas suburb is a mere 20-minute drive east of Frisco, where Jacob enjoyed success skating for the Texas Tornado. Among the many familiar landmarks was the visibility of loyal fans who closely followed their home team. The Dallas Cowboys may be viewed by some as America's team in football, but the hockey Americans were not to be shared and the fans made their feelings known. The players, in turn, were treated as celebrities.

At just 24 years old, Jacob still stood out as among the younger players in the league but quickly established himself as a leader on a team battling the Wichita Thunder for first place in the Central Hockey League's Barry

Division. Jacob found the spirited and competitive play in the cozy confines of the 4,400-seat Allen Event Center free of stress and soon regained his joy in freely playing the game he'd always loved. He embraced his role as the leader of the defense and his spirited mood soon expanded to increased activities off the ice. Since his marriage and therapy sessions where he learned the cost in always pleasing others, Jacob had temporarily cooled the wildness often displayed in his early years. But he retained his outgoing and friendly persona and his teammates easily convinced him to join in the social activities following and between games. He was drifting back into some bad habits. Along with the joy of playing hockey, the drinking, smoking, and partying slowly began to emerge. The same vices that gripped Jacob before his marriage crept back into his life, but he convinced himself that everything was under control and all was fine.

Jacob also tried his best to convince Annie, who remained in Cleveland, that the demotion was going to ultimately work out. He was regaining confidence and performing well. The team was winning games and it was just a matter of time before Colorado officials would take note and call him back up to Cleveland. Despite the confidence he tried to project, it was clear that Annie's patience was only going to last so long. While Annie's siblings were moving ahead in their more traditional lifestyles, her own life was filled with uncertainty. Jacob suspected that her growing frustration was fueled in part by her parents' continual acknowledgement of her siblings' success while covertly dismissing her husband's career choices. And Jacob getting sent down for the second time within months was not helping matters.

The Americans went on the road for back-to-back games at Dayton and Fort Wayne. The team was feeling upbeat with two wins and Jacob enjoyed beers and laughs with teammates on the back of the bus. Feeling a buzz and settling back to his seat, an itching temptation that had been haunting him finally overtook him. He pulled out his phone and went to contacts, searching for the name Meredith. A young lady from Frisco with whom Jacob spent some time while playing for the Tornado five years earlier. Was it possible that she was still in Frisco? Would it do any harm to meet up over a beer and share some laughs over old times?  To have a fun conversation void of arguments or a continual need to explain his career path?  He wrote and rewrote a text message on the phone, hesitant to send.  Following a brief greeting, he settled on: "... we have a home game coming up.  Would be great to see you if you're still in the area."  Hovering his hand over the phone for a period of time, he took a deep breath and hit the send button, closing his eyes in wonder if a reply would come.

Three nights later, the Americans hosted the Texas Brahmas.  Jacob looked up in the stands during warmups and waved to a beaming Meredith, sitting in the seat he had designated for her.  They hadn't seen one another in years and both looked forward to the postgame reunion.

The game was a hard-fought affair, typical of matchups with their crosstown rival located between Dallas and Fort Worth.  Reverting back to his proven disciplined approach, Jacob made continual stops as both teams found it difficult to score.  The scoring drought continued into overtime, before the Brahmas finally escaped with a 2-1 shootout win.

The locker room was mostly somber as Jacob dressed to go out for the evening.  Several teammates stopped by to gauge his interest in meeting up for a few beers after the hard-fought game.

"Not tonight, guys.  I have other plans."

Jacob stood at his locker and buttoned up his shirt.  There was a reflective pause before he slowly removed his wedding ring and dropped it into his pocket.  Closing his locker door, he slipped out of the room to venture into the evening.

** ** **

Jacob's fine play continued and he began hearing rumblings that he could be called back up to Cleveland at any time.  The American's schedule allowed for a weekend at home which enabled Annie to make the trip from Cleveland and finally spend some time with Jacob in Allen.  The two had much to catch up on and Jacob looked forward to having Annie with him for an entire weekend.

Once again, during warmups, Jacob looked up to see a smiling Annie wave to him from her designated seat in the stands. Skating toward the bench, he was totally unaware that another fan was paying him a surprise visit at the same game.

From her reserved seat, Meredith viewed the events unfolding before her with alarm. Who was the attractive young lady waving to Jacob in the same seat that she occupied just a week ago? Shaking, she took out her phone to do some investigation. Although they were not friends on Facebook, the two had many common friends from Jacob's time skating with the local Tornado, and she soon found photos of Jacob and the seated woman posing together. The happy couple at their wedding. Vacation photos. Posing together with former teammates. Meredith couldn't believe what she was seeing. From their time together following the Texas game, he gave no indication of being married. It was the same old free-spirited Jacob. After spending the night together, she was led to believe that perhaps there was something special between the two. Maybe he was approaching a point in his career where he was looking to settle down like so many of the other players who had come and gone over the years. Wishing to surprise him following the game, she even arranged to take Jacob to Frisco and meet up with some of the old gang who were looking forward to welcoming him at a local tavern. Now she sat in the stands humiliated and angry, watching the unknowing wife cheer on her husband.

The first period was winding down when Meredith decided there was only one thing to do. She got up from her seat and walked down the aisles and toward the section where Annie was seated. Upon reaching Annie's row, she got her attention and asked the startled woman if she was the wife of Jake Newton. Annie nodded. Meredith simply told her there was something important that she wished to discuss with her. As fans departed their seats to take an intermission break between periods, a concerned Annie followed the determined woman to learn what she feared was unwelcome news.

Jacob sensed that something was wrong as soon as he skated back onto the ice following intermission and noticed that Annie's seat was vacant.

He tried to get his head into the game as the second period got underway but his play was clearly distracted. Every time skating off the ice to finish his shift, he glanced up at her seat in the stands in the hope that she would be there. But the seat remained empty.

When the team returned to their locker room between the 2$^{nd}$ and final period, Jacob dared not look at the phone in his own locker. Something was clearly amiss and as tempting as it was to peek at his phone, he couldn't allow any more distraction than what he was already experiencing. Throughout the final period, he continually looked up at her seat in the hope that some miracle would bring her back, but it was in vain. The final twenty minutes dragged to the point that it seemed the clock would never wind down. The outcome of the game became secondary to an explanation of what had caused Annie's disappearance. As the final horn sounded, Jacob rushed off the ice. He could wait no longer.

As expected, his phone had exploded with missed calls and text messages. Not only from Annie, but calls and texts from his mother, sisters, and brothers. Everyone was trying to get in touch with him and Jacob had no doubt as to the reason why. Scrolling past the first of many angry rant-filled texts, his worst fear was realized. Annie had learned of his affair with Meredith. Fully clothed in his hockey gear, he put the phone away and dropped to the bench, covering his dejected face with both hands. He had made a huge mistake and there were no good answers for the many questions that were to come his way.

When Jacob finally reached Annie following a number of attempts and well after departing the Arena, she kept the conversation short. She had the car and was staying at a hotel for the night before flying to Cleveland the next morning. She was angry, upset, and humiliated. There was much to think about and Jacob had some serious explaining to do and actions to prove if there was any chance of their getting back together. And for the moment, she was not even sure if that was a possibility. Jacob simply listened and couldn't say much. Saying that he was sorry was not nearly enough. He had made a terrible mistake and wished he could take it all back but never wanted to hurt Annie or cause such pain. He tried to reason with her to stay with him for the night but her mind was made up.  Annie had no wish to see him and was determined to fly back the following morning.  She would tell him where the car was parked only when dropping it off at the airport.

Jacob's short time with the Allen Americans did not end on the high note that he had hoped.  His play and attitude were nowhere near the level they were up until Annie's visit, but he went through the motions and played out the season, hoping that he could work things out with Annie who had now returned to St. Louis where she was living with her parents.

When the season came to a merciful end, there were a number of challenges facing Jacob and Annie, not all of which were painfully obvious.

One, he was on the final year of his three-year deal and was now a free agent.  Based upon his limited playing time and uneven experience with the Avalanche organization, there was no guarantee that the Avalanche would bring him back.

Two, there were strong rumors of an upcoming labor dispute between the NHL and the NHL Players Association.  With the League's Collective Bargaining Agreement expiring at the close of the current season, the two sides appeared far apart and there was no guarantee that an agreement could be reached in time for the start of the new season.  This made his pending free agency extremely untimely.  Players without contracts were unable to talk or negotiate with any team.

Three, and most significant, Annie had suffered her third miscarriage.  The couple desperately wished for the miracle of birth.  Their remained obvious tension from the affair but both resolved to try and work things out.  The one thing that kept them together was the shared wish to raise a family.  But once again, they were forced to deal with a tragic loss.  As the challenges around them mounted, they collectively wondered if childbirth was simply not in their future.

And finally, even if they could make their marriage work, they now had no place to live. Jacob had no idea where he'd be playing next season.  And with no paychecks coming in for the foreseeable future, their funds were running short.  The options were limited.

After once again required to move their furniture into storage, Annie offered a solution. It didn't sit well with Jacob, but they had little choice. There was room for them to move into her parents' basement in St. Louis. Jacob, who had vowed to show her family that his hockey career would pay off handsomely and make them all proud, swallowed his pride to live rent-free for the summer in their basement. To make matters worse, they were all well aware of his affair in Texas. Jacob drove to St. Louis with the realization that it was going to be a long summer. He remained determined to achieve his dreams and find a way to make it back to the NHL doing the one thing that he truly loved. But convincing Annie grew more and more challenging. Her family, he was convinced, had already given up hope.

The reserved welcome and uncomfortable living conditions in St. Louis were everything that Jacob feared. The only time he felt free was away from the house where he could skate and get a good workout at the local rink. Their time spent in the basement was like walking on eggshells. In an attempt to get their lives back on track, the two decided to again seek support and work with professional therapists who had helped them in the past. Annie met with a local therapist in St. Louis, while Jacob went back to their couple's therapist in Syracuse. Once a week, he had a Skype session with Theresa, the lady who had helped him unlock the demon of his past. More memories of the abuse surfaced as Jacob came to the realization that he was spiraling on a path of continued destruction. He searched for answers to help get his life and marriage back on track.

Jacob also took the time to find a new agent to help him maneuver the changing hockey landscape around him. A number of opportunities were lost in the past year and it was clear that he could not count on Wade to represent him any longer. His former agent was never available when needed and was clearly more interested in seeking out or working with his big-name clients.

His friend Patrick Maroon recommended his agent, Alain Roi. The former goalie was a silver medalist on the 1994 Canadian hockey squad and Jacob found him to be personable and sincere in his stated effort to help Jacob find a suitable team to get his career back on track.

The couple sat in the lifeless basement with no way of knowing what lay ahead, but agreed to see what Roi could work out in his quest to help Jacob pursue his dreams of continuing his hockey career. Jacob had no way of knowing that he had yet to hit rock bottom. But the remaining challenges about to be faced would not appear without opportunities. And Jacob was growing increasingly prepared to accept those challenges in search of the light which remained hidden beyond the horizon.

# Chapter Ten

# Hockey in the Alps

2012 – 2013 season

## HC Eppan Pirates, Appiano Sullo Strada Del Vino, Italy

The village of Eppan, also known as Appiano Sulla Strada Del Vino, appears as a treasured postcard. Colorful stucco structures grace narrow streets and spacious plazas populated with charming cafes and ornate fountains. Beyond its walls and church towers lie the Italian Alps. Home to ancient castles, scenic lakes, and unspoiled forests. The entire region enjoys a moderate climate across a picturesque setting making it ideal for winemaking. Well-marked hiking trails are accessible all along narrow roadsides. This is the unlikely setting where Jacob and Annie found themselves for the 2012-2013 hockey season.

For the hockey guy from the San Jacinto desert who had only experienced the sport on the North American continent, it was quite a culture shock. Jacob's first sense of being far from home occurred at the busy Frankfurt airport where they hustled to catch their final flight after a full day of travel. Glancing up at the departures screen, names of foreign cities flashed on and off next to code letters which meant nothing to Jacob. Crowds milling about them spoke German or other languages which all sounded strange and foreign. He was unsure where to turn or how to even ask for help. Exactly what had they gotten themselves into?

Back home, the hockey world had stopped. NHL owners were not pleased with the expiring contract which saw players' annual salaries increase to an average of over $3 million with their revenue sharing agreement. Further, a number of teams were losing money in an environment where more established teams had an unfair advantage over the smaller market teams. The players union, which fought so hard to establish benefits for their players, was not about to cave in so easily to the owners. Both sides dug in and it appeared that a long and arduous battle was about to take place. The owners locked their doors on September 15 and fans worried that the entire season would be lost, as had occurred during the epic lockout of 2004-2005.

For the more established players and those under contract to report to a team once the existing labor negotiations were resolved, there was no immediate urgency to find a place to play. For Jacob, who was not under contract and unable to negotiate during the lockout, the situation was dire. His new agent Alain Roi had an idea. He worked the phones in a desperate attempt to find a European team which may have an opening with the season on the verge of starting. Teams in the more established leagues throughout the continent already had their rosters set. But there was a team in a small town of Northern Italy which was thrilled to bring in the young American with AHL experience. Jacob signed a contract and became a proud member of the HC Eppan Pirates.

The Pirates competed in the eight-team Coppa di Leaga of Italy's A2 division. All eight teams were located in the majestic setting of the Alps, separated by narrow roads winding around rugged mountains which added hours for the team bus to maneuver. Jacob often looked out of the window in wonder at how their driver, grinding gears continually, was able to escape from the steep drops hugging the road's narrow edge. He gradually grew more comfortable and confident that their skilled driver would get them safely to their destination.

Games were played in older arenas of small towns with just a smattering of fans. For home games, the Eisstadion Eppan Arena rarely filled the 500 seats, but the fans who did arrive were extremely vocal and passionate. And they quickly gravitated to the team's new star. Jacob became a fan favorite. The American from California was racking up the points and his spirited play was placing the team at the top of the league's standings.

Life and hockey in the Italian A2 division was a far cry from anything that Jacob had experienced before, but there were some unexpected perks that came along with the low salary and stress-free environment. The twenty thousand euros salary could be stretched much farther with the team picking up the rent for their furnished apartment, loaning a car, and paying for insurance and other small benefits. And of course, the setting was spectacular. Although focused on hockey, the couple did manage to spend some time away with old friends.

Living nearby during the lockout period were two former teammates with Anaheim and Syracuse. Nick Bonino joined Jacob in the A2 division skating for HC Neumarkt-Egna, and MacGregor Sharp found a home in the Italian A league skating for Bolzano HC. On a splendid autumn afternoon, Jacob and Annie joined their friends at one of the many famous wineries popular in the region. Nick made his grand entrance approaching from around a hillside with dust trailing his shiny Porsche, and the three couples enjoyed the afternoon drinking the vineyard's wine with a colorful assortment of grapes, cheese, homemade bread, olives, and pepperoni. Sharing experiences in Italy and reliving their time together in the States, the hockey couples felt far removed from the ongoing lockout back home.

Life in the small town of 14,000 inhabitants surrounded by mountains and lakes was slow and simple, but Jacob often found himself wondering just how he could have fallen so far from the precipice of making the final Anaheim Ducks roster just over two years removed. The joy of hockey had certainly returned, but he was sure that there were no NHL scouts anywhere remotely close to see first-hand how he was performing in a league made up of obscure players in this remote area of Italy.

When not practicing or playing hockey, he stayed at home most of the time to avoid the uneasiness of venturing out into unfamiliar territory. The town was so far hidden in the northern Alps and near the Austrian border that most of the residents spoke German in lieu of Italian. Even shopping at the local market brought out anxiety in Jacob. Although English was largely spoken by his Finnish coach and generally understood by the vast majority of players on the team, venturing out into public was much more daunting.

In his first visit to the market, Jacob stood in line and watched others in front of him check out while speaking a foreign language and exchanging in currency that he had yet to master. By the time he reached the cashier he was a nervous wreck. When they added up the total and asked for payment, Jacob just stared and motioned to write the total down on paper. The cashier looked confused and Jacob sensed that others in the long line were growing impatient with his inability to complete such a simple task. Finally, he just threw up his hands and dug in his pocket, then held out wads of bills and coins for the cashier to count and take. Thankfully, he didn't understand the litany of comments accompanied with chuckles that rang out behind him, but he made a point to collect his bags and rush out as quickly as possible. He had no idea what he ended up paying, but he was thankful just to get out of the store and back to the familiarity of home.

Life in the apartment was pretty much resigned to basic meals and watching familiar shows on Hulu or Netflix to retain some connection with life as Americans. The binge-watching may have brought some comfort and relief from the homesickness they felt, but Jacob and Annie were missing out on the rich local culture all around them. Then they met Dave.

Dave was a friendly middle-aged Canadian who had found his niche in this hidden corner of the Alps, and he had no intention of leaving. He headed a Junior program for the Pirates, introducing young skaters to the sport of hockey, and quickly made friends with the young American who had Canadian ties. Spotting Jacob rushing out the door after practice one day, Dave stopped him to join him at a nearby café. Sensing Jacob's hesitancy, Dave spoke up.

"You have no idea what you're missing. Come on, let's sit outside and enjoy the day."

The two spent the next few hours at a nearby café joined by a mix of locals and lazily watched the day wind down. Shoppers carrying wine and long loaves of bread purchased at the local markets. Young mothers pushing strollers. Couples young and old walking hand-in-hand to the deep chime of bells ringing from old church towers. Laughter heard all around them with expressive hand gestures from locals enjoying coffee or wine with tasty platters of food. Jacob noticed that outside of the one TV near the kitchen entrance, not one television set adorned the walls. There were no sports events or news flashes from TV screens to distract the patrons. Seldom was anyone idly looking down to read or scroll their cell phone. As the arriving winter sun gently faded beyond distant snow-capped peaks, Jacob made a decision as he got up to leave with his Canadian friend. The binge-watching was over. This was so much better for the soul than anything that the TV had to offer. Dave just introduced him to a love of local cultures that would remain with him for the remainder of his career and beyond.

With his newfound spirit for adventure, Jacob convinced Annie to partake in the Krampus festival taking place in nearby Neumarkt. Unaware of the origins of the festival, the two were in for quite a surprise. A Krampus is a frightening half-goat, half-demon figure, whose purpose is to punish naughty children before the feast of Saint Nicholas, complementing St. Nick's practice of rewarding good children with gifts. The Krampus tradition takes its roots in pre-Christian, pagan winter solstice celebrations. Over the years, the controversial festival has become quite popular along the Austrian and German Alpine regions, and its participants take great delight in striking fear among the visitors who venture out to witness the spectacle.

Walking along the historical arcades in the picturesque village, there was a demonic presence all around them. Scores of tourists and wide-eyed children looked on in fascination as creatures mingled about, ready to pounce on unsuspecting onlookers. Just when it appeared that they were about to clear the area unscathed, a demon appeared directly in front of Annie as she momentarily turned away from Jacob. A hairy black creature with a cloven hoof and the horns of a goat stood directly in her path.

He opened his mouth to reveal a long-pointed tongue dart out between threatening fangs.

Annie let out with scream unlike anything that Jacob had ever heard before. She clutched onto him in genuine fear as the creature continued his pursuit, as if seizing the opportunity to overtake his prey. Jacob was uncertain how to react, caught between witnessing the alarming spectacle and a need to protect his wife who appeared in genuine fear for her life. He tried his best to return a glare that minimized any further interaction while not overreacting to a scene intended to entertain the crowd. They gradually managed to separate from the demon who seemed just as intent to achieve his goal of exacting fear.

Returning to the safety of Eppan, Annie took comfort in befriending the wife of Jacob's Finnish coach and she also began to appreciate the local culture. On the ice, Jacob continued his fine play and was recording hat tricks, the first of his professional career. Home crowds gradually began to increase and the team grew hopeful for a championship in the Italian A2 division.

Shortly after the new year, the NHL and Players Association finally came to an agreement. Owners agreed to end the lockout on January 6, 2013, and an agreement was ratified on January 9. Players returned to their teams for play to resume on January 19. The revised season began over three months late with a shortened schedule from 82 to 48 games.

Nick informed Jacob that he would be reporting to Anaheim, where he made the final Ducks roster and would go on to enjoy a lengthy NHL career. MacGregor chose to stay in Italy and close the season with Bolzano in the top-level Italian league. Jacob chose to remain in Italy and finish what he started. He felt it was too risky to displace Annie yet again and report to a team without any guarantees. He would bring a championship to the Pirates and use the offseason to determine his next move.

With the season winding down, Jacob and Annie once again received the news. Annie was pregnant. However, they noted some differences with her condition compared to that from prior pregnancies. She found herself in good spirits and feeling fine. Maybe it was the mountain air, the fresh market food, or simply the lack of stress so often felt back home. But the couple remained cautiously optimistic that this time the miracle would occur.

The mood carried over to the ice where Jacob was enjoying the most productive season of his career. Of course, the level of talent was not the same as that back home. But he enthusiastically embraced the added responsibilities given to him. He became a prolific scorer, so unusual for a defenseman, and led the Pirates to the Finals in their playoff drive to win a championship. The team prepared to face off against the Vipiteno Broncos in their best-of-seven series.

In a series dominated by defense and close games, the Pirates won game 5 by a score of 1-0 to win the title. They were the A2 division champs, and would move up for the next season to Division 1. Immediately after the game on the Broncos' home ice, Jacob was presented with an impressive trophy at center ice for being recognized as the League's Most Valuable Player. The team returned home the following morning and Jacob fully expected a warm welcome from their passionate fan base back home. He did not expect the reception awaiting them as the bus pulled into the main plaza.

The entire population of Eppan appeared before them. People wildly waving and cheering in celebration as if they had just won an Olympic gold medal for the country. Jacob was surrounded by the mob as he got off the bus, hoisting the trophy high for all to see. For three days, the party continued nonstop. Colorful banners filled the area and horns blared to the evening sounds and display of fireworks. Jacob was offered food and drinks throughout the celebration and told to keep his euros to himself. Everything was paid for by the appreciative townspeople.

It may not have been a Stanley Cup, but the region's fans and locals celebrated every bit as much as fans of the most prized trophy in all of hockey, if not more. Jacob enjoyed celebrating and observing the happiness brought to the entire region, especially for those fans who remained loyal to the team throughout the season. Many of them showed up for every game from day one, including the treacherous trips to watch games on the road.

The reward and satisfaction of winning a championship in this remote area of the Alps meant so much to the proud locals, and Jacob's satisfaction was even greater in knowing that he helped to bring so much joy to them.

Adding to their own personal joy, Annie was having no complications with the pregnancy. As life slowly returned back to its normal pace in Appiano Sulla Strada Del Vino, the couple prepared for the long flights back to the States. Annie appeared fit and ready to go. The only dilemma facing them now was, where would they go?

Jacob was certain that he did not wish to go back to St. Louis. Although appreciative of Annie's family for taking them in, the memories from the past summer were not good ones. Moving back to California for the summer was appealing to both with Jacob's family and a number of close friends in the area, but rents in the Los Angeles area were sky high and their financial situation was hindering their options. Making matters more complicated was that Jacob was without a team. The majority of North American players stayed home during the lockout. And although their pay was hindered with no team to skate for to start the season, they eventually joined a team and established a place on the roster once the lockout ended. Because Jacob remained in Italy throughout the season, he was starting from ground zero. He had to find a team during the offseason.

Just when it appeared that they would be forced to dig into their savings to coordinate yet another move, an opportunity arose. And from a most unexpected source. Through a casual conversation with his old friend Russell, an idea came to light. Russell's mother learned of their dilemma and offered to take Jacob and Annie in for the summer. Mrs. Anderson. The same woman who drove Jacob and the group of eight on the road trip to British Columbia to kick-start his dreams for a hockey career once again stepped up. They had plenty of room at their home in Riverside and she would be delighted to host Jacob and Annie while he searched for the next leg of his hockey journey.

Jacob was coming back home. The year away in the Italian Alps, far removed as it was, brought a much-needed sense of peace and tranquility back to Jacob from both a personal and hockey perspective. They would be getting back into the grind and fast pace of Southern California but accepted the challenge. Mrs. Anderson assured Jacob over the phone that he and Annie would be welcome to stay for as long as they needed and assured him that everything was going to turn out just fine. Jacob hung up the phone with warm recollection of Mrs. Anderson driving the boys on the most memorable road trips. He looked over at Annie who sat next to him listening in on the conversation, and placed a hand over her slightly protruding belly.

"We're going to California. Not sure where we'll end up, but we're going home."

# Chapter Eleven

# Smurf

2013 - 2014 season

## Team 1: Ontario Reign, Ontario, California

The scrappy-looking coach tossed the contract on his desk with a smug expression. He assured Jacob that playing for him would enhance his play and open doors to the NHL. In reality, the coach spent more time promoting his own hockey exploits while proudly pointing to framed pictures from his playing days that covered the decorated office. Jacob silently observed not one NHL jersey among the many on display in team and action photos. Coach's colorful and detailed descriptions would have one believe that he was the most feared and successful skater on the ice. As if that would somehow translate into magically rubbing off on his players to become the same. Jacob feigned interest, but had his doubts that the short goateed man in front of him was the intimidating presence that he boasted. He spoke with confidence in a gruff voice as if to prove his point, but was on the pudgy side and Jacob couldn't really picture him striking fear into other skaters.

The idea of skating for the Ontario Reign actually had a number of advantages. The contract that Roi had worked out and now appeared before Jacob was for only $650 per week, but it did include an apartment and was affiliated with the NHL Los Angeles Kings. A far cry from the pay received during his first three years and on par with money received in the A2 Italian league when including all their perks. But it was close to home and there was no urgency to move and displace Annie yet again during this critical time in her pregnancy. Annie was now well into her second trimester and all signs were pointing positive. The only issue was with cravings and Jacob went out of his way to make sure that they were met. She was putting on significant weight, but healthy and excited for what lay ahead.

There were other options and offers on the table. He could have tried out for a number of franchises without guarantees or gone back to Italy. Several other teams across Europe were also showing interest. But for now, Annie and the expectant baby were the first priority and staying close to home was clearly the best option. The couple was still staying in nearby Riverside with the Andersons, which had been like a second home for Jacob ever since his childhood. There was no urgency to pack up and move out of state or country. This move was easy.

Jacob took a pen and signed the contract, sharing how excited he was to skate for the coach. Coach collected the documents with a look of satisfaction as if he'd just scored a game-winning goal.

The coach's eagerness to sign Jacob almost certainly stemmed from his actions in the lone preseason game that he participated in for the Manchester Monarchs. Jacob received a last-minute invite to camp for the King's AHL affiliate in New Hampshire, and the preseason game enabled him to test the fighting skills that he had diligently trained for over the summer.

After returning to California from Italy, Jacob took it upon himself to get over his fear of fights by taking boxing lessons. He had already learned to adjust to the triggers which he now understood, but felt it was time to properly learn how to both fight and defend himself in the event of finding himself in a brawl. Hockey fights were much more common in the NHL than what he had experienced overseas. So, Jacob joined the UFC (Ultimate Fighting Championship) Gym in nearby Corona, just thirteen miles from Riverside.

Jacob sought instruction from a professional UFC trainer, and request-ed the instructor to provide a workout that would guarantee he throw up by the end of each session. For two days every week during the summer, Jacob led a grueling workout for a group of young skaters in Riverside both on the ice and in the weightroom. Then he drove to Corona for an intense UFC workout to hone his skills in self-defense. Not once in any of the sessions, despite the continuous routine of running, jumping, and sparring in intense heat, did the instructor achieve the goal of getting Jacob to vomit. Although not achieving that goal, Jacob went into the season fully prepared for any fight that may come his way. He even grew out his beard in an attempt to appear more menacing. And the opportunity to fight came almost immediately.

The Monarchs were going up against the Portland Pirates in a game where all participants were eager to make a final impression before the final cuts. Jacob had arrived late to the camp but was given a chance to get on the ice. Throughout the game in what proved to be a physical contest, the Pirates noted enforcer Keven Veilleux was goading him for a fight. Jacob wasn't sure if it was the beard or his size that made him a target for the imposing six-foot-five-inch center, but he kept skating away from the invites to fight. Finally, while sitting on the bench during the final period, it hit him. *This is what I've been training for all summer. Forget his size. This is a test. If I can fight him, I can fight anyone in the league. If and when he comes at me again, the gloves are coming off!*

Within seconds after Jacob was back on the ice, Veilleux was right back at him. Slamming into him and taunting, "Come on Newton, let's do it!"

That did it! Jacob turned to face his combatant and threw down the gloves. Play immediately stopped as the two locked horns. Jacob's initial instinct was to grab and hold Veilleux close to avoid his ability to swing and connect with his long reach. With Veilleux doing much the same, the result was that the two were spinning in a slow-moving circle. All referees now circled around them and Jacob heard one of them ask, "What are they doing?"

The remark prompted Jacob to momentarily release and follow through with a heavy jab to his opponent's chest. Veilleux fell back and with the opening took a shot at Jacob's face which just missed its mark. The two now faced off with repeated jabs much to the delight of the crowd. The fight was a standoff and the referees were finally able to step in and separate the combatants, who gave one another respectful nods as they skated off in anticipation of the upcoming penalties.

Jacob sat in the penalty box fully satisfied. Even though he did not expect to make the final Monarch's AHL roster with their roster set and due to his late arrival, he was at least now convinced that he could successfully square off against any player in hockey.

Returning to California and with the contract signed, Jacob and Annie moved into an apartment complex managed by the team and just a half mile away from the team's game and practice facility. The complex housed the entire team and the Reign picked up all living expenses. The spacious Toyota Arena sat near parks and the airport just outside of the tidy downtown populated with palm trees. The Reign competed in the highly competitive Pacific Division of the East Coast Hockey League's (ECHL) Western Conference. A league that began in 1988 with just five teams was rapidly expanding with 22 teams now spread across the country and acting as a feeder system for NHL and AHL teams. The Reign was affiliated with the nearby Los Angeles Kings, and fans in the growing community were enthusiastic to support a competitive team filled with King hopefuls.

The entire region, located just 20 miles northwest of Riverside and hemmed in at the foothills of the San Gabriel Mountains, represents a sprawling corridor located in the Inland Empire region that serves as the gateway to Southern California. With a solid fan base and close proximity to the parent club, it was not unusual for Reign fans to fill the 11,000-capacity arena. Jacob found himself aligned with where he started as a high schooler playing at the Junior Kings Toyota Sports Performance Center in El Segundo.

During the early practice sessions, it quickly became apparent who was running the show. Coach had one assistant who actually had some NHL experience and helped to conduct practice sessions, but the assistant was seldom heard. Their spunky head coach who had signed Jacob to his contract was the one in charge. He barked instructions while skating with the intensity of an active player, making sure that everything was done right and everyone was well aware of his presence. Not only on the ice, but even after practice.

Jacob sat alongside his teammates in the locker room following an introductory practice. With his AHL experience, year overseas, time with the Ducks, and skilled practice habits, he was quickly gaining the respect of his teammates as a team leader. A number of players joined him in light-hearted banter when Coach barged into the room from his nearby office. Jacob suspected that he must have something important to share to so suddenly invade a revered space normally reserved for the players, but the coach had other ideas. He immediately broke into his own banter, chiding and joking with the unsuspecting players seated all around him. The players responded with smiles and some forced laughter, as if not sure how to take the lewd comments that were clearly intended to come off as one of the guys.

Jacob suddenly caught confused stares from those around him when Coach threw out a comment at one of the young players that initially left the entire team confounded.

"Hey, I saw you trying to talk to that young lady out there. You got square wheels, Dude. You need some game. Do I need to show you guys everything?"

It took some moments before the group responded with uneasy laughter while the targeted player offered lighthearted defense of his prowess in meeting women.

Coach just shook his head and left the room laughing and chiding, "Alright, see you girls at practice tomorrow."

His departure was initially met with silence. The players simply looked around at one another as if they weren't sure what they just witnessed. Then someone from the back repeated the words: "Square wheels?"

Everyone laughed. Another player broke in. "Well, you know, back in the day he was known as 'Smurf'."

The name caught right on. Everyone agreed in unison that it was a fitting name. From that day on, Coach became known to the players as Smurf. Of course, that name was never mentioned in Smurf's presence.

The Reign opened the season with a shutout victory before a packed house at the Toyota Arena. Smurf chirped throughout the game from his perch on the bench, encouraging his players while trash-talking their opponent. It was a recurring theme for the Reign. Jacob was dominating play on the defensive end and racking up points while participating in all power plays. The team's only losses to open the season came in either overtime or shootouts, and they stood comfortably on top of the standings. The energetic and packed home crowds made Ontario an outstanding place to play hockey. It was excellent hockey in an electric environment. The only negative was the constant chirping heard from the bench. Eye rolls could be seen as even opposing players often stopped to ask, "How can you play for this guy?" One factor could not be ignored; the team was winning and the coach was getting results.

Back at home, Annie was now in the third trimester of her pregnancy as the couple eagerly awaited the baby's arrival. Jacob had little time for socializing or spending time with the team after games or practice. He was also continuing with the therapy sessions that they began in Syracuse. When on the road with the team, he continually called to check in and keep up with Annie's condition. The due date was fast approaching and the couple was doing everything in their power to ensure a safe delivery. Particularly with knowledge of Annie's three prior miscarriages.

They were down to the final month when Jacob approached Smurf to request time away from practice to accompany Annie on one of her scheduled doctor visits. The coach gave him a blank stare before spitting into a nearby cup to deposit some of his customary chew. It was painfully obvious that the request did not sit well with the disgruntled coach, but he reluctantly agreed with a cursive nod as he turned to pack more chew.

The following day, Smurf approached Jacob with a smirk as he skated onto the ice from the locker.

"Hey Newts, so the wife is allowing you to practice today?"

Jacob played along with a short reply before skating away to participate in the day's practice session. His tolerance towards the coach was running thin.

Christmas break was approaching and the team entered a crucial stretch with three games in Anchorage to close out the year. The team began the trip with an outstanding record of 19-4-4. The Alaska Aces sported a 17-7-1 record and were battling the Reign for the League's best record. Both teams were looking to close the year on a high with a series win to make a statement for the upcoming playoff drive. Smurf was even more vocal than normal during practice sessions and the team was playing well with nine wins in their last 11 contests. Jacob was having another MVP-caliber season, leading the league in scoring among defensemen and anchoring the team's outstanding defense. Unfortunately, the timing for the five-day road trip to faraway Alaska was not good.

Annie was just weeks away from her due date and growing more anxious with the expected delivery day fast approaching. Jacob had a decision to make. He did not wish to risk being so far away and not there for Annie if an emergency arose. He chose to stay with Annie and miss the trip. When he met with Smurf to tell him of his decision the coach was visibly upset. He simply gave Jacob a look as if to say, "You have got to be kidding me", and walked away. Jacob had no qualms with his decision. As important as the series was for the team, Annie and the baby were now his top priority.

Six days later the Reign returned home after winning two of the three games. Annie was still expecting. The team now prepared for a two-game series in Las Vegas before returning home on January 5, which was right about the time of Annie's due date. Jacob reasoned that it would be safe to make the trip. He would stay in constant contact with Annie and if any complications occurred or he was needed home for the delivery, which he was prepared to be a part of, he could quickly get back home from Vegas. The drive with a rental could be made in under four hours if a flight was unavailable. Jacob prepared for all possible scenarios and packed for the trip.

The team was on the ice for their final practice session before the trip to Vegas when Smurf skated up to Jacob to ask the question that he already knew the answer to.

"Hey Newts, did your wife have the baby?"

"No, Coach. I'm good to go for the trip. We've got things worked out."

Later than night at around 11 p.m., a phone call came. It was Smurf.

"Hey Newts, just checking. Are your sure you're okay to come on this trip?"

"Yeah Coach, I'm good to go. If anything comes up, I'll be sure to let you know".

The following morning, with the equipment manager and players loading the bus with hockey gear and personal luggage, Jacob walked past Smurf. Again, the coach stopped to ask,

"So, you still good to go?"

"Yes Coach, as I've told you I'm good to go. If anything had come up, I would have let you know."

Smurf gave him a look as if biting his tongue. An exasperated Jacob climbed aboard the bus to join his teammates. He sat towards the back and they all patiently waited for Coach to join them before departing for Las Vegas. When Smurf finally boarded, he stared at Jacob and slowly walked towards him. His face reddened as he spat out:

"Oh! So, YOU will let ME know! Now you listen, I run the show here..."

Jacob had enough. He was tired of the continual haranguing and having to continue answering the same question. Moreover, these were life-changing decisions that were impacting his family and he was repulsed by the need to even have to explain his support. And now here stood the coach in a rage. Confronting him in front of the entire team when he could have easily met and discussed one on one if he was having a problem with Jacob's decisions or with what he now seemed to be perceiving as a disrespectful attitude.

Jacob got up from his seat and gave it right back.

"That's it! I've had enough! You can talk to my agent."

He walked right past Smurf. Brushing the startled coach as the entire team sat wide eyed staring on in disbelief. One player mouthed YES and others gestured with subtle nods or thumbs up as Jacob stormed off the bus.

He continued walking. Not even bothering to remove his gear from the bus that now made its way out of the arena parking lot. He walked back to their nearby apartment where a startled Annie opened the door in wonder of what happened.

Twelve days later Harper Joy Newton was born one week late in Riverside, California. The birth did not come without complications. Annie had put on 60 pounds from multiple cravings and developed high blood pressure. Some of the medication got into Harper's lungs and she spent three days in the neonatal intensive care unit. Three days after returning from ICU, the joyous family was finally united and home together in their apartment.

For Jacob, it was life-changing. Harper proved to be the dream baby. Alert during the day and sleeping most of the night. Beautiful soft skin and sparkling brown eyes. Jacob could barely put her down. He sang to her every night as she fell sound asleep on his shoulder. He understood for the very first time the real meaning of true love. He was alarmed by the outpouring of love that melted through his pores for his precious daughter. The middle name Joy so fitting. A tribute to his mother and symbolic of the feeling shared by everyone around her. He immediately looked at himself as a better person, father, and husband.

Jacob felt a peace unlike anything he had experienced in his lifetime. It was a feeling both pure and without bounds. He barely bothered to catch up on the Ontario Reign. But the itch slowly returned. He contacted Alain Roi to inform him that he was ready for a return to the ice.

# Team 2: Bridgeport Sound Tigers, Bridgeport, Connecticut

The Bridgeport Sound Tigers were suffering a season of turmoil. A rash of injuries coupled with promotion of their top prospects to the parent New York Islanders left the roster in disarray. The season represented a continuous shuffle of players between Bridgeport, Long Island (home of the NHL NY Islanders), and their ECHL affiliate in Stockton. The required shuffle never stopped and the team played an unheard total of 65 players throughout the season.

For head coach Scott Pellerin, who entered the season with high hopes for the team, the challenge was simply to get a collection of players unfamiliar with one another to compete and play together. The chaos did enable an opportunity for Jacob. Once he gave his agent Roi the signal to find a team in need of players, the Bridgeport scenario quickly surfaced. A timely promotion back to the AHL with an organization that was never on his radar.

Jacob left Annie and Harper back home to acclimate to the area before they would join him. The team was placing all new incoming players at a nearby Residence Inn, and the occupancy was filling fast. At one point, ten newcomers from outside of the organization were residing at the Inn. Among the new teammates that Jacob found was an old friend from Southern California, Scooter Vaughn. Scooter was from Placentia, just outside of Anaheim, and the two had competed against one another numerous times in the past. Including summers in California and the NAHL title in 2007, when Scooter skated with Patrick Maroon for the St. Louis Bandits. The three had reunited many times since then, and Jacob was pleased that he had at least one familiar face on the team.

The hotel wake-up call came at seven a.m., four a.m. back home. Jacob needed a moment to get his bearings and realize that he was not needed to tend to Harper. He rubbed his eyes and cleared his head. Now was the time for hockey and getting acclimated to life on the opposite coast. At least he had a rental car to get around.

The Tigers played their home games at the Webster Bank Arena, right next to the Bridgeport-Port Jefferson Ferry which takes passengers across the ocean's Long Island Sound and into New York's Long Island. A one-hour-and fifteen-minute trip across open water that docks in Port Jefferson. From there, a one-hour drive to the Nassau Coliseum in Uniondale. Home of the NHL New York Islanders and the intended destination for every player who dons a Tiger jersey. For most, like Jacob, a voyage wrought with twists and turns where the goal posts are continually moving and the destination can slip away just when it appears in your grasp. Jacob pulled into the Webster Bank Arena parking lot alongside the ferry dock. Now was not the time to get ahead of oneself.

Jacob immediately took to the coaching style of their young coach Scott Pellerin. He worked well with his assistants and treated the players like professionals. The problem was, the team was now largely a collection of strangers just getting to know one another and who represented a wide range of hockey backgrounds. Jacob did his best to fit in and contribute, hoping to salvage the season for the coach with some gritty wins. Pellerin recognized his skills and immediately placed him with Scooter and the top lines, including minutes with the power play unit.

In Jacob's first game with the team against Albany, he scored a goal on a power play to keep the game close. It wasn't enough. The Tigers' losing streak continued and more losses followed. The local press was coming down hard on the team and coach for their losing record, but Jacob took pride in the grit and determination that all players played with for their coach. Virtually every game was close and the players went into every game determined to get the win.

The win finally came. The Tigers secured a much-needed victory at home against the Adirondack Thunder. Scooter and Jacob each scored a goal, and Jacob added an assist on the game winner to bring some joy to the home crowd. Coach Pellerin gave Jacob a hug in the locker room after breathing a sigh of relief. It was going to be much easier addressing the media and Jacob felt happy for the likable coach who was dealt a rough hand. He joined his teammates in celebration, but the mood was heightened much more than simply a win for the team and coach. Annie and Harper were on their way to join him for the remainder of the season.

From the instant Jacob saw Harper at the airport in her mother's arms, he melted at the sight of her eyes growing wide with a gratifying burble of excitement. He held her high before holding her close as if to protect her from anything and everything that the world had in store. There was no better feeling and his happiness was once again complete. Once they got home, the Residence Inn accommodations were far from ideal. It didn't matter. The family was together and from Jacob's perspective, they may as well have been vacationing along the shores of the Hamptons across the Sound and along the southeastern tip of Long Island.

The Bridgeport season finally came to a merciful end. After the win against Adirondack, they lost 13 of their final 14 games, including two heartbreaking shootout losses in overtime. Again, it was not for a lack of effort as six of the final seven games were decided by one goal. But, the loss of so many players in such a short time through injuries and late season promotions was simply too much to overcome. After a season that began with so much hope, the Tigers finished the season with a record of 28-40-8, and failed to reach the playoffs.

Jacob grew hopeful that the team's management would take note of the replacement players' spirited play to close the season and bring back head coach Scott Pellerin for another season. He felt that with improved health of the many injured players and returning with Scooter and the team's upcoming draftees, he'd be positioned to make a name for himself in the Islander organization. Unfortunately, in a results-driven league, the coach was relieved of his duties. Jacob was hoping to come back and enter a new season with Coach Pellerin as part of the Islanders organization. Now, with his main advocate within the organization gone and an unlikely return to the Kings following his brusque departure in Ontario, he was back to ground zero.

The family left their temporary home at the Bridgeport Residence Inn for a return to California where once again, the Andersons welcomed Jacob and his family of three back into their home. A chance to catch up with family and friends, discuss future options with his agent Alain Roi, and get some practice and workout time on the ice. Jacob also took note of the ECHL playoffs to see how his former team was faring.

The Ontario Reign finished the regular season with a record of 44–20–0–7. Good for the second-most wins in the Western Conference and one win behind the Alaska Aces who did in fact catch the Reign by finishing their season strong. In their first round of the playoffs the Reign got swept in four games to the Stockton Thunder. Alaska advanced to the Finals where they defeated the Cincinnati Cyclones in six games to win the 2014 Kelly Cup. It was a disappointing finish to a season that began with so much hope for Smurf and the Reign.

As for Smurf, he would go on to become the winningest coach in ECHL history. To this date he has never been hired as an NHL head coach, but did serve as an assistant coach for three seasons with the NHL Buffalo Sabres.

Jacob was ready to put the 2013-2014 season behind him. Although the season did not go as planned, it was a success by the most important measure with the birth of Harper Joy, who was a constant presence at her father's side. Jacob sat on his chair in their temporary home in Riverside, Harper nestled against his shoulder. He contemplated the options that Roi had outlined for him and felt a strong desire for where he wished to continue his hockey career.

## Chapter Twelve

# Winter Wonderland

2014 – 2015 season

### Val Gardena HC – Selva di Gardena, Italy

A morning sun rising above distant peaks extended its rays towards the eastern face of a majestic mountain. The mountain's appearance sometimes described in poetic terms as carrying the weight of the heavens on its shoulders. A striking canvas emerged, as if curtains slowly opening to reveal a decorative stage that comes alive when the village of Selva di Val Gardena appears in the valley below. Jacob stood outside of their mountainside flat holding Harper to take in the miracle of another awakening. Below them lay a three-kilometer stretch of road which ties together three enchanting villages tucked inside the lush Val Gardena valley floor. Above and all around the valley stood the Dolomite Mountain range, offering spectacular views and challenging ski slopes which attracts visitors from around the world. If Jacob and Annie thought they were fortunate to live in the charming area of Appiano Sulla Strata Del Vino, which sat just fifty miles away as the crow flies, they were in for an entirely new treat upon arriving in Selva di Val Gardena.

The sport of hockey in this remote resort district of the Italian Alps was equally thrilling. Because of the team's proximity to world class ski resorts, visiting and local winter sports enthusiasts routinely filled the

2,000-seat Pranives Ice Stadium to cheer on one of Italy's oldest ice hockey organizations. The team competed in the Italian Serie A1 division, made up of 12 teams spread across the winter sport-loving region of the Italian Alps. Included among the teams competing for the title was Jacob's old team from Eppan, which had advanced to the A1 division upon their title win two seasons ago.

Jacob was pleased to be reunited with his Finnish coach from the Eppan Pirates championship team, Jarno Mensonen. He was also reunited with the Italian goalie from the Pirates, and joined by one fellow American and two Canadians. During early practice sessions, it quickly came apparent that the North American imports would be the ones to bring hope of a winning season. Coach Mensonen was also leaning on Jacob to take on the role of scorer in addition to leading the defense, and on the top line for all power play situations. Jacob embraced the opportunity.

Jacob readily agreed to the modest salary of twenty-seven thousand euros with not only the knowledge that playing in Italy's A1 division would attract more attention from higher-level leagues spread across the European continent, but equally from their wonderful experience of living in this region during the 2012-2013 season. Just as in Eppan, the team was most generous in picking up virtually all living expenses, and even offered a few unexpected perks.

For the automobiles, the team provided the four North American imports with what turned out to be flashy travelling billboards. The team owner proudly handed Jacob the keys to his silver Fiat Punto and Jacob had to do a double take before entering the car. Plastered across the back of the car was a bold American Flag below the name "Newton" and his number "55". The front hood was emblazoned with the hockey club's logo: the head of a white stallion poking through a bright red G in front of a blue hockey puck. There would be no doubt who was driving the colorful car in the Val Gardena valley of South Tyrol, Italy.

The Italian-made Fiat enabled Jacob and his family to tour the many attractions available to them when not practicing or playing hockey. He gradually mastered the standard gear driving over narrow roads snaking up and down statuesque mountains which offered spectacular views. They came upon a railroad station offering tours which took them near the top of a peak. With Harper strapped to his back, they hiked across rugged trails and found themselves lost in nature. Hand gliders were sometimes spotted soaring alongside rock cliffs in the distance. Occasionally, seemingly out of nowhere, a rustic hut appeared offering generous portions of goulash and cheese platters with beverages that included samples of local wine from nearby vineyards.

Back in town, the experiences and ambiance were equally enjoyable. Gone were the days of freezing to pay for groceries at the market; Jacob seamlessly blended into the culture. Although the natives spoke a Romance language unique to the region known as Ladino which Jacob strove to learn a few words in, most people either spoke or understood basic English. And as a tourist area, it was not unusual to hear the English language spoken in public places. One venue which became a regular for Jacob was the popular Ristorante Lamm, a bar and pizzeria restaurant.

The two Canadian teammates who lived in the upper floors of the restaurant introduced Jacob to the pizzeria. Lamm's featured a tidy outdoor seating area which offered a panoramic view of the village and mountains, and specialized in generously-sized pizza servings which could feed an entire family. Known among friends and teammates for his voracious appetite, Lamms became a staple for Jacob on game days. Six hours before every home game, Jacob was served one pound of pasta and one pound of beef to go along with two chicken breasts on the side. A pitcher of water and side servings of warmed homemade bread completed the setting. The owner joined patrons who watched in wide-eyed wonder as the young American loaded up on carbs and protein for the upcoming game.

On the ice, Jacob was equally impressive. He was not only leading the defense, but also the team in scoring. On defense, he anchored the top line with fellow American Derek Eastman, while also scoring goals at a rapid pace. Jacob was not only leading his team in scoring, but among the league leaders. A very unusual and impressive feat for a defenseman. As for the team, they were enjoying limited success. The team was young and the North Americans led by Jacob kept them in most games, but the wins were few and far between. That did not keep visiting scouts from taking note of Jacob's fine play. Among the organizations showing interest was a club from far north in the upper reaches of the European continent. In a country considered a hockey powerhouse with a strong national presence and a significant number of players competing in the NHL.

Vaasan Sport was in their first season in the Finnish Liiga, which represents the top-tier hockey league in the hockey-crazed country of Finland. The team was young and driven to move up the standings following their recent promotion to the top league, and were looking for players throughout the continent to sign and ensure their standing in the league. Jacob was at the top of their list and they offered him a contract to finish the season with the team in Finland.

Jacob was thrilled! A chance to not only compete in one of Europe's top leagues, but also a significant increase in salary. Of course, it meant another move and leaving a region that they were quickly falling in love with. The decision was not easy, but Jacob felt that it was just too good to pass up and would provide a stepping stone on the journey for his goal to get back to the NHL. He discussed with Annie and after weighing all pros and cons, they agreed. Go for it!

Coach Mensonen was visibly disappointed when Jacob approached him with the news, but he also readily understood and supported Jacob's decision. Being from Finland and having played eight years in the Finnish leagues, he was well aware of the opportunity awaiting Jacob. The trick now was to get the Val Gardena owner to see the same and agree.

The owner immediately responded with a flat-out "NO". Jacob was his top player and he was not about to simply let him walk away. The contract was for one season and he was not going to relent. Jacob's initial reaction was more anger than disappointment. How can the owner be so selfish and not see this as an important career opportunity for his star player? The team was likely not going to compete for a championship and the Finnish league was considered to be one of the best in all of Europe. He considered walking away. Going home. A rash decision acting upon his raw emotions.

Jacob needed time to pause and reflect. With the help of the therapy which he held onto from the past several years, he was well aware that his emotions too often continued to get the best of him. Memories flashed back. Walking out of the boxing ring in Boston. Slamming his drink on the pavement and storming away from the conversation with a Ducks coach upon learning that he would not be called up as a late-season replacement. And last season, walking off the team bus in anger following the confrontation with Smurf. Arguments could be made for each and every one of his actions. But was he hurting himself in the process? Was he running away just as he had previously during fights? Before he understood what caused the triggers and learned how to handle himself in those situations?

Following an initial desire to demand his release and walk away if that was not accepted, he made the decision to stay. He would continue the season and perform to the best of his abilities in an attempt to finish what he started and achieve his goals.

The end of 2014 was fast approaching. Jacob and Annie excitedly prepared decorations and made plans for the upcoming holiday season in the Alps. It was going to be special. Harper was nearing her first birthday and continuing to bring joy with her brightness and evolving personality. The team had some time off and the idea of spending their first Christmas with Harper in such an idyllic setting was everything that Jacob had dreamed of. And to make the entire situation even more perfect, his parents were on their way to join them. Jacob rushed out the door to pick them at the Bolzano Airport. They would be exhausted after a long day of travel and his excitement grew with the idea of having the family all together for the holidays.

Watching his parents walk out of the terminal, Jacob rushed to greet them and the three embraced in a long heartfelt hug. He grabbed their luggage and shared upcoming plans for over a fortnight in the Alps. His mother expressed relief that the travel was over and now she just wanted to get to the house and see her granddaughter. Jacob didn't think to warn her that the real travel excitement was just getting started. He totally forgot about his own trepidation on those winding bus trips during his first year in Italy.

Having mastered the standard transmission driving and maneuvering in his compact Fiat, Jacob flew out of the airport and soon found himself winding along the narrow roads now packed with ice and snow. The snow-capped mountains were striking to view but Jacob's mom could only grab onto the seat in front of her out of fear that the car would slide off the road at every turn. Jacob continued sharing updates and plans as the two quietly listened, and it was only when they pulled into town that he noticed his mom through the rearview mirror make a sign of the cross and breathe a sigh of relief. Their silence was suddenly explained. Jacob down-shifted into first gear entering their driveway and realized that he should have warned them about the narrow winding roads throughout the Dolomites.

The entire Val Gardena valley came alive for the holidays. Bright lights and colorful decorations welcomed the scores of tourists who flooded in from nearby ski resorts with holiday travelers who took up every available space in the region's hotels and travel inns. Horse carriages pulling sleighs provided a birds-eye view of the area's charms for families looking to step back in time. Heavenly aromatic scents filled the air from sausages and slabs of meats cooking on outdoor grills. People lined up for the mouth watering food and warmed beverages at the rustic decorative kiosks which now populated the streets.

Jacob and his family took it all in, their excitement further buoyed by the glitter of amazement in Harper's sparkling eyes. There was no need to wait in the long lines. The owner of Lamm was awaiting their arrival. The only choice to make was to sit inside, or outside under heated lamps to take in the fireworks display scheduled for later in the evening. Jacob looked over at his parents who appeared lost in a rare moment of innocence and happiness, his mother now holding Harper. He smiled reflecting on their own journey. The tireless hours of driving to hockey practices, spending hard-earned money to ensure that Jacob could compete on the ice. Diffi-cult decisions and sacrifices made which impacted the entire family. He remained unable to take care of them in ways that he hoped to with a lucrative NHL contract, but there was something to be said for the visual unfolding before him at that moment. They were together, they were at peace, and they were happy.

The holidays sped past them far too quickly. The calendar turned to a new year as life in the valley eased back into its normal pace. Mom and Dad appeared in no rush to get back and grew delighted in the pure joy shown from Harper who now approached them with her first steps. Following a full day of masterful packing to find space for exotic gifts, the entire group squeezed into the car for the ride back to the airport, filled with the vivid recounts of the amazing holiday they just shared. Jacob even noticed that Mom appeared more at ease with his driving, though he did note that she still held on firmly to the front seat around every turn. The group hugged and tears were shed as Mom and Dad disappeared beyond the departure terminal. Jacob waved his goodbyes and turned around with a new focus. It was time to get back to hockey.

There was a special buzz in the air for the upcoming January game on the home ice. United States Olympic gold medalist Lindsay Vonn was competing at a nearby slope for the World Cup of skiing, and would be among the international celebrities in attendance for the evening game. But she was not the reason for Jacob's excitement and anticipation. Several scouts from Vaasan Sport were also expected to be in attendance. They had not given up on signing him and he saw the game as a final opportunity to cement their interest in hopes of a contract offer for the following season. As Jacob finished his meal at Lamms, the owner wished him luck and asked to make sure that he'd be back in the morning. He had a surprise planned.

The excitement carried through right onto the ice. Val Gardena HC put on their best performance of the season with an impressive win, led by their American star Jake Newton. Jacob finished the game with two goals and two assists on a night where everything seemed to go right. The players basked in the atmosphere as Vonn and other winter sports celebrities were recognized during the game and cheered on by the throng of alpine enthusiasts. Jacob looked up in the stands to see Annie holding

Harper and raised his hands in celebration for the three. For one of the few times in his career, they knew well in advance where they would be settling for the following season.

The following morning, Jacob walked into the Lamm Ristorante expecting his double expresso and croissants, but the owner had a grin on his face as he guided Jacob to his favorite spot. Sitting and sipping his expresso, he viewed a savory breakfast platter brought out to him in ceremonial fashion. Four fried eggs surrounded by pastries and a pile of chopped potatoes fried a golden brown. A separate plate holding rolled pancetta lined up neatly alongside cuts of cheese. A generous bottle of his favorite carbonated water to go with a cup of fresh orange juice. Jacob looked on in amazement. This rivaled the best American breakfast, which he recently shared with the owner as the one thing he missed while in Italy. Jacob looked up and the owner and waiter who simply said, "Buon Appetito!" before walking away. Jacob picked up his knife and fork and proceeded to enjoy an American-style breakfast.

From that day on, the specialized breakfast at his favorite restaurant became a daily fixture for Jacob. While other patrons looked on approvingly with their more modest servings to go with shots of expresso or other steamed beverages, Jacob alone enjoyed the full breakfast platter. And when he tried to pay, he was continually rebuffed. The breakfast servings were on the house. Perhaps some sort of reward for the large dinner portions that Jacob always enjoyed on game days. Or perhaps it was for the generous tips that were always included in his payments, a gesture not common or expected in the local cafés.

More good news followed. As expected, the contract offer arrived to play the next season in the top Finnish league for Vaasan Sport. In truth, it was not going to be easy to leave the Val Gardena valley and if the team could only pay a higher salary, the decision to stay would be much easier. But the reality was the level of play in the Italian leagues was not on par with that across much of the European continent. Indeed, the Finnish League was one of the best in Europe, on par with the hockey played in North

America. If he was going to achieve his goal and make it back to the NHL, Vaasan Sport was the required stepping stone.

Another jolt of good news was Annie. She was once again pregnant. For the second time in three years, the couple conceived a child in the clear mountain air of the Italian Alps. As with Harper, the couple remained cautiously optimistic and took all precautions to ensure that the pregnancy would proceed without complications. Harper had proven that the miracle was indeed possible.

The season was winding down. Jacob remained the top scorer on the team and among the league leaders, and the team was positioning for a spot in the playoffs. Excitement grew, both before and after games at the Ristorante, when the owner came up with an idea. A challenge. Before a packed house one evening at the pizzeria, he challenged Jacob to eat two of the family-sized pizzas in one sitting. If able to do so, the pizzas were on the house. Jacob was immediately spurred on by several teammates to take the challenge as bets could be seen taking place throughout the restaurant. Jacob stood and raised his stein of beer, "You're on!" A date was set.

The night of the challenge arrived. Jacob took a seat at his favorite spot as the waiters rushed into position to serve with the proper formalities. A number of his teammates were in attendance, including the Canadians who lived upstairs and fellow American Darek Eastman who brought along his Italian girlfriend. Annie sat holding Harper nearby, his daughter looking on in more wide-eyed amazement than fear as many in the crowd now circled her father.

Jacob was well prepared. He had now fasted for 24 hours and was completing his order as the crowd hushed.

"Let's start with toppings of Prosciutto fungi. And for the second, just pepperoni."

The order raised loud murmurings with considerable debate and scrutiny. "What is he thinking?" "Why not just go with a plain?" More bets came on the table as the music picked up and Jacob awaited the first serving.

After some time, three servers came out and ceremoniously slipped off the first oversized pizza from its expansive iron holder and onto a raised plate. Jacob was handed a large napkin and a smaller plate to receive the portions from above. Two large bottles of carbonated water were placed at his side. The owner entered to formally announce: "Let the challenge begin!"

Since there was no time limit, Jacob simply dug in and enjoyed. Most went back to their tables and occasionally stopped to get an official count or update of his progress. He was nearing completion of the Prosciutto fungi when someone announced that it was time to get the pepperoni going. The odds were turning in his favor. This was going much faster than most anticipated. Still, doubt lingered.

"He can't keep up this pace!'

Jacob wiped his mouth and took a swig of the carbonated water, awaiting the pepperoni. His confidence grew.

As the pepperoni pizza slowly disappeared from view, more and more patrons circled the table to get a close-up view of the proceedings. Jacob was definitely slowing down but the end was in sight. Now just a few slices to go. An unsuspecting family sitting at the opposite end just shook their heads in amazement. How was he doing this when they were taking leftovers home from the one pizza ordered for the family?

Excitement grew. The crowd now chanting over and over in unison: "One more slice!' The owner stood at the head of the table boldly extending his arm and peered at his watch as if it played some factor in the outcome. Jacob took the final bite and chewed as the crowd erupted. Even Harper joined in the applause with claps and laughter as she was now held just behind her father. Jacob leaned back in his chair. As exhausted as he'd been from any workout. He acknowledged the crowd and felt relief that there would be no game this evening.

The team made the playoffs. They defeated Faasa in a best-of-three to advance to the quarterfinals, where they squared off against Rittner in a best of seven series. The Rittner Buam Sky Alps had just won the Division A championship the prior season for the first time in their long history and were looking to gain another for their passionate fan base. In Game One, Jacob took a vicious hit and fell hard on the ice. His entire hand was in terrible pain and he was unable to even hold his stick. He was out for the game.

Jacob learned later in the locker that he suffered a bad break on his index finger. The team owner hoped to get him taped up and back into the lineup to continue in the series, but Jacob had little desire to do so. For one, he was in great pain and could not even grip with his left hand. This would not only hinder his play but could lead to further injury which could impact his career down the line. Another factor was the team's long shot in advancing. The Sky Alps were clearly the better team and any chance of an upset was slim, even more so after the game one loss. And finally, the fact that the owner had not even considered allowing Jacob out of his contract to compete in the higher-level Finnish league. He did not feel compelled to risk further injury in sacrificing for the team. His season was over and the team was ultimately swept in four games to the Rittner Baum Sky Alps.

Jacob returned to Selva and the couple made plans for the offseason. Vaasan Sport invited Jacob to join the team for one week to officially sign his contract and get acclimated to his new team and home. Annie and Harper would go to St. Louis to spend time with her family, where Jacob would join them before driving back to California. The Andersons once again agreed to host the family for the summer. Before leaving for Finland, Jacob had one important task to complete.

Jacob entered the Lamm Ristorante a final time to present the owner with a gift. He handed over a wrapped package which the owner held onto like a prized possession. He laid the package on a table and slowly removed the wrappings of decorative paper. Out came a gleaming white game jersey, the colorful stallion emblem below his number and various sponsor names listed on the front. Blue and red bands on the arms displaying the number "55" in bright white print. And the name "Newton" proudly displayed on the back of the jersey above the number "55" which took up most of the space. Between the name and number was a written note and signature signed with a black marker. The statement read:

*I love you all and am so grateful for all your love and support,*
*Jake Newton "55"*

Tears flowed from the owner's eyes as he grabbed Jacob and held him close for the traditional touching of left and right cheeks. Jacob thanked him for everything and told him that he would never forget his generosity and hospitality. The restaurant and the entire community had become his home. He was leaving the Val Gardena valley, but the region would forever remain in his heart.

After seeing Annie and Harper off at the Bolzano airport for a full day of travel back to the States, Jacob boarded his flight north for Finland. There was much reflection on the trip, and he was filled with wonder of what to expect in the hockey-loving culture of Finland. He was interested to learn from his reading on the plane that the Scandinavian peninsula derived its name from a word of German origin that can be loosely translated to "dangerous islands". The countries tied together with a rich culture that dates back to the Viking Age, where rugged tribes participated in large-scale raiding, conquests, and trading throughout the European continent and beyond. Their vast nautical skills and daring for exploration even made them the first Europeans to reach North America. He was also surprised to learn that large areas of Finland are not considered by all to be Scandinavian due to a combination of geographic, linguistic, and historical factors.

He closed the pamphlet and gazed out the window from his airline seat. Annie and Harper would now be halfway home. There was much uncertainty regarding what awaited them all. Two things that he could count on were there would be a love for hockey all around him, and the experience would likely be far different from what they had just lived in Italy. Jacob closed his eyes in hopes of getting some sleep before his arrival.

Touching down in Vaasa, Jacob was struck by the vast concentration of islands that appeared just off the city's jagged coastline. The area was mostly flat, but there seemed to be water everywhere. Team officials were on hand to greet Jacob and explain all the arrangements for the upcoming week, including a drive back to the downtown hotel where he would be staying. Two things stood out to Jacob as he settled in for his first night in Finland. One, it was freezing outside. The calendar may have been pointing to early spring, but the weather was not cooperating. The darkness also came quite early. And two, why was there a sauna in his hotel bathroom? Did they give him a special room? Not sure what to make of the sauna and unfamiliar with its operation, Jacob chose to ignore it for his initial stay in Finland. He would soon learn that saunas are everywhere in that country, and it would become an important part of his daily routine.

It felt good to get back on the ice. Jacob's finger was healing nicely and he was able to participate in some light practices as the team prepared to close out the season. He fit in easily with the other players who all either spoke or understood some English and was introduced to fellow American Mike Brennan. It was clear to see that this was a good group of guys and Jacob looked forward to joining them on the bench for the final home game of the season.

Once seated on the bench, Jacob made several observations. The team was struggling to get wins. They were still young and relatively inexperienced, playing their first year in the higher division. That didn't stop spirited play. Jacob observed everyone skating hard and doing their best to play as a team. Also, the environment was definitely hockey friendly. The fans were loud, knowledgeable, and passionate about their team. The organization was very good with promotion and the press was visible and active in their coverage. Team officials even went so far as to introduce Jacob to the fans on the ice during one of the intermissions.

Following the first period, Jacob was asked to stay on the bench, from where he was called out to center ice. The introduction was heartfelt and followed with an interview conducted in English. The announcer read out his impressive stats from the Italian league to the approval of the crowd, and Jacob voiced how excited he was to join the team and bring a championship to the city next season. He skated off the ice waving to the appreciative crowd and felt a stirring and wish that he could suit up for the upcoming period. It was definitely going to be fun playing in Finland.

Before heading back to the States, Jacob entered the team office and went through the formality of signing his contract in front of several photographers. Taking pen to paper, the realization struck him for the first time that the contract arranged for him might be in the team's best interest but certainly not his own. Was forty-thousand euros in the respected Liiga a fair contract for a player of his caliber? Jacob signed with a smile for the cameras but couldn't hide a nagging feeling that the contract and numbers were on the low side for the league he was entering.

# Chapter Thirteen

# Sauna on Ice

2015 - 2016 season

## Vassan Sport – Vassa, Finland

Beads of sweat dripped profusely from his lowered face. Jacob fought internally to hang in there a bit longer before rewarding himself with a tantalizing plunge in the crystal-clear water that beckoned him just beyond the closed door. For the hockey guy who grew up in the California desert, heat had always been something to avoid rather than seek. Seated all around him were a number of his new teammates, appearing much more relaxed in their enclosed quarters. In fact, it would be fair to say they appeared in heavenly bliss and in no rush to exit. A teammate seated towards the front dipped a large wooden spoon into a bucket of water and poured the contents over a clump of rocks. The entire room filled with yet more heat to a hissing sound accompanied with gestures of approval heard above the masculine exchanges which filled the room The dry smoky aroma of cedar enveloped the steamy sauna. Jacob glanced at the clock to gauge if he could last the 20 minutes before bursting out into fresh air. He had barely made it halfway. He took a gulp of beer and forced his mind to reflect on where he was and how he got there. It seemed the best way to ignore the heat and train his mind to adapt to what those around him so eagerly embraced. He broke away from the talk around him to focus on his thoughts.

From the moment that Jacob arrived in Finland with Annie and Harper, he noted a drastic change from the city he departed. Gone were the frigid cold and long nights, replaced with mild summer temperatures and almost eternal daylight. The hours of daylight had noticeably decreased since their arrival in mid-summer, but it still remained light for much longer than Jacob had ever experienced. The city and team offered a number of other pleasant surprises.

Although few views could compare favorably with those seen from their home in the Val Gardena Valley, the two-level apartment was much more spacious and comfortable and just a half mile from the Gulf. He was gradually growing familiar with the eight-seat sauna that once again took up a prominent space in their bathroom, though he barely used it. Getting around was also much easier in the roomier Czech-made Skoda. After mastering the compact Fiat in the Alps mountainside, driving the Skoda around Finland was a breeze. When handed the keys, Jacob wasn't sure if he was more pleased than disappointed upon observing there was no team name or eagle logo plastered on the car. Annie was certainly relieved. But memories of driving #55 around the resort town remained most fond in Jacob's memories of Italy.

In addition to the perks available through the team, Vassa certainly had its charm. The coastal city of just over 70,000 was considered an educational, cultural, and tourist center of Western Finland and an energy hub for all Nordic countries. In addition to the many outdoor activities available to residents in the community, the city boasted the University of Vaasa among a number of other institutions of higher learning. Jacob quickly picked up the energetic vibes of a college town. He also observed many Swedes living in the community. With a string of islands populating the narrow strip of the Gulf of Bothnia as the only separation between the two countries, it was not surprising to observe so many natives of Sweden living and speaking their language in Vaasa. One element that was somewhat surprising was the number of refugees present in the community who were flooding into Europe from across the Mediterranean Sea. Finland had been part of a resettlement program, and with the Syrian crisis growing in the Middle East more and more asylum seekers were now being accepted across the country.

As for hockey, it seemed to be the talk of the town. Even more popular in Finland than the continent's beloved sport of football. Jacob quickly learned from his early days in Italy that the term soccer was never used across the European continent. Whenever referring to the game of football played in North America, Jacob made a point to be very clear that he was talking "American" football so as to avoid any confusion. It seemed that to the rest of the world, the game which Jacob always knew as soccer was simply referred to as football. And while Vaasan Palloseura competed locally in the top tier of Finnish football, the locals couldn't seem to talk enough about Vassan Sport for their upcoming second season in the Finnish top division Liiga.

The young team had been practicing hard and they were eagerly embracing a true test with the upcoming Pitsiturnaus tournament leading up to a new season. The annual hockey extravaganza would let the team and coach know where they stood. Jacob approached the season with the utmost confidence. He had a great summer of training back in California, once again leading the group of young workout buddies at the UFC gym in Corona, and his new coach with Vaasa had given him a vote of confidence. Following a recent practice, their Polish coach Tomek Valtonen had all his players fill out a questionnaire. Included among the questions was space for the players to write down their own personal goals for the coming season, along with goals for the next three and five years. The coach called Jacob into his office the next day to discuss his responses with him.

"Do you know, you are the only player to write down the NHL as a personal goal. I know that you're one of only four foreigners on the team, but I want you to take a leadership role on this team. You are my best defenseman and I encourage you to follow your dream."

The words encouraged Jacob to step out of the shadows felt as a foreigner joined by only a fellow American, Slovakian, and Frenchman, and take a more vocal role in practices and team meetings. Glancing around at his teammates, Jacob looked up at the clock and saw that his 20 minutes in the steamy sauna was nearing. He was ready to take the plunge.

Stepping out into the bright sunshine and grabbing a towel, fresh air burst into open pores like a shot of adrenalin. All around him was an inviting display put on by the team. Long tables under shady trees filled with decorative trays of tasty entrees and appetizers. Bottles of beer in coolers stacked in ice alongside a makeshift bar holding refreshments and top-of-the-line liquor available to reward the players for their hard offseason work. A team photographer looking to capture team-friendly photos followed the American import sprinting and jumping into the refreshing waters of a lake that would be frozen with ice in the not-too-distant future. He felt confident that the photo, along with others taken throughout the day would make for excellent team marketing.

As if Jacob needed any more proof of the importance of hockey in Finland, it was completely confirmed during the annual Pitsiturnaus Tournament held every year in Rauma, Finland. The tournament always takes place during the Pitsivikko around the end of August and early September, a city festival that fills the courtyards, parks, and stages of Old Rauma with culture, crafts, and music. For the hockey tournament, the local Lukko club annually hosts six teams from across Europe every year who are drawn into two divisions. Teams within each division play one another, with the top two teams from both divisions advancing to the semifinals. The winners then advance to the finals. The tournament had grown to such popularity that it was a main source of income for the local club. For the hockey-starved fans of Finland, it was nonstop hockey from morning until evening. And for the 2015 Pitsiturnaus, Jacob and Vassa Sport were invited to participate.

For one entire day during the festive holiday, the Aijansuo Arena was filled to over capacity with vocal fans hungry for hockey before the start of a new season. Fans from each of the represented teams wore their team colors while screaming and singing in unison to outdo the opposing fans, adding yet more vitality to the raucous atmosphere. Jacob had grown accustomed to the sound of whistles to voice fans' displeasure in favor of the boos heard in North American arenas. Now it sounded like nonstop cheering and whistling that filled the arena from fans representing all sides.

Vassan Sport, no doubt spurred on by their travelling fans and the hard work put in during the summer, won their first game of the tournament designed for fast-moving action. There wasn't much time to rest between games. When not on the ice, players relaxed in the locker rooms while the cycle of games continued throughout the day. The team won their second game to advance to the second round. Jacob's primary focus was on defense but also helped to secure wins by scoring points with a goal and several assists. They advanced to round two with growing confidence.

Jacob was in his element. He was always one of the best if not the best conditioned athlete on the ice, and he was thoroughly enjoying the fast-paced format. His fine play continued in the semifinals and Vassan Sport put on an impressive performance to advance to the finals. They were going up against the host team Rauman Lukko for the title game.

Both teams skated out to the ice clearly exhausted for their fourth and final game of the day. Even the fans needed some time to recharge after a full day of emotions. But the atmosphere soon changed. From the moment the puck was dropped the hitting was fierce. The intensity increased as fans grew louder with anticipation of a goal as both teams struggled to get the puck into the net.

It was Lukko who finally scored the game's first goal. Their fans went wild as both teams prepared for the final push to either leave with a win or send the game into overtime  The clock was ticking down and Sport pulled their goalie to press with an all-out assault. It was like two boxers flailing with punches in the fifteenth round of a punishing heavyweight fight. Jacob scrambled and took a shot on goal with just seconds remaining but a Lukko defender barely blocked the puck with his stick before it could reach the net. The horn finally sounded and every player bent over in near-exhaustion.

Vassan Sport did not win the championship but accounted for themselves quite well in a preseason tournament designed to test their will and fortitude. Coach Valtonen was visibly pleased with the team's performance and felt they were well prepared to compete in their second season of Liiga play. Despite the team's youth and low budget, the coach was optimistic about the upcoming season.

The coach's optimism was warranted. The team came home and won their season opener against JYP by a 3-2 score. Back home, things were also moving fast. Annie was just weeks away from her due date and they prepared for Jacob's parents to join them for a visit and help with the baby's arrival. Jacob took note of the schedule and felt relief that all games were just a bus ride away from home. The Finnish Liiga is made up of 15 teams located across the country and all travel was by bus. If Jacob was on the road and needed home for any reason, he was prepared to make arrangements to get there as quickly as possible. The team was also much more accommodating in working with Jacob than what he experienced with Smurf and the Ontario Reign.

Unfortunately, a frightening incident occurred just before the baby's arrival that only added to Annie's growing unrest and apprehension. The family was at a local supermarket and waiting in line with groceries when Harper grew restless. Annie decided to take her outside in wait by the car while Jacob stayed in line to complete the transaction. The longer the wait occurred, the more unease grew inside Jacob's stomach. By the time he paid up and bagged the groceries, he felt a need to get outside as quickly as possible. Something did not feel right.

Just as he rushed out of store, he heard a scream and knew instantly it was Annie. Jacob sprinted towards the car and there was Annie clutching onto Harper, fear in their eyes. Jacob got Annie to settle down in an attempt to learn what happened. They had been approached by one of the many refugees who were known to be staying in the area. He put his hand on Harper and spoke in broken English something to the effect that she was so beautiful and he wanted to take them with him. When Annie screamed the man ran off just as Jacob exited the store. Following the incident, Annie did not want to leave the house alone.

The big day finally arrived. Just two weeks into the season, Nash Jaakko Newton was born into the world one day before Jacob's twenty-seventh birthday on September 21, weighing in at 8.8 pounds. He could not have been more different than his sister Harper.

Where Harper was the dream baby, Nash was the polar opposite. He spent much of his time crying and would wake up at all hours of the night, letting everyone know that he was awake and in need of attention. Having Jacob's parents with them for a few weeks was a blessing, especially in caring for Harper who was just approaching her second birthday. Nash's big sister expressed a generous degree of excitement in his arrival but was also in need of her own attention. Meanwhile, Jacob and Annie were getting virtually no sleep at night. They were continually getting up to tend to Nash, and despite all their efforts he was almost impossible to get back to sleep. Jacob did manage to get some serious core workout during the ordeal. In an attempt to quiet his son, he would hold him while bouncing on the yoga ball throughout the night. Just when he thought Nash was sleeping, he'd slowly stop to lift him back into the crib. And Nash would go right back to crying, requiring Jacob to continue the bouncing.

The sleepless nights were having an adverse effect on Jacob's play. But more concerning, the ordeal was having an impact on Annie's outlook. She was suffering from postpartum depression, made all the worse by the darkness now covering Finland and the unsettling incident with the refugee. The arrival of winter was met with extreme cold and only glimpses of sunshine barely peaking beyond the distant horizon. Jacob tried to pick up Annie's mood with outdoor views of the spectacular Northern Lights often visible on clear nights. Nature's most spectacular light show, the Aurora Borealis can be viewed from Finland's northern Lapland region for roughly 200 nights during the year. And now, even in Vaasa with little light pollution and clear skies, the spectacle was often visible in spectacular fashion. Vivid colors of green, blue, red, and yellow lit up the sky. But nature's light show only went so far in raising her spirits. Nash often appeared wide eyed at the colorful display viewed outside in the middle of the night with Mom and Dad, but Annie could not seem to shake her depression.

On the ice, the team continued their solid play. They were hovering right around the .500 mark going into the new year and in position to make the play-in tournament, if not the playoffs. To make the play-in, the team needed to finish no lower than 10th place in the 15-team league, and they were in good position with over half of their 60-game schedule played.

Fighting through the sleepless nights, Jacob was inspired by the home crowds and doing his part to lead the team's defense. However, Annie was growing increasingly depressed and Jacob could sense that the growing demands coupled with darkness so far away from home were taking their toll. Further, with half of the games on the road and Jacob not always available to help out, more and more of Annie's time was required to care for a demanding newborn along with a toddler. Jacob could sense that she was growing more and more restless, and the final straw occurred while Jacob was skating with the team during a practice session.

The equipment manager ran out toward the ice telling Jacob that he needed to get home right away. His wife called and sounded frantic. Jacob raced home in wonder of what could possibly be happening. Rushing into the apartment, he saw a frenzied Annie clutching Nash who was crying. A frightened Harper stood nearby. On the floor was a toppled child's seat which they would often place Nash in so he could bounce and settle down. Next to the seat were traces of blood on the hardwood floor. Jacob tried to calm Annie down. What happened?

It seemed that Annie put Nash in his seat and momentarily placed it on the counter so she could tend to Harper. While bouncing, Nash shook the chair so hard that be bounced right off the counter and fell face first on the floor. Annie saw the whole thing transpire, unable to reach him before the fall.

They rushed Nash to a nearby hospital where he was kept overnight to check for any permanent damage. Jacob called his coach to say he would be unavailable for games or practice until they learned more of Nash's condition. He stayed the night with Nash, and was relieved to learn the next morning that Nash was fine.  Nature's laws enabling children to manage and survive such falls proved a saving grace.

Jacob was back at the team facility after missing one game, and able to make the upcoming trip to face the KalPa Kuopio.  On the ice, Jacob had perhaps his best game of the season, scoring a goal and named player of the game in an impressive 6 – 2 victory.  He wasn't sure exactly how he managed to perform so well after all the emotions and drama they had just experienced over the previous few days, but pondered if there was indeed any correlation between the excitement experienced and his stellar play.

When Annie broke the news upon his return of her desire to go home for much-needed help from her family and support group, Jacob had already anticipated the request.  As much as he hated to see his family leave him, he agreed that it was all too much for Annie and in her best interest.  Towards the end of January, Jacob dropped Annie and the kids off at the airport to join her family in St. Louis.  He told her that he'd join them as soon as the season concluded in a few months.  It was going to be a long two months.

For Jacob, hockey proved to be his salvation.  The team facilities became his home and his teammates his family.  Six hours every day and endless hours on the road, the time spent playing hockey and interacting with teammates provided the support needed to get through the long winter. There was always a small group or someone available from their close-knit group to spend time with at a local pub or restaurant after practice.  And several local restaurants became favorites for pregame meals or morning caffeine.  Among his favorites was the nearby Svenska Klubben restaurant. The cozy Swedish-inspired restaurant, featuring large windows offering panoramic views near the city docks, provided a most delicious breakfast which became a favorite of Jacob's: pannkakos.  The Swedish-style pan-cakes, similar to French crepes, were served with sweet toppings of jam, whipped cream, and fresh fruits.  At times, Jacob even experimented with smoked salmon as a special topping.

The tasty food in eclectic settings and social interaction with teammates proved a saving grace for Jacob but it was not the same without his family. It took some time getting used to the silence every time he entered the lifeless apartment, and the resulting insomnia found himself longing for nights with a chance to hold and bounce his months-old son.

The season was winding down and the team continued their solid play. Jacob appreciated the finesse style of play in the Finnish Liiga. Technique and strategy were prioritized over physicality, which played right into his skills and strength. However, there were the occasional fights. In a game against Porin Assat, left winger Josh Gratton was continually goading Jacob to throw down the gloves. The burly Canadian, with five years of NHL experience and a reputation for fighting and penalties, was doing everything in his power to take Jacob out of the game. Rather than taking the bait, Jacob focused on frustrating Gratton with deft positioning and stick handling to help secure a win. Years later, after their playing careers were over and sharing their hockey experiences in a live podcast, Josh shared with Jacob his memory of the game. He finally gave up on goading Jacob into a fight but could not forgive himself for doing so after the game. With the game winding down, Jacob scored a goal to help secure the win for Vassen Sport. To Gratton's chagrin, "If I got you in the penalty box with me, we might have won the game."

Vassan closed the season with three straight wins to make the play-in tournament in just their second season in the demanding Finnish Liiga. Unfortunately, Jacob felt something pull during the game and was unable to get a burst while skating. Every time he tried to push off to explode into action, he felt excruciating pain in his groin. He gingerly skated off the ice in search of the trainer. His season was over. He was suffering from a double hernia that would require surgery before getting back onto the ice.

The inability to participate in the play-in and chance to advance in the playoffs were disappointing, but also enabled Jacob an opportunity to get back to St. Louis and rejoin his family. He quickly made arrangements to join Annie and the kids who were staying with Annie's sister.

Jacob was thrilled to be reunited and observe the fast growth in Nash over just a few months. Meanwhile, Harper was growing even more beautiful. Jacob prepped for the surgery and some time off before getting back to training. This allowed time to plot out his next course of action. He met with his agent Roi to review their options and develop a strategy following a successful season in the Liiga.

Upon closer inspection, there were several issues with the existing contract. The team-friendly contract he signed also contained a team-friendly option for year two. The second year was for fifty-thousand euros, which was still well below the average salary in the league and across much of Europe. Jacob signed the original contract for an opportunity to prove himself, but the year two was even more team friendly given the season he just enjoyed. Further, Jacob was receiving interest from several other teams across the continent that would likely pay significantly more than the fifty-thousand euros from Vasser Sport. Another issue was legalese language which kept him from playing for any other team in the IIHF (International Ice Hockey Federation) unless he paid a penalty to get out of the existing contract.

His agent Roi was somewhat apologetic in not being better versed in language that appeared hidden in European contracts and IIHF rules. He suggested that an overseas agent who he could recommend would be more capable in finalizing future contracts from Europe.

However, another reality quickly sunk in. Annie made it clear that she and the kids were not going back to Finland. The trials and tribulations of a hockey wife and mom had finally caught up to her. Although not her first choice, she was okay with settling somewhere in the States, but not leaving her family and support group yet again to upend her living across the ocean.

Jacob was running out of options. And time. Developmental camps were taking place across the States for organizations that were finalizing their rosters for the upcoming season. Jacob was still recuperating from the surgery and had no team on their radar in America. Meanwhile, he knew he could not leave Annie and the kids and do it alone in Finland, or in any other country where teams that could possibly get him out of the Vassan contract were showing interest. He asked Roi to see what he could find in the States.

Roi found interest. The Idaho Steelheads were thrilled to sign Jacob. It was a step down from the Liiga and a move back into the ECHL, which is the same league he played in for the Ontario Reign. But the ECHL was still considered premier AA professional hockey and an opportunity to get back on the radar for the NHL Dallas Stars. Or for any other team with the vast network of scouts at every ECHL game.

The contract was for $950 per week with an apartment in Boise, the home of the Steelheads. In the middle of June, Jacob and Annie packed their bags and rented a trailer to move their stored furniture once again to a new home on their hockey journey. Annie was clearly not thrilled, but it was a compromise from travelling across the pond to Finland. And Jacob kept his dream alive to play in the NHL. Why not the Dallas Stars?

# Chapter Fourteen
# Czech-ed Out

2016 – 2017 season

## Team 1: Idaho Steelheads – Boise, Idaho

The move to Boise brought Jacob almost full circle from where he began his career skating for the River City Jaguars in the North Pacific Junior Hockey League. The entire metropolitan area, sometimes referred to as the Treasure Valley, boasts a thriving food and arts scene with plenty of outdoor activities available to the public. Right at the top of Jacob's bucket list for things to do was the Boise River Greenbelt, a 29-mile tree-lined pathway on the Boise River that flows right through the heart of the city. The problem was finding the time to enjoy the region's amenities.

Their first issue upon arrival was finding a suitable place to live. The team apartment was not fitting for a family of four, and there was barely room to move around once their furniture and belongings were all unpacked and arranged. To make room, Nash's crib had to be placed in the confined bathroom. The entire apartment complex also had a dirty and unkempt appearance. They arranged to find a more suitable place to live near downtown. Jacob and Annie were required to pay $100 monthly for an upgraded apartment and the team picked up the rest.

During her apartment hunting, Annie was able to find employment at the local Lululemon store. The work not only provided some additional income but also got her out of the house and drudgery of caring for two young children. This did, however, require sacrifice on Jacob's part.

Throughout the summer, the only rink with available ice time for practice and conditioning was 6 a.m. to 7 a.m. So, Jacob awoke at 3:30 every morning to work out in the apartment complex before getting an hour on the ice. He could then be home to watch the kids while Annie worked her daily shift at Lululemon. By the time she was back home for dinner and some family time, there was little time or energy left to explore the area.

Once practices started, they needed to rework their schedules and modify Annie's shifts to make sure that someone was home with the kids at all times since they didn't know anyone in Boise to help out. It was a challenge that afforded little opportunity to get out and socialize.

The Idaho Steelheads were coming off a 38-24-10 season and hoping for a shot at the Kelly Cup in their first season as a member of the league's Mountain Division. Their young head coach Neil Graham was entering his second season and looking to enhance his name and reputation as a riser in the Stars organization. He was looking for a physical team that played with speed and quickness, and viewed Jacob as the player to lead the defense.

What the coach didn't realize was that Jacob was just learning of a team in the Czech Republic that was making a tantalizing offer. His new agent Jacob Muzzatti, who spent years playing in the Italian Leagues following a stint in the NHL, had an intriguing proposal for Jacob. The Canadian-Italian, who represented Italy in the 2006 Winter Olympics, enjoyed a vast array of contacts across Europe and was very familiar with the IIHF rules and requirements. Just as the challenges of playing at a low salary in another new city were becoming exposed, an opportunity to play in a highly respectable league at a sixty-five thousand euros salary arose. Before he could commit, there were several issues that needed to be addressed.

The existing contract with Vassan Sport included a penalty clause if he were to sign with another team in the IIHF. Muzzatti got the Czech team to speak with Vassan in hope of arranging a buyout that would be suitable for all parties. After several days, Muzzatti met with Jacob to discuss the outcome and offer. Vassan Sport would not back off of the buyout penalty. The Czech team, Mountfield HK, agreed to pick up 2,500 euros of the penalty but Jacob would have to pay 7,500 euros out of his contract to finalize the buyout. Having to do this did not sit well with Jacob, but there was one additional factor that was playing into the Czech club's favor. They were scheduled to play in the Spengler Cup for the upcoming season. The annual tournament in Davos, Switzerland, is the oldest Invitational tournament in hockey and fields both club and national teams from across Europe, Russia, and Canada. Six days of nonstop hockey in an atmosphere that is considered almost on par with Olympic hockey for its pageantry and national/club pride. The lure of playing in the Spengler along with more than doubling his salary in a highly respectable league was almost too good to pass. But, how would Annie and Coach Graham take this news? The new season was fast approaching and all contracts had to be finalized before the start of the season. He had only days to make his decision.

As expected, Annie was not thrilled with having to move yet again. And understandably so, especially considering this meant yet another city and country across the ocean. At the same time, she was sensitive to the need to work given Jacob's lower salary and they were facing difficulties in working around their conflicting schedules. And it was not like they were able to see and enjoy what Boise had to offer. Further, the excitement Jacob displayed in playing in the Spengler could not be hidden. "Think of the Christmas vacation we can enjoy in the markets and beauty of the Swiss Alps."

Annie finally relented. She would take some time and remain in the States before taking the kids to join Jacob in the Czech Republic. Coach Graham was not as understanding. Just days before the start of the season and deadline to finalize all contracts, Jacob asked for a meeting with the coach. As Jacob entered the office, Graham smiled and asked him amicably how the move was going. That's when Jacob broke the news. He was taking an offer to play in the Czech Republic.

Jacob could understand why the coach was upset. Coach Graham had no idea of the offer and was counting on Jacob to be a big part of the team's upcoming season. Jacob tried explaining his reasoning and felt that the coach could understand his position and rationale, but that did not hide his visible displeasure in hearing the news. Jacob thanked him for everything and wished him and the Idaho Steelheads luck before walking out the door. There was no turning back.

Jacob and Annie packed once again. They placed the furniture in storage and drove to California where their trusted refuge away from home awaited them. The Andersons opened their doors to Annie and her one and soon-to-be three-year-old. Jacob had little time to stay and thank the family. With help from his new team, he booked a flight to Prague. A new season was getting started and Jacob had some catching up to do.

## Team 2: Mountfield HK Lvi (Lions) – Hradec Kralove, Czechia

The historic city of Hradec Kralove has been regarded as the regional capital of Eastern Bohemia since the tenth century. The city's historical significance is largely owed to its strategic location, lying at the crossing of old trade routes from the Baltic Sea to the Danube River and from Prague to Krakow, Poland. The eclectic mix of old and modern architecture is on display all along a long triangular plaza and tucked inside narrow streets which wind around the Elbe and Orlice Rivers. From the top of the Renaissance White Tower, one can view the entire city and catch glimpses of distant peaks representing various mountain ranges. Just south of the White Tower along the banks of the Orlice River sits the CPP Arena, home of the Mountfield HK Lions. In the city of just over 90,000 inhabitants, they had no problem filling the Arena on game days.

Mountfield HK competes in the top Czech league, Tipsport Extraliga. And Jacob could see early on that their rabid fan base was unlike anything that he'd ever encountered before. During games, the noise never stopped. There were organized chants, flag waving, drum beating, raucous cheering, and whistling. It was nonstop noise. Every game was played before an over-capacity crowd of over 7,000 which required about half of the fans to stand. And even those with seats remained standing throughout almost the entire game. Another surprise soon hit Jacob. He unknowingly adopted several loyal fans.

The first was the local BMW owner. The team owner greeted Jacob after a team win with the news. The burly owner who had the appearance of an Eastern European gangster waved his cigar and shared in his broken accent, "BMW owner really like you and want you drive brand-new car."

The other fans were a middle-aged couple who had season tickets about ten rows above the penalty box. After Jacob scored his first goal of the season, the entire section erupted as if they had just won Game Seven of the Stanley Cup. Jacob knew he had to meet and speak to his new fans.

As was tradition following all wins, the team skated around the Arena and waved to the appreciative crowd immediately following the game. After completing a lap, the players grouped together and bowed to the crowd. The fans loved it. Following the ritual, Jacob skated up to the couple to introduce himself. He learned that the husband had spent 15 years in Canada as a hockey referee and he enjoyed the passion and style of play that Jacob brought to the team. Jacob signed their banner and told them that he'd be looking for them at every game. True to his word, he sought and waved to them before every home game. And true to their support, they were at every game waving their American flag and Newton banner.

The atmosphere in the locker room was not as pleasant. Jacob was one of only two North Americans on the team, the other being a French-Canadian, and it seemed that nobody on the team got along. Outside of the North Americans, there was only one other import on the Czech team. English was rarely if ever spoken, and there was an atmosphere of coldness and distrust all around them. The players were led by team captain Jaroslaw Bednar. The grizzled veteran had a long and distinguished hockey career which included three seasons in the NHL. Bednar was the established star on one of the top teams in the Liberec, and he clearly knew it. His attitude eventually spilled onto the ice.

Jacob and Bednar were both on the ice during a power play. Every time Jacob got the puck in the pressure penalty situation, looking for a teammate or open net to attack, he could only hear Bednar screaming angrily for the puck. When play finally stopped and they returned to the bench, Jacob had enough and yelled his displeasure at Bednar.

"Shut the fuck up and let me play!"

A photographer captured the moment perfectly. What was probably seen as an intense moment of the game showing a player's desire to win was actually frustration voiced at a teammate. The team's winning ways continued but the atmosphere was growing toxic and it was affecting Jacob's mood. Fortunately, he was heartened by the fact that Annie and the kids were on their way and the Spengler Cup was fast approaching.

The arrival of his family was exactly the tonic Jacob needed to once again view life through a positive lens. It was disappointing that he was no longer in the spacious hotel room that the team provided upon his arrival, but they would find a way to make do. The BMW owner certainly helped out. Aware of the family's arrival, he upgraded Jacob's car from a BMW 128 hatchback to a 2-series Active Tourer. The new family car was perfect for trips around the area. They soon found a favorite destination just barely over an hour away: Prague.

The captivating city of Prague took Jacob back into another time. Once the car was parked, they allowed themselves to get lost walking around the Old Town and finding gems throughout the city. Crossing an ornate bridge over the Vltave River, they were surrounded by picturesque churches and the Prague Castle proudly overlooking the city. Lively cafés populated open plazas and the Christmas markets came out early in preparation for the upcoming holidays. With Nash now over a year old and Harper proving to be a responsible toddler, it was relatively easy to get around with a stroller and they enjoyed watching their children take in the sights and sounds with innocent amazement. The family would continue visiting Prague every weekend unless there was an away game that took Jacob on the road.

As the team prepared for the trip to Davos, Switzerland to compete in the 2016 Spengler Cup, Jacob received some unexpected news. Despite an earlier promise that he could bring his family, the team was not paying for accompanying family members. It would be impossible now to book accommodations during the busy season. Jacob's promise to Annie was broken. He would be going with the team alone while Annie and the kids were stuck in their cramped apartment during the holiday season.

The unsettling circumstances put a giant damper on the upcoming experience, but Jacob was overwhelmed upon the team's arrival in Davos. It only made the absence of his family hurt even more. The city was alive with color and pageantry. He had a taste of the festive hockey atmosphere while in Finland, but this was the Pitsiturnaus tournament on steroids.

For the 2016 Spengler Cup, host team HC Davos hosted another Swiss team, two Russian clubs, Mountfield HC, and a Team Canada made up of Canadian imports competing professionally all across Europe and Russia. The eyes of the hockey world were on Davos, Switzerland, between Christmas and New Year's Eve of 2016.

Fans decked out in their team garb were seen all over the resort city, mingling around trucks containing satellite dishes to televise the event from around the world. Every café in the charming region was packed with fans, and the snow-capped Alps which towered over the entire area added an aura of mystique that blended with the holiday spirit. In this cozy picturesque setting, the Vaillant Arena was the center of the hockey universe.

On the team's first full day in Davos, they were conducting warm-ups in preparation for their opening game when a reporter grabbed Jacob to conduct a live interview. With the bright lights shining on them under the arena's iconic chalet-style wooden roof, he was being interviewed on TSN, the popular Canadian sports network comparable to America's ESPN. They apparently learned of Jacob's Canadian background and were interested in getting his observations of playing overseas and competing in the Spengler Cup. All around him, more interviews were being conducted and Jacob could see that this was not just any hockey tournament.

Mountfield HC faced off the following evening, the second day of the tournament, against a Russian club from Yekaterinburg. Fans from both teams were vocal a full 30 minutes before face-off, chanting in unison and waving flags. The atmosphere was electric. The Arena's cathedral-like enclosure featuring layers of broad wooden beam captured the noise which was at times deafening. The intensity on ice matched that in the stands. Jacob skated off the ice following his first shift and noticed that his lungs were burning and his legs heavy. Was it the intensity of the action or the elevation? He observed in the warm-up the previous day that the higher elevation brought about some shortness of breath, but now with the game and hard-hitting taking place the feeling was amplified. Jacob suddenly understood why the host club Davos was so successful in their own tournament. There was definitely a home ice advantage for the Davos club.

The game stayed close throughout as Jacob and his teammates slowly acclimated to the thin air and lack of oxygen. When the final horn sounded, it was the Lions who survived with a 4-3 victory. Their fans were banging on the boards and chanting a victory song as the team skated up to acknowledge them and further excite the crowd.

The following day, they went up against the other Swiss Club, HC Lugano. This time, a 4-3 loss. The Lions were now required to face off against Team Canada for a shot to compete in the semifinals. For Mountfield, playing their third game in three days in the challenging elevation of the Swiss Alps, the Canadians proved to be too much. Team Canada skated off with a 5-1 win and would go on to win the 2016 Spengler Cup.

The experience of playing in the Spengler Cup was everything that Jacob had ever imagined it would be. If he could describe in one word, it was simply: "incredible". The only problem was that it did not include his family. He headed with the team back to Hradec Kralove with hope that the new year would see an improvement in both the hockey climate and harmony on the home front.

The situation did not improve. The team was winning games and near the top of the standings in the competitive Liberec, but playing for the Lions was not the enjoyable experience that Jacob had come to expect with the hockey brothers throughout his career. English was almost never spoken and there was very little interaction between the players. Some of the interaction with team officials were also a bit unsettling. Although he continued receiving pay, most was now coming in the form of cash seemingly under the table. This begged the question, was the team having financial problems and choosing to hide the disclosure of all payments? Further, the winter blues were also being felt at home and Jacob feared that Annie was once again contemplating leaving Europe to go back home to the States. There was relatively little to do in Hradec Kralove during the winter months and they mostly just stayed at home in their cramped apartment. The final straw likely occurred during a family outing with the kids.

In an attempt to get out of the house and let the children burn some energy, they searched and drove to a large indoor playground. While there, Jacob received a disturbing call. A team official explained that he received a frantic call from a neighbor in his apartment complex and there was some problem with his unit. They decided to give the kids a bit more time to play and enjoy themselves before rushing home to see just what was going on.

When they walked inside their apartment, they were met with flowing water covering the entire floor. Jacob searched in desperation for the source of the leak and found the water hose from the dishwasher had somehow gotten disconnected and was now spewing water everywhere. Water was leaking from their own apartment down to the unit below and causing damage.

They shut off all water valves and called the apartment manager for help in addressing the problem. It took days to clear and dry up the dampened apartment, and there was a good amount of damage in the aging structure.

The wooden floors were all water logged and would require repairs, along with clean-up and mold removal. Jacob had to pay one thousand three hundred euros to help repair the damage. The cold winter had grown even darker.

Around mid-February, Annie finally had enough. For the second time in two years, she decided that it was too much struggle living on the road taking care of two young children, and flew back to California and the Andersons where she felt more comfortable and settled. Jacob was unable to convince her to stay and in fact was beginning to question his own decision to stick the season out with the Mountfield Lions. But he was under contract and even if he was able to buy himself out, it was growing increasingly difficult this late in the season to sign with another team. His agent informed him from time to time of interest shown from other clubs in countries where it was not unheard of to change clubs midseason, but he also cautioned that some fine print in the contract would likely make it very challenging to part ways with the Lions. There was one glaring difference in his feelings with Annie and the kids leaving, from their departure the year prior. Some doubt was creeping in for the first time as to whether their marriage was strong enough to survive the mounting challenges confronting them.

The season was winding down and several strange occurrences took place which added yet more uneasiness to Jacob's frustration with the team and the season. Just about the time that the team owner was going on a late winter vacation along the Spanish Mediterranean coast, star player Jaroslaw Bednar came down with an undisclosed illness. He returned back to the lineup around two weeks later right about the time the owner returned from his vacation. The physical appearance in Bednar was un-mistakable. Despite the drab and cold weather felt all across the Czech Republic, Bednar came back with a suntan every bit as noticeable as that of the team owner. He was also back on the ice with no hint of any illness, and no questions were asked.

The team also found themselves on a losing streak. They remained near the top of the standings but were not playing their best hockey. Just before skating onto the ice for one of the final regular season home games, the team captain gave a hushed warning to all the players. For Jacob, it was translated into plain English.

"If we lose tonight, it's not going to be good. We need to play our best and get a win."

The dire warning did not deliver the intended result. The team lost and the losing streak continued. As the players dejectedly trudged into the locker room, they were met with a most unexpected scene.

Seated in the middle of the locker room was the city mayor, and standing behind him was the team owner. Both wore a serious expression, and the players knew to keep silent and take their place to hear what the two had to say.

After the final player settled into his space and the owner knew that all eyes were on him, he made a gesture which ensured that everyone had his attention and understood his intentions. He took a puff of his ever-present cigar and made a show of knocking the ashes onto the locker room floor. The pristine space traditionally viewed as sacred ground to the players was desecrated. The owner then put one hand on the mayor's shoulder while holding his cigar with the other and fell into a loud tirade that echoed across the entire room for a full fifteen minutes.

Although Jacob did not understand the Czech language, he was able to pick up certain words and the message was clear. The players all simply looked down with blank stares but then suddenly looked up with surprise and shock as the owner concluded his tirade. What could possibly have been said? The mayor then got up from his chair and the two brusquely walked off leaving a pile of ashes behind them. The players looked at one another with puzzled expressions.

Jacob immediately sought out and received the shortened translation. The team's recent performance was an embarrassment to not only the team but for the entire city. They are all simply stealing money from the team and not playing to win. Such uninspiring play is not up to the standards of the contracts that they had agreed to, and if they cannot prove their dedication and commitment to the team, then there will be penalties to pay.  Therefore, every player is required to take a VO2 max test, and if a desired level is not met, there will be unnamed consequences.

The requirement to drive two hours away to take such a physically demanding test at this point in the season with the threat of penalties seemed unthinkable.  Every team goes through its ups and downs, but to question the players' dedication and put such demands on them was not only an unnecessary task but downright disrespectful to professional athletes who give so much of their time and energy for the team.  The strewn ashes along the locker room floor further symbolized the disrespect which the owner obviously intended to project.  Jacob went to speak to coach Tomas Martinec to determine if the owner could actually get away with doing this.  The coach was sympathetic to the players' requirements and concerns, but he was now facing his own problems and convinced that there was nothing else he could to do to change the owner's mind.  Jacob and the others had no choice but to relent and make arrangements from their busy schedule with the season winding down to take the test.

The VO2 max test is designed to measure the maximum rate of oxygen consumption attainable during physical exertion.  The measurement provides a quantitative value of endurance fitness, thereby measuring one's cardiovascular fitness and endurance capacity.  To put the measurement into perspective, men aged 20 – 29 fall into the 90th percentile with a score of 58.6 or higher, and ages 30 – 39 fall into the 90th percentile with a score of 55.5 or higher.  To avoid penalty, players were required to attain a score above 58.

Jacob and the others drove the following day to take the test.  He was fitted with a tight-fitting mask and taken to a treadmill.  This brought about immediate angst.  He was not accustomed to a treadmill and never considered himself a runner, preferring the stationary bike which is also used to conduct the VO2 max test.  For this session, the treadmill was the machine to be used.  Jacob had no choice but to submit to the machine and hope for the best.

At the end of the day when all the players had completed the test, it was learned that only two players scored above the required 58.  Jacob and the others were told that they would face a 10% penalty for all subsequent pay. During a season which already saw him pay 7,500 euros to get out of the Vasser contract and 1,300 to repair the apartment, Jacob was now subjected to a 10% reduction in his remaining salary. The 65,000-euro salary that Jacob agreed to at the start of the season now seemed far removed. Jacob's mindset was quickly changing to just surviving the season and getting away from the Mountfield Lions.

The Lions got over the losing streak and finished the regular season in fourth place with a record of 29 – 16 – 7. They opened the playoffs with an impressive series win, defeating HC Verva in five games. They then went up against HC Kometa with the home-ice advantage, but lost in the semifinals to the eventual Extraliga title champs four games to two.

Jacob did his best to help bring about a title for the home team and their passionate fans, but it wasn't to be. He skated up to greet his personal flag-waving couple one final time and was astounded by what he saw. The two appeared even more upset than Jacob for the season's end, and they presented him with a small package.

The package was wrapped in the team colors of maroon, black, and gold. Inside, a home-made photo album with the Mountfield team logo of a lion on the cover. Jacob opened to the first page and couldn't hold back the tears. Written neatly on the left page were the words:

*We don't have to speak the same language to understand each other...*
*For Jake Newton*

*#4*
*Defenseman with Offensive Skills.*
*April 2017, Hradec Kralove, Czech Republic*

To the right was an extreme close-up of Jacob. Likely taken while sitting nearby in the penalty box. A look of intensity as if he couldn't wait to burst back onto the ice.

Page after page, the same format. Beginning with the next page titled: *How I met Jake Newton,* followed by *Our Hero in Action.* The trip down memory lane took him to Christmas, a family photo with their two teen daughters donning team gear in front of an American flag, with the words: *Merry Christmas for #4, From 4 of us.*

More and more pages with colorful photos accompanied with personal messages. On the final page, another family photo with a final message:

Dear Jake!

We would like to thank you for your ice hockey skills and your attention and wide smile which you often dedicated to us. We wish you good health, much happiness, and joy from ice hockey. We wish the best to Annie, Harper, and Nash too. Do not forget you have friends in Hradec Kralove....

Bartonicek family. Lenka + Milan + Eliska + Lenka

*Jacob posing with the Bartonicek family at a team function.*

Jacob thoroughly enjoyed interacting with the family for every home game, but had no idea how much his presence meant to them. Their precious gift made him realize the importance of not taking anything for granted and taking the time to reach out to others.

It was a long season. Despite the personal challenges and not scoring many points in a league focused on defense and with a team that promoted scoring for their offensive stars, Jacob once again stood out as the defensive leader. His agent shared at various times throughout the season that several teams across the continent were expressing interest, particularly during the Spengler Cup. But the long grind of the season was just too much to overcome and Jacob was actually relieved to end it and return home to California, free of any further contract obligations with the Mountfield HK Lions.

One thing that could always be counted on was the love and support of the Andersons. Jacob returned to their family home once again where he joined Annie and the kids. Both Jacob and Annie had done lots of thinking, separately, about their futures, and the one thing they could both agree upon was the need for a fresh start. Annie was offered an opportunity to work at a brand-new Lululemon which was opening at the Crocker Park location in Westlake, Ohio, a suburb of Cleveland. She was adamant that this was her final move and if he was serious about remaining in the marriage and working on their relationship, he would need to join her and the kids there where she had a job waiting. Jacob readily agreed to the move.

Annie also requested some time alone and they agreed for her to drive to Boise where their furniture was in storage. Jacob flew with the kids several days later to join her. They rented a trailer to haul their furniture and belongings to their final destination in Avon, Ohio. Jacob loaded the furniture onto a trailer hitched to their Mazda CX-90, and the family of four set off on a multi-day journey to their new home.

For Jacob, the long drive across the northern part of North American relieved some of the stress of the long season. It was wonderful to see his children's joy and once again be close to Harper and Nash, and to see Annie with a sense of purpose. So different from her mindset stuck in their overseas apartment during their past two years.

Jacob did most of the driving, and felt invigorated watching the land-scape change around them and feeling familiarity with America's road stop eateries. By the time they entered Ohio and closed in on Cleveland, Jacob was struck by the lush foliage that was greening all around them with the arrival of spring. He wasn't sure where the journey would lead but at least for now they had an apartment to settle in and a place to begin anew.

## Chapter Fifteen

# Happy Jake

2017 - 2018 season

**Team 1: KooKoo HC – Kouvola, Finland**

Jacob was lost in a sea of symbolic memories. Some of which he packed away while others he left behind as nostalgic mementos. Article clippings alongside colorful jerseys neatly folded and spread across the bedroom floor. Visible were reminders of his first season in Juniors with the River City Jags. Adventures from Boston with the Northeastern Huskies. The championship and MVP trophy with the Eppan Pirates. So many of the memories tied to Annie from over eight years of time spent together. The Lincoln Stars jersey he wore in Nebraska where they first met, the Val Gardena jersey with such fond recollection of their time in the Italian Alps. He could easily drown in the vivid evocation.

However, there was a somber backdrop to the entire packing ritual. Was this leading to the end of their marriage? Would leaving once again prove to be the final gesture to convince Annie that there was no hope? Annie remained defiant that she was not leaving her job and moving the kids, and Jacob respected her decision. But it became painfully obvious that he was equally unprepared to give up on the only thing that he had ever known and what had remained a passion from his earliest memories. Further, he viewed himself as in the prime of his hockey career entering his twenty-ninth birthday. His NHL dream remained alive. It was not out of the question for players entering their thirtieth year to finally make the jump to the NHL following success overseas. It just took one injury or unexpected event to create an opportunity, even if just for a partial season, to receive the reward of a modest (by NHL standards) but lucrative payday that could make an impact in all of their lives. If he walked away now, he would likely regret the decision for the rest of his life.

It's not like he didn't try. Living in a small town 20 miles from Cleveland's city center provided easy access to everything the family needed. A handful of jobs were available, from selling autos to working at a local athletic training facility. But the thought of not playing hockey and competing at a high level with his hockey brothers who all shared so much in common left a void which felt more like a giant crater. He was starting at ground zero in a world which seemed as foreign to him as that of a stranger arriving into a new country fresh off the boat.

Despite all efforts to stay together, the biggest telling sign was his relationship with Annie. The intimacy was fading, replaced with growing responsibilities and layers of trust levels which needed to be restored. Following the cheating affair in Allen, Jacob remained loyal to Annie. Even during the periods where she left with the kids during the long winter months, he socialized little and chose to stay in most of the time, calling home almost daily. But the prospect of getting back to what they once had was vanishing and Jacob felt like a duck on dry land trying to fit into what was expected of him.

When Muzzatti called with an offer from Finland, Jacob was immediately intrigued. A salary of seventy-thousand euros going back to the respected Liiga. Jacob's hockey experience with Vassan Sport was a good one, hindered only by the lower starting pay and unexpectedly losing Annie and the kids during the middle of winter. Playing for an established team without the drama experienced in Czechia would enable him to get back on solid footing and make a final push to achieve his lifelong dream. He would come back during holidays and maybe have them join him for a stretch of the season to enjoy a nice apartment in Finland. He continued packing the necessities that would get himself through the season while continuing to soak in the memories.

Jacob picked up a photo of him holding his two children with the Northern Lights in the background, and squeezed his eyes shut to stifle a tear. The biggest challenge was leaving Harper and Nash behind. Nash had grown into a two-year-old dynamo who was all boy. He could not get enough of the roughhousing and getting bounced around by Dad, and Jacob enjoyed reading and singing him to sleep every night. Harper was growing even more beautiful and continued bringing joy to everyone around her. Jacob loved how she could roughly tussle with her little brother in one moment and then have a thoughtful discussion which revealed her sense of humor and inner beauty. The elevated vocabulary that came out of her mouth never ceased to amaze him. Because of his own experience of abuse as a child, he did everything in his power to protect the two and build their confidence to handle any unwanted or questionable encounters. To leave them now at an age similar to his own age when the abuse occurred was a continual reminder of their vulnerability. He would remain in constant touch with them and make sure that they were always safe and protected, and he was confident that Annie would do the same.

With more time spent alone, he was also having further reflection of the abuse suffered as a child. The therapy over the years proved invaluable in understanding his actions and managing bad choices that were made, but that did not stop unanswered questions from continually surfacing. Why did it even happen? And could the little boy have done something different to change the outcome? How different would his life be today if the abuse had never occurred? Jacob was convinced that the triggers from fights on the ice played a factor in not making the final cut for the Ducks. And the endless drinking and partying to please others blocked him from achieving his dream during a time when rejoining the Ducks was right within his grasp.

Jacob could not help but feel that there was some unfinished business. More to accomplish. He was not yet to the point of learning from his past to take control of his life. There was so much more that he could and needed to do, even if not in the hockey arena.

Jacob made one last round to ensure that he had everything packed. For his carry-on bag, he double-checked for his passport and travel documents. Just before heading out of the bedroom for his final goodbyes, he noticed a book on the dresser: *the untethered soul*. He picked it up to admire its cover. A graceful chestnut-colored stallion running on a desolate beach, standing out against the grayness of sand, sea, and sky. Upon closer inspection, the horse appeared to have a horn. It was a unicorn. Below the title a tagline stating, *'the journey beyond yourself.'* And above, a quote from a critic proclaiming, *"Read this book carefully and you will get more than a glimpse of eternity."*

Annie had purchased the book some time ago but the pages remained unopen, as crisp as the day it was brought home. She had been more preoccupied recently with home and garden readings so likely wouldn't notice the book's disappearance, and he would return it after finishing. Plus, the book was mysteriously sitting there directly in his view as if to say, "Take me with you". Jacob found room to squeeze the book inside his carry-on. Perhaps he'd find some time to read on a full day of travel to Helsinki. Now came the hardest part. Saying goodbye to Annie and the kids.

** ** **

The city of Kouvola lies in Southeast Finland, a mere 40 miles frum the Russian border. The region is made up of a string of natural lakes and marshes, but any drive outside the city of 78,000 inhabitants would easily get you lost in narrow roads connecting the few small towns appearing across the coastal lowlands.

KooKoo was coming off of a respectable overall season of 26 – 24 – 10, although only 15 of those wins came in league play. Improvement was needed to get the team back into the playoffs and Jacob embraced his role as the defensive leader to bring the team back to respectability. He was committed to making an impact.

Beginning on the first day of practice Jacob arrived early, a full 30 minutes before the second arrival. He had the locker room set up with his own selection of lively music geared for inspirational energy and bodily movement. As his new teammates slowly began to filter in, they couldn't help but join in the dancing and soon the entire room was filled with laughter and an electric buzz that resembled a postgame celebration. The coaches rushed in to see what was happening on the first day of practice, a day normally quiet and reserved with anticipation for the upcoming season. The shirtless American stood surrounded by all his new teammates who suddenly stopped as if schoolkids caught in the act of breaking a rule. Jacob never broke stride and the coaches concealed smiles before leaving the room to begin day one of meetings and an organized practice.

Jacob continued the ritual, and it soon became as natural as lacing up the skates to engage in friendly greetings and perform dance moves to prepare for the daily grind of preseason. With Jacob greeting every player by name upon their morning arrival, it was only a matter of time before the reply most commonly heard became his moniker. Some used the name Mr. Sunshine, but most throughout the organization now referred to the lone North American as Happy Jake. A name that would eventually go on to be adopted by even the fans of KooKoo.

Happy Jake's own tap into mindset training began days before his arrival into the locker room. He was thrilled from the moment he stepped inside his furnished apartment. The only pause was the realization that Annie and the kids were not with him to enjoy such comfortable accommodations. Walking around the new digs to learn what he was acquiring he came upon an unexpected find. And, one which would have a profound impact on his life throughout the season. A whiteboard, complete with dry-erase markers and an eraser decorated the main wall of the living room. Jacob picked up a marker and immediately produced the first words which would become daily reminders to his mindset training.

In neat bold lettering in the upper right corner of the board he wrote down, "You will be fine". Below that he wrote, "Be HAPPY!". And then, "GRATEFUL!".

Moving to the upper left, he wrote down the names of Annie, Harper, and Nash.

The white board blended perfectly with another tool at his disposal. During the summer, Annie purchased for Jacob a workbook titled, *Creative Mediation and Manifestation (CMM): Using Your 21 Innate Powers to Create Your Life.* From the day of his arrival in Finland, Jacob began the process of reading, journaling, and meditating using the guiding principles of the book. The workbook outlining 21 days of reflection and exercises to cover everything from gratitude and trust to forgiveness and visualization.

Jacob sat back on a comfortable chair in the room and stared at the board, thinking of what else he would add. The white board would reflect his CMM exercises to serve as both a constant reminder of what was most important to him and a path for his destiny. There were no excuses or any room for negative energy. He was freed to detach from the past, readily accept all challenges, and find peace in the present by surrendering to the rhythm of nature.

Week one of practices came to a close when Jacob received the call from Danish teammate Patrik Bjorkstrand on a Sunday morning to join him and his wife at a nearby sauna. Just two miles from his apartment, Jacob pulled his colorful brown and orange team car into the parking lot for Tykkimaem sauna. Walking through the entrance and onto an expansive boardwalk along the edge of Kayralampi Lake, Jacob was met with a bustle of activity.

With a forest of pines lining the distant shore, patrons in comfortable white robes either lounged or moved between neat wooden stalls containing showers and different-sized saunas spread throughout the area. Jacob now noticed that not everyone was robed. Some enjoyed the sun's rays without cover, and it was clear that all were free to enjoy their liberation without judgement or discrimination.

Patrik spotted Jacob and introduced him to his wife, and soon several other teammates who happened to be in the area joined them. Jacob paid his 15 euro and dipped into what was to become an almost daily ritual in Finland.

After showering, they decided to meet up in the large sauna which was the main attraction of the complex. Over two tons of dense rocks were used to keep the vast enclosure steamed at just the correct level. The 90-person vacancy was almost always filled to near capacity with people continually entering and leaving, and Jacob noted an interesting phenomenon take place while in the sauna. The normally reserved and quiet Finnish people suddenly opened up. As challenging as it was to get even a simple response to a hello on the street, he now saw people chatting freely with whoever happened to be seated around them. Family information proudly shared, medical updates, nothing appeared taboo in sauna conversation. When word got out that "we have players from KooKoo in the room", interest piqued to an even higher level. Team members took that as their cue to depart and shared that they hoped to see all their new friends at the upcoming season opener,

Leaving the excitement behind, they rushed out to dive in the lake's refreshing waters. One teammate informed them that he was swimming out to claim a floating sauna. Each floating wood-burning sauna seated six and Jacob eagerly swam to enjoy another new experience. Sauna life was growing on him.

There was a buzz in the locker room the following week, well beyond even their normal greeting and dancing routine, and Jacob once again found himself in the middle of the spirited conversation. One of the KooKoo players was approached by a Finnish Sports magazine looking for six athletes and celebrities across the country to pose nude for a special edition celebrating the human body. The player expressed that he was not interested in posing nude, prompting a teammate to blurt out, "What about Happy Jake?"

Before he could even react to the suggestion, the entire team joined in unison of Jacob posing for the magazine. Comments could be heard that he was always walking around shirtless anyway and he had the right physique. All eyes were on him for some affirmation of his interest, which to his teammates already seemed a done deal.

"Sure. I have no problem posing for the magazine."

The music was cranked up even louder and laughter spilled out with dance moves choreographing runway shoots, complete with towel spins and exaggerated poses. Everyone was having fun with the possibilities as Jacob began to wonder for the first time just what he was getting himself into.

Things for the photo shoot were moving fast. Jacob was contacted by the magazine within days to collect info and set a date that worked for all. The shoot would take place at a lake and Jacob would be one of six celebrities, including athletes from football, track and field, and another, Finnish-born, hockey player.

Shoot Day quickly arrived and Jacob found himself growing nervous when Patrik stopped to pick him up for the drive to the lake. His nervousness had nothing to do with posing nude. Jacob was always very comfortable with his body. He viewed the human anatomy as a treasure which everyone should be proud of and respect with the proper nourishment and exercise. He had always taken the utmost care of his body and encouraged others to do the same. There was no reason to feel shame or embarrassment. But a sudden realization hit him. What if the photographer was an attractive woman? How embarrassing would that be if he has an unexpected reaction and they are unable to continue in what is a serious and professional operation? Patrik initially laughed off the concern but proceeded to provide some helpful hints when it became clear that Jacob's anxiety was not subsiding.

"Look, it's probably some dude but if it is a woman and she's hot, just think of your most matronly teacher from grade school. Or imagine her as an old hag who has some terrible disease. And hey, if worst comes to worst, at least she'll know how you feel and will likely take it as a compliment."

Patrik's words brought little relief but Jacob's fears were all for naught. After everyone arrived and settled in the organizers informed them all there was a slight change in plans. All but two of the models expressed discomfort in posing nude so there would be no nude shots exposing private parts. The shoot would include various stages of undress and continue its aim of celebrating the male body, but they could all relax in knowing that they would not be exposed in any way that would make anyone uncomfortable.

Jacob dove into the shoot with the same energy and intensity of a hockey game. It felt liberating and rewarding to work with a professional photographer, which made posing in nature both enjoyable and natural. Whatever anxiety that may have arose from posing nude was removed, and the photographer was indeed a man.

The 2017-2018 Liiga season saw KooKoo get off to a surprisingly fast start. One month into the season, the club made history by briefly leading the SM-Liiga standings for the first time in their 52-year history. Jacob was named an Assistant Captain who anchored the defense and was racking up points with power play goals and assists. Fans were showing their appreciation, filling the Lumon Arena to near capacity for almost every home game. The team was riding high with energy introduced from the very first practice. But it would not last.

For starters, it was not readily apparent who was in charge leading the coaching operations. Head Coach Tuomas Tuokkola was rarely seen due to what was rumored were medical issues. For over a month he never entered the locker room, was rarely visible during practice, and there seemed to be some disconnect between him and the assistant coaches who were now conducting most of the practice sessions. The team was slowly evaporating into a rudderless ship and despite all the players' best intentions, it was little surprise that the losses began to mount.

November introduced extended darkness and Jacob found himself overjoyed to get out of the house on a dreary Sunday to spend the day with his old coach, Jarno Mensonen.  Coach was back home in Finland for a short break from his coaching duties in Italy, and Jacob looked forward to catching up with the man who helped bring so much joy and success for Jacob's two years there.

Jacob pointed south to enjoy the morning drive, but after an hour began to grow apprehensive about where the narrow and desolate road was taking him.  The GPS was not picking up clear connection and there were few signs or towns to provide any reference to where he was.  He continued on the hope that he was indeed going in the correct direction, but doubt coupled with fear of being suddenly stopped on the Russian side of the border began to haunt him.  He felt relief upon viewing hints of civilization as the coastal city of his destination came into view.

It was good to catch up with Coach and his wife and share all the news of family back home and life in Finland.  Following dinner, Jacob shared how much Annie would enjoy seeing them, and arranged for a FaceTime with her and the kids.  Although he and Annie continued corresponding on a regular basis, Jacob had observed that the frequency and duration of calls were diminishing.  Further, FaceTime was no longer the favored medium for communications, replaced with simple messaging.

Jacob knew from the moment that Annie accepted the call that something was amiss.  There was little emotion or interaction, simply going through the motions of showing the kids and some small talk to get through the call.  When they said their goodbyes, Jacob knew that he needed to get home and have a deeper discussion to learn what was going on.

That evening, he learned what he both expected and feared.  Annie wanted a divorce.  There was no room for discussion, her decision was final. Jacob braced for a sleepless night and thoughts of what he needed to do in the morning.

Jacob texted in the early morning that he needed to meet with the coaches well before the nine a.m. team meeting.  He arrived at eight, and all the coaches were there to hear what he had to say.  For 45 minutes they allowed him to spill out his feelings and emotions.  Jacob broke down in tears almost immediately but received only support and encouragement to let out all his frustration. It was nearing nine and they all knew the players would be wondering what was going on. Happy Jake was not there to greet them and the closed door to the office was meant to ensure that nobody entered the coaches' quarters.

The coaches escorted Jacob into the locker room, which now resembled more of a funeral wake. Every player looked up in concern and wonder.

Coach Tuokkola took the lead and brought to everyone's attention the need for family and to always be there for one another in tough times. He equated the team as a family and told the players that one of their brothers had something he'd like to share.

Jacob walked to the middle of the room and everything stood still. For a moment, he wasn't sure if he had the courage to muster up the words before a room full of over 30 men who stared on in total silence. He started by thanking Coach Tuokkola for this opportunity to speak and shared that he may not be Happy Jake for some time as he dealt with personal and legal matters related to the termination of his marriage. The words began to flow and he openly poured out his feelings. He concluded with assurance of how important every teammate was to him and vowed that Happy Jake would soon be back and better than ever.

When he concluded his remarks, he looked up to realize that he was not the only one crying. Players approached with unconditional support and assured him that he was never alone. Whatever he needed, all he had to do was ask. They were there for him just as they knew that he was always going to be there for them.

Jacob sat back in his chair that evening staring at the whiteboard. Despite the emptiness, he felt a strength and power unlike anything he'd experienced before, and tried to understand how this was even possible. A day that began with such pain, doubt, and uncertainty had evolved into a lightness which eliminated all the heavy matter that was steadily suffocating him. He read the words "you will be fine" and smiled knowing just how grateful he truly was. What was it? How was it possible that he could sit here free of the negative energy that earlier consumed him?

The day was indeed a powerful stream of emotions. He had fully exposed himself to his coaches and teammates with the pain he was feeling. But his vulnerability had somehow become his liberation. To a man, he received love, support, and now this gift of freedom. He recognized the significance of everything happening where and when it did. How different the outcome would have been had it occurred the previous season with Mountfield, their locker room rife with distrust and discord. He focused on the moment with no excuses for what happened in the past and free of worry for what may happen in the future. There was a purpose and anticipation for the journey that he was travelling.

Jacob's gaze returned to the whiteboard. The names Harper and Nash constant reminders of who and what was most important to him. The name Annie now erased from view. There was one other change on the whiteboard. An open space on the lower left section of the board now prominently revealed the words, "USA Olympics!". Team USA had named a preliminary roster to compete in the upcoming Games, but the roster was still in flux. The Team, made up of non-NHL American born skaters competing professionally across North America, Europe, and Russia (with several college athletes mixed in), had just finished a disappointing last in the four-country Deutschland Cup. Although Jacob was not invited to compete in the tournament, there was still time to make an impression with Team USA scouts known to be flooding hockey arenas in a final push to upgrade the roster.

Jacob reached for the CMM handbook and turned to the exercise for Day 10, Visualization Drawing. He drew a scoreboard in the background revealing a final score of: USA 4 – Russia 2. The bottom of the scoreboard read: "Last goal scored by J. Newton". In the foreground, the back of a hockey player donning the number 5 and name "Newton" raising his stick in celebration. Before him a goalie in the net, helpless to stop the puck slipping past his shoulder. Jacob turned his gaze to the whiteboard.

*The whiteboard was now a backdrop of ice in sharp contrast to a deep blue and red jersey displaying the letters "USA" in bold white. The jersey comes alive with measured movement towards the goal, the number "5" now visible.*

*The player suddenly flicks the puck above the goalie's extended reach, just catching the corner of the net. The horn blares to a bright red light and a wild celebration ensues.*

Jacob's daily journaling also set the tone for another new opportunity. Writing his first blog. During a conversation with his agent's assistant, who was working with Jacob on filling out some contractual paperwork, he shared a little about his past and the journey he was going through with his CMM program. She was intrigued and suggested that he share his experiences in a blog, explaining the process in setting up a social media platform from which he could reach others in sharing his experiences. Jacob liked the idea, figuring it was a natural extension of his daily journaling and meditation, and wrote his first blog. Little did he realize the impact it would have later that season.

With just weeks to go before the holiday break, clubs across the European continent were competing against one another in games that did not count towards their league standings. This twist in the schedule enhanced the scouts' ability to single out players available to upgrade the final Olympic roster. The 2018 Games were taking place in Pyeongchang, South Korea, and with opening ceremonies set for February 9, there was little time to make a final impression.

Jacob was not just making an impression; he was setting the ice on fire. He scored a three-goal hat trick in KooKoo's first interleague game, and it didn't stop there. Following a two-goal one-assist game, the team's equipment manager approached him in the locker room with a startling observation.

"Happy Jake, you keep this up and soon you'll be wearing the golden helmet."

All across the Finnish Liiga, the team's leading point producer wears a golden helmet on game day. The idea of wearing the golden helmet never even entered Jacob's thinking. Defensemen are never a team's leading scorer, but Jacob now viewed the figures shared by the equipment manager and was shocked to learn that he was only points away from this distinguished honor.

Nothing was said among his teammates, at least not to Jacob, but it appeared that everyone was looking for him on the ice to ride his hot streak. Skating effortlessly, the puck always seemed to find him at the right time and in the right place. The goals and points continued piling up.

Sure enough, it happened. Just before departing for the holiday break, Jacob was awarded the golden helmet. His teammates surrounded him in celebration as Jacob proudly held up the coveted helmet, placing the black one in his locker. He skated onto the ice that evening fully aware that the many scouts in attendance could not miss the American skater at any time throughout the game. His confidence soared, as if the helmet somehow radiated a magical power. But it was Jacob's own work and perseverance that placed him here. He had done his part, now it was up to nature to run its course. Skating with determination, he fully embraced the moment.

Jacob returned to Cleveland to spend ten days with his family. He grew excited in anticipation of delighting the kids with exotic gifts from across his foreign travels. As expected, Harper and Nash were thrilled to see Dad and Jacob held onto them as if he never wanted to let go. Annie was cordial but without feeling or warmth, and Jacob naturally settled into the spare room in their Avon apartment.

Within days he received a call from his agent with the good news. Team USA was interested in his services for the 2018 Winter Olympic Games. Jacob raised a fist into the air and let out a yell that was likely heard across the entire apartment complex. However, his agent quickly informed him that there was an entire page of protocol and requirements to be met before the deal could be finalized. Drug tests, vaccines, medical checkups, documentation with proof of clearance related to a variety of matters. And time was running out. They were barely over a month from the opening ceremonies and all testing and paperwork needed to be finalized well in advance of leaving for South Korea.

The two went through the list in painstaking detail to determine if they could meet the deadlines. With the holiday season upon them, it would be another week before they could even begin scheduling for tests and exams to be conducted at specific destinations, and the required paperwork included some documents that required Jacob to go back to Finland to re-trieve. And they would have to meet with the team to rework the contract for any provisions which would allow him to leave the team. After much consideration, they concluded that there was simply not enough time to complete all activities in the required timeframe. One week earlier they likely could have made it. Two weeks for sure.

Jacob flew back to Finland one week later resigned to the fact that he would not compete for Team USA in the upcoming Games. But he also felt a strange sense of power and comfort. He had proven to himself, against all odds, that he was capable of willing his vision to come to life. Simple readings from *the untethered soul* served as a roadmap and writing on the whiteboard became the reality of his manifestation. He asked for nothing but received only unconditional support from everyone who he now consciously accepted into his sphere of life. Was life, which at times appeared brutally complex, really this simple? With nothing but the ocean far below, he closed his eyes and fell into a dreamless sleep.

Following Christmas, KooKoo returned to Liiga play and the loss-es predictably returned. Just as they had experienced earlier, there was disconnect with the head coach who was barely visible during practice sessions, and seemingly only a figurehead on the bench during games. The players began running their own plays and switching strategy in-game in an attempt to compete. When it was learned that coach only played several years in the lower Finnish leagues and received most of his hockey knowledge from academies, it made some sense in explaining why he was so unrelatable with his players. But now, even the assistant coaches were becoming impacted.

They approached Jacob and the other team captains following a practice with a most unusual request. "To save our season, we're asking you guys to meet with the team owner and request that Coach Tuokkola be fired."

The coaches reasoned that the request would carry more weight coming from the players, who had no personal interest other than winning games. And it was clear that Tuokkola had already lost the locker room, with players basically coaching themselves. The request did not sit easy with the team, but they agreed the situation was dire enough to warrant a meeting with the owner. The younger captains looked up to Jacob, who had become the unofficial team leader in both the locker room and on the ice, to take the lead in making this difficult request with the owner.

Several days later the meeting was set. Jacob did most of the talking with full support from the co-captains, and they left without any promise from the owner, who mostly just sat and listened to what the players had to say. Although cordial, he tipped his hat in no way regarding his thinking and concluded the meeting by standing up to lead the players out and thank them for their time.

The players learned of the outcome the next day. Following practice, Coach Tuokkola made a rare appearance in the locker room to make an announcement.

"It has come to my attention that my players are demanding my firing. Well, let me be clear, if I go down, I will make sure that some of you go down with me."

Jacob listened, enraged. That was his response? Rather than find a solution he was looking to cast revenge on young players who perform to the best of their abilities for their livelihood? Further, he was sure that Coach was directing his anger and gaze at the young captains who were only taking direction from the assistant coaches. Feeling a need to say something to protect his teammates, he stood up and all eyes were on him.

"Coach, your words no longer carry weight in this locker room. Every single player in here is doing everything they can to win games for you and for this team to help salvage the season."

The defeated coach stood speechless. He looked down, muttered something inaudible, and stormed out of the locker room. The losses continued.

Losing games in the long winter months of Finland while dealing with the realization of losing Annie and the kids so far away was wearing on Jacob. He did his best to maintain the Happy Jake image and spent all his free time reading when not at the sauna. One evening, Patrik and his wife stopped over for a visit and offered a suggestion to help relieve some of the winter blues. They introduced Jacob to a world that was brand new to him: dating apps.

"Come on, Jake. It's time to get back in the game. Let's get some photos and we'll get your profile started."

Just like that, Jacob had his first profile set up in a popular Finnish dating app. Patrik's wife put on the finishing touches and sat back with a look of satisfaction.

"You're all set up. This is sure to get a ton of attention."

One week later, Jacob found himself sitting across from an attractive Finnish woman at an elegant restaurant outside of Kouvala. The two had seemed to make an instant connection, intrigued by one another's background and career aspirations. Jacob listened intently as his date shared her recent experience of finishing second place in Finland's version of The Voice television program to discover new talent. Her penetrating eyes framed by arching eyebrows and dark wavy hair emanated a passion that Jacob found both relatable and enticing. It didn't really matter if the reason for not winning was due to her decision to sing the final song in English vs. Finnish. She obviously had talent and Jacob enjoyed discussing life's challenges and accomplishments with someone who shared his passion for life. The two parted ways that evening with a warm embrace and talk of experiencing more new things together in Finland. Jacob didn't hold any expectations with the divorce still not finalized and this being his first date in years, but it felt good to enjoy a wonderful evening of female companionship.

Jacob's fine play on the ice continued but team victories remained few and far between. The season was approaching the latter stages with teams battling for playoff position when KooKoo made the decision as a non-contender to sell off marketable players to contending teams. As the second-leading scorer among all defenseman in the Liiga, Jacob was drawing plenty of interest. So, it was no surprise when the GM called Jacob into his office to inform him that his contract was being purchased by JYP. It was now up to Jacob and his agent to finalize the deal with JYP for him to begin playing meaningful hockey in preparation for the 2018 playoffs.

Happy Jake said his goodbyes to the teammates who'd proved so supportive of him during this tumultuous season.  It was a most memorable stop along the path, but time to move on to the next leg of the journey.

## Team 2: JYP – Jyvaskyla, Finland

A three-hour train trip north brought Jacob into the heart of Central Finland's Lakeland region.  The city and entire region are surrounded by scenic lakes created by continental glaciers carved from the Ice Age 10,000 years ago.  Just like in Kouvola, the sauna culture was alive and well in Jyvaskyla.  What differed was the dynamic energy.  The city of 150,000 inhabitants boasted a renowned university which created a vibrant atmosphere and offered numerous amenities and nightlife in the city's lively surroundings.  Jacob was provided with a luxurious apartment, complete with a sauna, right in the middle of the city center.  He eagerly prepared for an exciting period of hockey and life in this colorful setting.

His arrival into Jyvaskyla aligned with a break in JYP's schedule.  There were no games scheduled for the weekend and the team held a Saturday night party at a popular night club in town: the Revolution.  Jacob's excitement for the evening was buoyed even further by the contract which he and his agent had just finalized with the team.  By removing a clause that would allow him to leave the team for the Kontinental Hockey League (KHL) following the season, Jacob opted for an increased guarantee to close the year with JYP for forty-thousand euros, with a condition that the team make the playoffs.  The playoffs were virtually a lock, so Jacob eagerly signed the contract.  Further, he was now under contract for the following season for one hundred thousand euros.  The decision to not opt out at the end of the season would come back to haunt him, but he went out that Saturday evening with the knowledge that he'd be earning over one hundred thousand euros for the current season.  His biggest career payday to date.

Jacob walked the short distance from his apartment to a bustling area alive with students and young people filling the streets.  His teammates were easily recognizable upon entering the club.  Several tables with attractive ladies surrounding the outgoing hockey players made for a festive scene which kept the waitresses and other staff fully occupied.  Jacob joined his new teammates with his trademark friendly greeting and was immediately drawn to the steady beat of music which had the dance floor near capacity. It was obvious that the women around the tables were eager to dance, but his teammates appeared more content to mingle or simply take in the eclectic atmosphere.  That was about to change.

With the dance floor filling, several young ladies at a nearby table took it upon themselves to clamber up on an empty table to dance.  They smiled at the friendly American who hadn't stopped moving since his arrival, and gestured for him to join them.  Jacob needed no further prodding. He raised his drink and took a step to join them before he was brusquely grabbed from behind.  He turned to see a teammate who informed him, "Jake.  We don't do that here."

Jake put an arm around the teammate and smiled.  "Well, this is what I do."

He proceeded to join the girls on the table, much to their delight and that of others around them.  Jacob barely sat for the remainder of the evening. And before the night was over, most if not all of his teammates had joined him and could no longer say, "We don't do that here."

Jacob had only been with the club for a short time when he received an unexpected call.  Finland's largest newspaper, Ilta-Sanomet, reached out to him for a story.  They came across the blog he wrote earlier in the season while with KooKoo, and now gauged his interest in having his story shared in their daily tabloid which reaches millions across Finland in both print and digital media.  Jacob jumped at the idea.  He met with a reporter and in no time his story was displayed in a four-page spread, complete with photos, for all of Finland to see.  There was no turning back.  In a season where he had grown exponentially by exposing all of his vulnerabilities, he had just shared his story of overcoming abuse for an entire country to see.  He had no fear or second guessing.  Only hope with the belief that countless individuals could now come forward and begin their own healing. It gave him added strength.

On the ice, Jacob blended in and did his part to keep the team's championship aspirations alive. He was not provided with the same scoring opportunities as he was with KooKoo, but focused on defensive stops to make his mark and help bring a third championship trophy to the city.

The team closed the season with an impressive 5 – 1 victory in Kouvala, and returned to Jyvaskyla in preparation for the playoffs. Because JYP finished top four in the standings, they advanced directly to the quarterfinals where they faced off against HIFK. The defensive-minded club from Helsinki finished just below JYP in the regular season standings, and was a formidable foe for any team in a seven-game series. Every game turned out to be a playoff battle, but JYP fell short, losing in six games.

It was a long eventful season that saw much growth and personal gain, coupled with the most profound pain. Jacob packed his bags heading back to the States for the summer. He could not contain his excitement in reuniting with Harper and Nash, and braced for a reckoning that he knew he must face to continue his growth.

** ** **

Jacob's arrival to Annie's house rental in the eastern suburb of Cleveland Heights was brief. He now entered a new experience in traveling alone with one energetic toddler and a four-year-old. As experienced as he was with both international and domestic travel, this new adventure proved daunting. By the time they arrived at the LAX airport, Jacob was relieved to see his parents there to greet them and heap attention and responsibilities on their grandkids.

That same attention was also much appreciated for the children's first trip to Disneyland. Jacob initially thought that he'd manage the day alone with his kids at the popular theme park in Anaheim which he enjoyed so much as a boy, but soon came to realize that grandma's presence made the day so much more manageable and fun. The next trip, motivated by the CMM Handbook, was one that he knew he had to do solo.

He was at the San Jacinto home of his boyhood alone when his parents left for a full day to spend with Harper and Nash. Jacob had given much thought about this moment, and the time had come for him to face the demon of his past. There was no turning back.

He entered the room where the abuse had occurred for the first time with the full intent of bringing back all the memories that he had consciously removed as a child. The bathroom which was the place of so much pain and suffering was now hoped to be the source of his healing. If he could confront and destroy the demon which had plagued him on and off for a lifetime, then he could free himself of the chains which had tied him down. He wished for freedom to pursue his true meaning and aspirations.

*Jacob closed his eyes and felt a heaviness upon his chest. His cousin John, who was once imagined as an intimidating shadow of evil now appears weak and frail. Conniving, fighting to control an innocent young boy with wispy blonde hair who is lost and frightened. The child feels helpless and is forced to do things that he knows are wrong. There is no escape. The scales of intimidation and control are stuck in complete favor of John and the child has no recourse. But somehow, it is John who appears defeated. His hollow eyes reveal a cold emptiness as if there is no soul. In his efforts to exact abuse, he in some way projects a tortured forlorn figure.*

*The innocent child stands still and afraid. A tear rolls down his cheek as he looks up for some type of support or comfort that he expects does not exist. Jacob squats down and rests his right hand on the boy's left shoulder. He smiles a reassuring smile and simply says, "I love you. You have done nothing wrong, have nothing to fear, and you are perfect just the way you are. You are freed from any more pain. I've got if from here."*

*The boy's face radiates with a brightness that fills the room. Jacob hugs him tightly as tears flow freely down his face. The boy returns the hug and the two remain locked in an embrace that generates a collective strength which consumes them. All energy is momentarily released from Jacob's body. At the same time, he feels a freedom unlike anything he has ever experienced.*

# Chapter Sixteen

# Detour on the Autobahn

## 2018 – 2019 season

**Team 1: Beyreuth Tigers – Beyreuth, Germany**

Jacob sat in the passenger seat of a luxury German-made automobile in complete fascination. The Bayreuth Tigers team owner proudly shared his excitement in having Jacob join the team for the upcoming season, but Jacob was more focused on disguising his lean to discreetly read the speedometer. Since being picked up at the Nuremberg airport, he was expecting a leisurely ride to his new home. But road signs on the Autobahn showing driving distance in kilometers to Bayreuth were diminishing almost as fast as he could count. Just how fast were they going? And how cool to drive at this speed without worry of a siren to pull them over!

Jacob decided to give up on the reading and simply take in the Bavarian landscape while reflecting on the unusual turn of events that brought him to Germany. When he received a call from the JYP GM to see how his summer was going, the last thing he expected to hear was the unforeseen realization that his contract had an unexpected clause which made him unavailable to the team until January 1, 2019.

It was time to once again secure a new agent. He would still receive the full pay and in fact additional money from Bayreuth, but such an oversight was impacting his personal plans. As much as he embraced every moment that summer with Harper and Nash, the living situation at home with Annie was growing increasingly toxic. And joining a team midseason without any practice or playing time would be extremely challenging. Individual workouts only go so far. Nothing can replace the participation in live performance on ice. He turned to former NHL star Michael Nylander to represent him for future contracts with a hope that the Swede may one day find him a home in the coveted Swedish Hockey League (SHL).

Nylander's investigation resulted in several difficult pills to swallow. Two teams in the KHL made offers, but due to removal of an out-clause in Jacob's contract with JYP, he was unable to accept either one. HC CSKA from Moscow offered four hundred thousand euros and Dinamo Riga (Latvia) offered one hundred ninety thousand euros. Jacob's decision to go with more guaranteed money from the prior year seemed a good idea at the time, but now he realized how costly that decision had been.

Time was running out to find a team and JYP was not helping matters by continually changing their collective mind on whether or not they would allow Jacob to play with another club before January 1. JYP finally gave the green light for Jacob to sign with another team for games up to the end of 2018.

As for Jacob, he was well aware that the temporary move to the lower-level Bayreuth Tigers would be a far cry from Finnish hockey in the competitive Liiga. The final selling point to accept the proposal was the promise to participate with the parent club Nuremberg Ice Tigers for their invitation to the 2018 Spengler Cup. Jacob reasoned that playing with two clubs in the Spengler would look good on the resume, and the opportunity of playing in the Tournament was such a sublime hockey experience.

Without any more time to think or reflect on the journey, they found themselves entering the historic city of Bayreuth. The owner proved to be a wonderful tour guide, driving through cobblestone streets in Old Town and past the Oberfrankenhalle Sports Arena where home games were played. He made a point of showing off the Wagner Museum, displayed in the former villa of the famous composer, Richard Wagner. Handing Jacob a key as he dropped him off at his new home near the Roter Main River, he promised future visits to show Jacob much more of his new Bavarian home in the city of Bayreuth.

Competing in the second tier of German hockey was in fact a far cry from life in the Liiga.  The workout facility next to the team's locker room was so small and cramped that they could barely fit five people in the dimly-lit room at one time.  The lone equipment manager had difficulty keeping up with the constant demands and lacked the expertise to sharpen skates.  Fortunately, the team had two Finns who were both quite experienced in the art of skate sharpening, and they took it upon themselves to conduct this important task for their teammates.  As for the playing surface, that was another issue.  The Arena had openings at both ends which enabled birds to constantly fly inside.  It was not at all uncommon to see bird droppings on the ice during practice and on game days.

Jacob did not allow the conditions to deter him.  He continued the practice of arriving first to create an atmosphere of fun and winning.  As in Kouvala and other stops along his hockey career, the American became the team leader both on and off the ice.

The fans were also a joy to play for, and true hockey fans.  The atmosphere was much like that in the Czech Republic.  Every game was a sellout with the fans who barely sat holding banners, flags, and chanting or whistling throughout the entire game.

There was one game that stood out for Jacob in his time with the team.  And it had nothing to do with his play on the ice.  He was on the ice in pregame warmups when the bus carrying the visiting team from Freiburg finally arrived.  Jacob looked on in anticipation as the visiting players hurried to their locker room, but one player made a point of rushing directly on the ice to greet Jacob.  It was fellow Californian Alex Miner.

Alex contacted Jacob for the first time during the 2017-2018 season while Jacob was with JYP.  He arranged a FaceTime call and had lots to share.  Alex was born in the foothills of the San Gabriel Valley in the city of Glendora, just 25 miles northeast of downtown Los Angeles.  He had been closely following Jacob's career since his time with the Junior Kings and made a point to come out to watch his games with the Ontario Reign. He was drawn to the style of hockey as well as the passion which with Jacob played and was inspired to take up the sport himself, modeling his game after Jacob's.

After graduating from Quinnipiac University where he honed his hockey skills, Alex went on to Strasbourg to play professionally in the French League.  On their call, he explained that he had been wanting for years to contact Jacob to introduce himself and discuss life and hockey, but for some reason could never make the call.  Alex had countless questions, and the two hit if off like long-lost brothers.  Now they stood together in an embrace on center ice, meeting for the very first time.

Jacob played the game with extra motivation as if to pave the way for the younger brother he never had.  For his part, Alex played with the same intensity as if to prove himself as Jacob's protégé.  The need to prove himself was not necessary.  The two shared a common bond and mutual respect that would go on to serve not only as mentor and mentee, but lifelong friends.

There may have been no fan more dedicated than the team owner who was doing his part to keep Jacob on this team for the entire season.  As promised, he came back to show Jacob more of Bayreuth.  The Christmas season arrives early in this region of Germany and he wanted to make sure that Jacob enjoyed every aspect of the festive surroundings.  The main square was alive with rustic wooded huts offering an array of traditional Bavarian crafts and culinary delights.  The two stood at a strategic spot to take in the crowd while enjoying mulled wine.  Jacob found the warm spiced beverage absolutely perfect for the setting.  The only thing missing was having Harper and Nash with him.  Jacob vowed that he would one day bring his children back to enjoy this cherished tradition with him.

Jacob's time with the team was winding down.  The owner came through once again to speed Jacob back to Nuremburg on the Autobahn. Although he would not be going back to skate for the Tigers, Jacob was sincere in his thanks for all the team owner had done during this unexpected transitional period of the hockey season.

Although excited for the opportunity to skate once again in the Spengler Cup, there was somewhat of an empty feeling in making the trip with his new club. Jacob got just one practice in with his unfamiliar teammates before they departed for Davos.

The electric atmosphere of the Spengler was everything that Jacob remembered from his first visit. The difference was his involvement in the games, appearing in only one game against Team Canada. A loss that saw the Nuremburg Ice Tigers eliminated from the Tournament. A team familiar to Jacob from the Finnish Liiga won the tournament. KalPa Kuopio defeated Team Canada in a shootout to claim the title. It was time for Jacob to get back to Jyvaskyla, where he would close the season with JYP.

## Team 2: JYP – Jyvaskyla, Finland

Jacob was happy back in the dynamic city and with the team and teammates with whom he had closed the prior season. However, the darkness that now covered Finland was casting its shadow inside the locker room. The team won their first three games to open the new year and traveled to KalPa with a respectable record of 17-15-6. It may not have been up to the club's high expectations, but Jacob felt the team was playing well and he was eager to help get them into the playoffs. That evening, following a 3-2 loss to the Spengler Cup winners, Jacob and his teammates sensed something different in the air. Two days later, it was announced that their head coach Lauri Markivi was relieved of his duties, to be replaced by Risto Dufva.

For Jacob and his teammates, the move was consequential. The new coach was definitely old school. From the moment they skated out for their first practice under Dufva, the change was crystal clear. Here they were, midseason, and the coach ran the practice session as if it was a preseason conditioning camp. Jacob retreated with the others to the locker room following practice with the realization that things were definitely going to be different.

In addition to the more rigorous practice sessions, the coach seemed to be confusing the players with mind games. Suddenly changing instructions or showing displeasure for unknown reasons. It was keeping the players off balance. One thing the coach was clear about was his demand for everyone's attention to detail.

The team was in playoff contention when Jacob learned that Coach was unavailable for a home game against the Pelicans on February 6 due to an illness. For Jacob, it was like the stress and weight of the world was suddenly lifted from his shoulders. That evening, in a game where everything seemed to go right, he scored three goals for the hat trick in an impressive 6-2 win. The entire team played with a passion and joy that they had not felt for some time. Coach was back at his spot on the bench for a loss at Vassan two nights later.

*Jacob celebrates his third goal for the hat trick.*

The season was coming to a close when JYP travelled to KooKoo for their final game of the season, needing a win to make the play-in tournament. KooKoo was out of the playoffs but looking to play spoiler by ending JYP's season. The game was on and Jacob's old team was on top of their game, making life difficult for JYP in their bid to reach the postseason.

Jacob was also on top of his game. In a game that JYP had to win to finish above Vassan Sport, he scored two goals in the 5-4 shoot-out win. JYP would now face off against Lukko in a best-of-three play-in series with hopes of making the playoffs.

The team traveled to the coastal city of Rauma for game one. In a game where JYP never seemed to get on track, Jacob took a hard hit on his knee and was unable to continue for the duration of the series. JYP lost the game and ultimately the series in three games. Jacob and the JYP's uneven seasons were over.

Jacob traveled back to Cleveland determined more than ever to make a final push for a pivotal season in his hockey career. He would go into the 2019-2020 season as a thirty-one-year-old. Time was running out and this may be his last opportunity to achieve his hockey dream. He informed Nylander of his desire to compete in the SHL. If the Swede could use his connections to get him into the Swedish Hockey League, that could be the break that he needed. As good as the Liiga was, the SHL was arguably the second-best league in all of hockey behind only the NHL. Perhaps exposure to the SHL could even lead to a late-season call up to an NHL team looking for last minute replacements in their playoff push. Whatever it took, Jacob was focused and determined to make it happen.

Jacob had two goals for the summer. One: get in the best shape of his life; and two: spend as much time as possible with Harper and Nash. Every morning, he made breakfast and entertained the two before driving them to daycare. After dropping them off, he fought the tears along the twenty-minute drive to Life Time Fitness Center in the Cleveland suburb of Beachwood. Dropping them off was a trigger of despair that he knew would be final when ultimately leaving for his next hockey destination in late summer. He prayed for the strength to not expose the tears to his children, showering them with joy and love from Happy Jake. It was indeed a wonderful and rewarding summer with the now three- and five-year-olds who were growing into everything that Jacob could have possibly hoped for.

Jacob received a call from Nylander with the good news. IK Oskarshamn was moving up to the top-tier league of the SHL and offering Jacob a contract for ninety-thousand euros. A chance to compete in the coveted league and make a name for himself for a team with much to prove.

He was ready. In the best shape of his life and determined to make his dream come true.

# Chapter Seventeen

# Scandinavian Finale

2019 - 2020 season

### Team 1: IK Oskarshamn – Oskarshamn, Sweden

The city of Oskarshamn lies on Sweden's southeast coast along the Baltic Sea. Accessible from the scenic shoreline are ferries which take visitors and locals alike to nearby islands and the Damen Oskarshamnsvarvet shipyard. Outside of that, a handful of cafés and eateries, and the community's sports complex including the Be-Ge Hockey Center, there's not much activity in the small town of just over seventeen thousand inhabitants. A drive through the commercial area takes mere minutes if you time the lights just right. This served Jacob perfectly in his quest to focus on hockey and make a name for himself in the coveted SHL.

Jacob picked right up where he left off and continued his practice of being the first to enter and warm up the locker room with music and greetings. He was joined by a fellow American import and several Canadians, blending in with their Scandinavian hockey brothers to bring winning hockey to the club in their inaugural SHL season.

Jacob got his first taste of SHL hockey in the team's first preseason (friendly) game against the Vaxjo Lakers. From the opening face-off, Jacob was astounded by the precision and puck handling that the Lakers displayed in controlling the game. They dominated play with IK constantly on defense and rarely even having the puck in their possession. In all his years of hockey, Jacob had never seen such a display of timing and precision. Despite Vaxjo's dominant play, it was Oskarshamn who took advantage of a penalty and scored the game's first goal.

The game remained tight and the two teams found themselves deadlocked with the game winding down in a 1-1 tie. Jacob was on the ice in a power play possession when he took a pass and slapped the puck past the goaltender to secure the win. In IK Oskarshamn's first game in the SHL, albeit a friendly which does not count in the standings, the team came away victorious. The player's celebration in the locker room was proof that the game meant more to the players than just a friendly victory.

One week later, the club faced off against the Malmo RedHawks. Jacob's assist helped to tie the game, but Malmo scored in the third period to come away victorious, 4-3. Jacob was playing excellent hockey and believed the team's competitive play would have them ready to compete in the upcoming regular season. He was excited to get the season started and experience hockey in the SHL.

Several nights later, the unthinkable happened. Jacob awoke around 4 a.m., feeling a strange sensation as if forced to swallow. He sat up and turned on the light to gather his senses. Looking down, he observed a stream of blood dripping on his arm. He was swallowing blood.

He tried everything to stop the bleeding. Tilting back his head, pressing a wet cloth against his nose. Nothing worked. Several hours passed and panic began to settle in as he could not only not stop the flow but now his nose was bleeding profusely. He called to wake up the trainer and see what he should do. One hour later, the ambulance arrived at this house to transport him to a nearby hospital. He had lost a significant amount of blood and needed immediate care to both stop the bleeding and receive blood infusion.

Jacob remained in the hospital through the next night, and was slowly getting his energy back when he walked into the team's practice facility several days later. The team had two acting head coaches, Hakan Ahlund and Per-Erik Johnsson, that inaugural season in the SHL. Expecting to receive some form of concern or interest in how he was recovering, Jacob was surprised to see that none of the head coaches even acknowledged him. It was no surprise that he didn't suit up for the team's next game, but the reaction he received on the day following that game was a total surprise.

The team's GM walked out of the coach's office and approached Jacob. "The coach would like to talk to you in his office."

Jacob immediately sensed something was amiss. Earlier he watched his American teammate David Goodwin exit the coach's office and he did not look happy. Jacob didn't have the opportunity to ask David what happened, but now he entered the office expecting to hear the same message.

The exchange was brief. Ahlund bluntly informed Jacob that the team was going in a different direction and he was free to join another team. He was still under contract and would continue receiving his pay with the apartment and car until he was able to find another club. He could also use the team and practice facilities for as long as it took for him to secure a new team. He wished Jacob luck and escorted him out the door without even allowing for an opportunity to ask for further explanation.

Jacob was stunned. He came into the season in the best shape of his life, had two excellent preseason games, achieved the highest athletic test scores among his teammates, and was determined to realize his lifelong dreams. Now here he was, just days removed from a medical emergency which could have sidelined him indefinitely, showing his dedication to be back with the team, and suddenly told that his services were no longer needed. It made no sense.

Jacob met up with David over the next few days and it was not lost on them that the two Americans were suddenly removed from the team. Was there some kind of discrimination against American imports? It was also not lost on them that the coaches never once spoke English during team activities or meetings. The two had to continually ask their teammates for a translation. David had already put feelers out and through his agent was looking to find another club. But before leaving, the two agreed to get away from Oskarshamn and treat themselves to some reward for all the troubles they had been through.

On a perfect September morning, they packed their bags and drove the five hours to reach their destination in Copenhagen, Denmark. They crossed a bridge from Sweden to enter the picturesque city standing on the coastal islands of Zealand and Amager, and left all their troubles behind them as they prepared for a weekend of fun.

After checking in at the luxury hotel that they decided to treat themselves to, they took an Uber to the city's popular meatpacking district to get the weekend started. It was a weekend of bliss. On Saturday, they rented scooters to see as much of the enticing city as possible. Massive canals spread all across Copenhagen provided a bevy of opportunities for relaxation and entertainment. People sitting and tanning all along the canal, many of them naked. There were even volleyball games taking place in the canal's lower waters.

During the evenings, they went out and discovered the city's active nightlife. Meeting attractive Danish women and dancing in the underbelly of exotic clubs making up the city's unique nightlife scene. It was the perfect way to get away from the uncertainty which had just thrown a curve at their respective hockey careers.

Shortly after returning to Sweden, David accepted a demotion to play for Mora IK in the second-tier Swedish League. Jacob was not ready to make a move. He was tired. He had worked relentlessly since leaving Jyvaskyla to make this push and get in the best shape of his life for the upcoming season. He needed a break. He had an apartment and a car so would continue to work out but take the time to read, relax, and enjoy the local saunas. It was time to work on the mental aspect of his conditioning to catch up with the physical. The answers would come.

Jacob settled into a daily routine of exercise, reading, journaling, saunas, and of course his morning coffee. One morning at his favorite spot in the Oskarshamn Espresso House, Jacob was approached by a fellow patron who introduced himself as Andreas. Andreas had overheard some of Jacob's phone conversation in English with his agent, and was intrigued by his story. The two sat down to chat, and before long learned that they had much in common. Andreas' wife was from California, he knew of

San Jacinto, had two young kids, and was an avid hockey fan. What Jacob found interesting was that Andreas knew of Jacob and shared the rumor he heard of why he was cut. Apparently, the club was letting out in leaks to the press that Jacob was cut from the team because he was "out of shape".

Jacob could only laugh at the absurdity of the leak. Of all the reasons they could have provided, this was probably the least plausible. He remained confused as to why he and David were so unceremoniously removed from the team. But the mystery was not going to impact his outlook.

Jacob and Andreas would go on to meet almost daily to sit and chat at the Espresso House, sometimes also meeting up at a local sauna. They soon learned that they also shared a passion for music, and Jacob was thrilled at the idea to record a song together at Andreas' in-house recording studio. Following a few practice-runs, Andreas got out his guitar and the two nailed Dante Bowe's spiritual song, "Your Majesty." For Jacob, it was a first and an accomplishment that he was most proud of.

Coach Ahlund did not appear too thrilled that Jacob was without a team and still using the team's equipment and practice facilities. They amended the workout agreement to say that Jacob now had to use the training facilities over 64 kilometers up the coast with the Vastervik IK club. Jacob made the fifty-minute drive every day to Vastervik where he resumed his role as Happy Jake and was sometimes invited to join the team in their practice sessions. The coaches and young players in the second-tier Swedish League certainly enjoyed and appreciated Jacob's contribution to their team development and practice sessions, but when it became apparent that Jacob still wasn't seeking another club, Coach Ahlund made yet another change.

Jacob was now relegated to working out at the practice facility for the local 16 and under Youth Hockey League Team. Jacob skated around the young players lined up in drills to learn basic hockey skills and was more amazed than perplexed as to the steps the team was going through to get him out of Oskarshamn. He suspected that it may have something to do with the poor start that the Club was having in their inaugural season in the SHL. They were languishing in last place with only a few wins and it wasn't a good look having the player removed for being out of shape so visible and looking fit to play.

Jacob was ready to move on. He reached out to his agent and asked what was available to get back on the ice to close out the 2019-2020 season.

## Team 2: Storhamar Dragons – Hamar, Norway

Jacob was appreciative of the opportunity to join one of the top clubs in Norwegian hockey over the last 30 years. Professional hockey was first introduced to Hamar in the 1950s. For decades, the club played their home games outdoors on natural frozen ice. Despite this modest infrastructure and limited budget, the club found success and reached the second level of Norwegian hockey. Things really opened up in 1981 with a new arena, and the club's outstanding play moved them up to Norway's top level of hockey. But, an even bigger break was soon to take place.

When it was announced that nearby Lillehammer would host the 1994 Winter Olympic Games, lobbyists successfully arranged to have a world-class arena built in Hamar. The hockey club moved into their new home in 1992, setting the stage for increased revenue with Hamar now a desired destination for the country's top talent. The Storhamar Dragons won their first Norwegian title in 1995, and entered the 2019-2020 season looking for their eighth national title. The club was also an annual contender who found success competing in the European Continent's Championship Hockey League.

In addition to a love of hockey, the scenic city of 33,000 inhabitants nestled alongside the country's largest lake holds unmistakable ties to its Viking culture. The Hamar Olympic Hall stands prominently along the shoreline, resembling a Viking ship which gives it the name Vikingskipet (The Viking Ship). Remnants of longhouses and other structures remain in the area, providing evidence of Viking settlements which date back to the ninth and tenth centuries.

The local hockey fans expected the Dragons to bring that same Viking-like ferocity to the ice. The club did not disappoint. Following a fast start to the season, the club was positioned near the top of the standings in the ten-team GET-Ligean (now known as EliteHockey Ligean). Jacob was immediately accepted by his new teammates who all shared a common goal of bringing home their eighth Kongepokal trophy. It may not have been at the level of the SHL for which he had prepared the entire offseason, but it was good hockey.

His first game with the Dragons got off to a memorable start. The club faced off against archrival Lillehammer IK in the 2019 Norwegian Hockey Classic. The game was televised across the entire country in a neutral site at an arena which was unlike any Jacob had played in before. The arena sat almost completely underground and was filled to capacity for the nationally televised game. Jacob went all out for his initial shift on the ice. It was his first action in months and it felt good to be back playing competitively. By the third shift, his legs felt heavy. By the third period, he was fighting exhaustion. It was going to be a battle getting through his first game back of competitive hockey.

The hard-hitting play on the ice did not come without verbal exchanges. During one scrum, a player for Lillehammer made a point of shouting in Jacob's face, "You need to quit spending so much time writing on Instagram!"

An exhausted Jacob smiled and retrieved the energy to push the player away. But not before answering, "Thanks for following me."

The final horn finally sounded and it was Lillehammer IK who skated away with a 3-2 victory.

The opposite end of the spectrum for Norwegian hockey that season occurred in Oslo. Norway's capital city boasts much to be proud of, but hockey in 2019-2020 was not on the list. Dragon players arriving in Oslo looked forward to the game, dubbing it the "points game". A reference for the chance to accumulate points against the undermanned Gruner IL club.

A sparse crowd that could probably have been counted in Jacob's head showed up for the game at the Grunerhallen Arena, and it was indeed a points game with Dragon players padding their hockey stats. From Jacob's perspective, it was a far cry from hockey in the SHL.

It was growing increasingly difficult to stay motivated in a season that Jacob had put so much hope into. He enjoyed the city of Hamar and appreciated the opportunity to play with a club competing for the best record in the GET-Ligean, but he was also facing the reality that his hockey dreams were coming to an end. This season was his last chance to make it big competing in the second-best league in the world with hopes still alive for the NHL, but here he was playing before a crowd that may not have even numbered one hundred. And what was making it all even more difficult was the extended time away from Harper and Nash.

The divorce was finalized the prior year while Jacob was in Germany and he was paying $4,000 in monthly alimony, working an agreement to FaceTime his kids every day. But even that benefit was growing more challenging. Because of a six-hour time difference between Hamar and Cleveland, the only guaranteed time available to talk to the kids was early morning as they were preparing for school. Nash was now four years old attending preschool and Harper was in kindergarten. It was not the best time for quality communication without interruption, but Jacob did his best to maintain a positive attitude and make sure they knew how much they meant to him. It certainly didn't help that now the boyfriend could be heard from time to time yelling out that the kids needed to get to school. It finally reached a boiling point during a Saturday morning conversation with Harper.

Jacob had been mulling an idea. Perhaps he could play for one more season and convince Annie to give him primary custody of the kids. A year overseas could be an invaluable experience for Harper and Nash, and he would be with them every day and do everything in his power to make it work for everyone. He picked up Harper's mood by throwing out his idea and she grew excited at the prospect of maybe spending an entire year overseas with dad. Just then the boyfriend walked by and picked up the phone with words that filled Jacob with rage.

"You need to stop putting crazy ideas into your kids' heads. It ain't gonna happen!"

Jacob could barely contain his emotions. If it was possible for him to transport his body across the internet and ocean to confront this intrusion, he would have given anything to make it happen. Upon later reflection, he realized that it was probably best that he was not there to act upon his instinct. His entire body shaking in anger, Jacob fought to control his emotions as a startled Harper now looked on with the boyfriend nowhere in sight. The idea of someone he didn't even know living in, and telling him from the home that Jacob was paying for, what was best for his kids was beyond insulting. He needed to get away and let out his anger and frustration.

Having gained experience with breathing exercises and their benefits, Jacob took a deep breath. He told Harper that everything was going to be fine and closed the call before any further damage was done.

Jacob considered leaving the club to return home and get his family life back in order. Time to pause for reflection coupled with a love of hockey and conversations with his trusted hockey brothers convinced him to hold off before making such a rash decision.

The Storhamar Dragons were playing excellent hockey, entertaining their passionate fans with exciting play which had them in second place for the playoff drive. With the first-place Stavanger Oilers coming into town for a crucial matchup, Hamar came alive in anticipation of a game that was sure to be played with playoff-level intensity. For Jacob, there was an added incentive. The chance to reunite with his former teammate and longtime friend, Greg Mauldin.

Jacob and Mauldin had become best of friends since their playing time together in Cleveland with the Lake Erie Monsters during the 2011-2012 season. As with Jacob, Mauldin's career turned to the European continent following the NHL strike in 2012, having played professionally for clubs in Switzerland, Germany, Croatia, and Norway. The two had much in common and often turned to one another in dealing with both their professional successes and personal challenges. Greg had the added challenge as an African American competing in a sport dominated by white athletes and front office personnel, which could be magnified even further when playing overseas. Like Jacob, Mauldin always maintained an upbeat attitude and the two often leaned on one another to help get through difficult times.

Now they competed against each other for the first time overseas, and the only thing better than competing on the ice was meeting up to spend time together at one of Hamar's finest restaurants after the game. Mauldin listened to his friend with complete empathy and understanding. He had found himself many times in the same situation, wondering if it was time to hang up the skates. He offered Jacob words of encouragement, telling him to find the strength to do what was right, and they discussed the likely possibility of going up against one another to compete in the Norwegian Kongepokal Trophy Finals. It was a scenario that was both enticing and incentive for Jacob to remain in Norway.

Perhaps the words that most convinced Jacob to stay with the club came from his California protégé, Alex Miner. Alex asked Jacob a pointed question which landed squarely and convinced him of what he had to do.

"If Nash was a grown man, and in your shoes, what advice would you give him?"

Jacob knew what had to be done. He was a professional athlete who was under contract to play to the best of his abilities for an entire season.

He would do everything in his power to make the season a success. There would be plenty of time moving forward to spend with the kids and sort things out at home.

Jacob's decision to remain in Norway paid off handsomely just one week later. He was invited to a well-known retreat one hour north of Hamar in the hinterlands of Norway. A couple in the area had started a Siberian Husky retreat and offered sleigh rides through the Norwegian wilderness. The Siberian Husky was always Jacob's favorite dog. As a boy, it was the only dog the family owned, his father also being a fan of the friendly breed known for their thick double coat and striking eye colors. The only problem was that the California desert is not an ideal location for the energetic thick-coated Husky. After one year, they reluctantly returned their dog to place him in a more suitable environment.

On a clear afternoon, with the sun peeking from the north to reflect an appearance of diamonds covering a snow-covered pine forest, Jacob stepped into a winter wonderland. The trail crunching below him, he was led into a rustic hut to enjoy a warm beverage before the ride and learn about the amazing creatures who eagerly awaited their duties. There, Jacob learned the true story of perhaps the most famous Siberian Husky of all time. But it came with a twist.

Balto was the Siberian Husky who became an American hero in 1925 for leading the final leg of a 674-mile relay to deliver medicine and save the townspeople of Nome from a deadly epidemic. Because this courageous feat took place in the most treacherous conditions and impacted so many lives, his name became known worldwide. He was even commemorated with a statue in New York City's Central Park.

However, it was not Balto but Togo who was the true hero of the story. Of all the lead dogs, Togo covered the longest and most treacherous stretch of the journey. Most harrowing was a perilous crossing over the frozen Norton Sound. By the time Togo reached his end of the journey, he collapsed, unable to go any further. The courage, loyalty, and sheer determination that Togo displayed to help save human lives is almost beyond comprehension. A true testimonial to the unique bond between humans and animals, and a model for anyone looking to achieve goals that appear beyond their grasp.

Jacob stepped out with the others, eager to begin their adventure and with a whole new appreciation for a breed of dogs willing to give up their lives to save their owners. It made the scenic journey across the most beautiful wilderness that ended under the spectacular Northern Lights even more memorable. The problems that had been bogging Jacob down for so much of the season suddenly seemed far away.

The Dragons' fine play continued and with the playoffs approaching, the club was a lock to finish in second place behind the league-leading Stavanger Oilers. The possibility of the two teams squaring off in the Finals was appearing more and more likely, just as Jacob and his friend Greg Mauldin had anticipated.

The question now was, would there be a playoff? Rumors of cancelling the season were growing, and the heightened concern spreading across the entire planet was headed into an even more dire direction.

It began earlier in the new year with news of an epidemic in Wuhan, China. The virus, which would go on to become known worldwide as COVID-19, was quickly spreading and now reaching other countries. It had grown into a pandemic. Scientists were working feverishly to find the source and potential cure for the virus, which was easily transmitted through respiratory droplets produced from sneezing, coughing, or even talking.

The initial strain of the virus was also proving deadly. While most infected individuals experienced fever, cough, and muscle aches often associated with the common cold, the symptoms were indeed more severe and also included loss of taste or smell. And for some, especially the elderly and those afflicted with existing health conditions, complications such as pneumonia or respiratory failures were leading to organ failure and death.

Perhaps what was most disturbing was simply fear of the unknown. News of earlier pandemics were being reported. The 1918-1920 influenza pandemic, also known as the Spanish flu, resulted in death tolls estimated to be anywhere between 17 million and 100 million people. Several countries outside of China were now reporting deaths, and every country around the planet braced for the worst which was yet to come.

In an effort to stop infections before they could multiply, countries were taking precautionary steps to isolate citizens and cancel events with large public gatherings. The sporting world was among the first to take action. With the hockey and basketball seasons coming to a close, leagues across every country made the difficult decision to suspend their seasons. The GET-Ligean season was over. There would be no playoffs.

Dragon players received news of the announcement from the coaches in their locker room. Players sat stunned at the news. Even though rumors of cancelling the season had surfaced, it seemed surreal to think that everything could so harshly end just as they were preparing for the most exciting part of the season, the playoffs. Adding to the somber realization, the entire community and world around them was shutting down.

The coaches departed, but not before informing the players that they were free to stick around and take whatever time was necessary to collect their gear and leave the premises for an unknown period. The mood was somber, but the players made a unanimous decision of how they would close their season. A handful of players went out to make a run, bringing back an assortment of bottles for their consumption. The Storhamar Dragons 2019-2020 season would end not on the ice, but in a locker room filled with alcohol.

# Part 3

# Chapter Eighteen

# The Transition

March 2020 – February 2022

The city of Cleveland in March of 2020 appeared as a ghost town. Much like the rest of the country and all around the globe. At least Jacob was able to get out and reunite with Harper and Nash while seeking out living arrangements and job opportunities. That was not the case everywhere. In addition to a lockdown in China, a COVID outbreak in Italy caused the Government to impose a quarantine across the entire country, restricting all movement of the population with the exception of health and emergency matters. Several stateside news outlets expressed possibilities that if the virus could not be contained, the same could happen here.

As an athlete who was in peak physical condition, Jacob was not overly concerned with his own personal well-being. He was rarely sick, blessed with the conditioning that built an immune system which kept him from seldom contracting even a common cold. But he could see the concern all around him, and was worried for his family. Driving around the city to find a place to live, he came upon an Airbnb home in the inner suburb of Lakewood which seemed an ideal location for a temporary residence. However, the city was virtually shut down with people wearing masks and generally avoiding one another. On his car radio, the normally sports-crazed Cleveland fans were not discussing sports, but bemoaning the cancellation of the NBA season and the realization that there would be no opener for the Cleveland Indians. They were even wondering if the upcoming NFL draft would take place. Popular restaurants and bars all along Lakewood's normally busy streets were now empty. Some displayed signs that they were open for take out, but most simply shut down with their doors boarded up. Even the schools were closed.

Two areas that remained open and proved to be havens for Jacob were the nearby Winterhurst Ice Arena and a destination which Jacob viewed as the region's jewel; the Cleveland Metroparks. As viewed on a map, a network of 18 nature reserves connecting along Lake Erie and the area's winding rivers form a distinctive green space. The resulting 325 miles of trails gives the Park District a name proudly referred to among locals – "The Emerald Necklace" – due to its resembling an ornamental chain hanging below the city on Lake Erie's north coast.

Jacob delighted in exploring the Park's many attractions with Harper and Nash, and the endless trails were perfect for two youngsters needing to burst out of the house and constraints imposed by COVID. Jacob also introduced them to the Arena and came upon a welcome surprise. Both took to the ice like it was their birthright. Nash in particular. He couldn't get enough of skating around the rink and in no time mastered the moves exhibited by Dad and the few young boys seen working on their hockey skills. He badgered Jacob relentlessly to get him involved in the hockey program which Jacob read to him from the bulletin board.

"Not yet Nash. I promise we'll get you signed up later in the year after you turn five."

The other promise that Jacob made to both Harper and Nash was that he would never again leave them. Regardless of what happened down the road, whatever offers may become available, he vowed to stay close to his two children.

In an effort to do just that, he moved from his desired location on Cleveland's near west side to an apartment on the city's east side nearer to Annie. The location in Highland Hills was not only close to her, but right near the Park's North Chagrin Reservation, enabling new explorations for Jacob and the kids. Their favorite spot was the Squire Castle. While much of the city remained in their own isolation, Jacob and the kids spent hours fantasizing their own Game of Thrones in the 1890s gatehouse modeled after German and English baronial castles.

The move was short-lived. Several months after moving into Highland Heights, Annie moved to the west side suburb of Rocky River. Jacob followed once again, finding a place close to the lake and in the shadow of the Park's Rocky River Reservation.

It was time to get a job. His first outside of professional hockey. Jacob's initial offer came about from a serendipitous meeting. Jacob's workouts on the ice caught the attention of a fellow retired hockey professional who was an advocate for hockey with a focus on player development and enhancing the sport's landscape in the Cleveland community. With that mission, Russ Sinkowich founded the Ohio Hockey Project (OHP) and was committed to it full time upon his retirement in 2015.

With the Project operating out of the Winterhurst Ice Arena, Jacob and Russ had a chance to meet and the two learned they uncannily had much in common. Like Jacob, Russ played in the Juniors for the Lincoln Stars, and both played professionally for the Lake Erie Monsters, Bridgeport Sound Tigers, and Idaho Steelheads. Although never on the same team at the same time, several of their seasons were spent just one season apart. Jacob's availability aligned perfectly with OHP's goal of providing premier training from a team of coaches which included former professional players. Jacob had always enjoyed working with and mentoring the younger players, so the idea of coaching youngsters in such a positive structure that the OHP provided was a natural fit.

The coronavirus was not going away. Despite all efforts to contain the virus, there were significant outbreaks and differences of opinion between elected officials of both political parties and health experts regarding how to handle the crisis which was causing confusion and angst among the population. One thing which was not in question; the United States was now the leader of deaths being reported worldwide. Talk of a vaccine becoming available was viewed by many as a saving grace, while others felt the best thing to do was get on with their normal lives and allow the virus to run its course.

As for Jacob, he remained confident in his own well-being, continuing to take care of his body and now looking to bring his family closer together. He reached out to his sisters and mother and shared the idea of having them move to Rocky River. They were open to the plan, making a few visits to acclimate to the area, and Jacob looked forward to having the family back together.

As the year wore on, subtle signs of normalcy began to surface. Restaurants and bars began to reopen on a limited basis, and professional sports came back in a restricted manner. Major League Baseball (MLB) returned for a shortened 60-game season which began on July 23. It came with a catch. Fans were not allowed to attend games. Sports fans celebrated for the chance to once again view live action, but could only watch games played in empty stadiums from the television sets in their own homes. Things loosened up slightly with fall's arrival of the National Football League (NFL). Due to the low infection rates among staff and players, twenty of the thirty-two NFL teams allowed varied numbers of spectators to attend home games during the 2020-2021 season.

The upcoming NBA and NHL seasons were also set to begin on schedule with a series of safety protocols set up for the players and their fans. At least there would be games with fans in attendance. Jacob's agent began receiving calls. Offers were coming from Finland, Norway, Italy, and more countries where leagues were returning to play. Jacob remained steadfast that he would not accept any offer requiring him to leave Harper and Nash.

One afternoon, Jacob drove by Serpentini Chevrolet of Westlake and observed a number of people shopping outside on the expansive lot. The outdoors was generally considered a safe place during the pandemic and Jacob, who always had a love of cars, felt that selling cars could provide a good source of income. He met with the owner who was immediately drawn to the positive energy and athletic presence of the recently retired athlete. Happy Jake seemed a perfect fit and was hired on the spot.

The COVID vaccine finally arrived.  Following months of speculation, the first doses were administered on December 14.  People lined up for the chance to remove the fear of infection and get their lives back to normal.  Availability of the vaccine arrived just as the winter season was showing an increase in cases among the population, particularly the aged.  Several months after the first vaccines were introduced, the number of reported cases and deaths reduced significantly.  There was a sense that the worst was over, and spring's arrival of 2021 brought a sense of hope and renewal.  Even the schools, which had closed their doors and were teaching remotely, were now expanding to a hybrid or in person format to close out the school year.  Harper and Nash were thrilled at the prospect of rejoining their friends.

As for Jacob, he chose not to take the vaccine.  From a combination of his strict workout regimen and daily regimented breathing exercises which he began in the summer of 2018, he hadn't even experienced a common cold in years and did not wish to take any chances with an immune system which was working just fine.  He supported efforts of the Center for Disease Control (CDC) to eradicate the virus, but felt that for him it was in his best interest to avoid the vaccine.

Back at Serpentini Chevrolet, Jacob was enjoying success.  The local population, spurred by the arrival of spring and a growing confidence that came with the vaccine, were lining up for test drives.  Jacob was in his element, easily engaging in conversation and learning the stories and backgrounds of potential customers.  They in turn showed interest in his own background, assuming that he must be an athlete of some sort, and delighted in learning that he once played for the local Monsters.

Jacob enjoyed the many conversations, eventually learning enough to walk a customer directly to the one automobile that was placed on the lot just for them.  "This rugged SUV will enhance even more that cross-country trip you're planning for your growing family.  You'll be the most popular dad on the block".

"With your divorce almost final, this is the look that will get you back into the game. Sporty, fun, and with just the right touch of adventure. It suits you perfectly."

"Imagine the impression this will make on your clients, driving in such luxury. Once you settle into these soft leather seats, they won't want to get out."

The late evenings at Serpentini were leaving Jacob in a conundrum. He felt a sense of satisfaction in handing keys over to customers who were genuinely excited that they were getting the right car and relief in that his own commission checks were growing. But there was also the creeping realization that he was spending less quality time with the kids and a dose of reality in that the bonus checks were needed to maintain his financial obligations. Between selling cars and coaching for OHP, he fought to maintain the same positive energy for time with Harper and Nash. Hastening the challenge, the monthly child support and alimony payments he was required to pay were based upon the healthy contract he signed with JYP. Any earnings significantly less than that would negatively impact his own financial needs and quality of life.

The Rocky River Reservation trails remained his saving grace, whether alone or with his children. Jacob seemed to be increasingly attracting the attention of fellow hikers who took an interest in a professional hockey player's unusual path to arrive in Cleveland from the desert of California. People seemed to enjoy his genuine sincerity in reaching out to help others coupled with the positive vibes which he projected. Several young men asked if they could join him in his strenuous workouts at an area with 155 steep steps, and Jacob was struck by the strange coincidence of receiving an almost identical query from multiple hikers. Following a brief conversation with a woman he had passed numerous times running up and down the steps, she left with the words, "There is a beautiful gift awaiting you."

Just one week earlier, someone told him that God had a special gift for him. And others left similar messages. Why was he receiving these messages? After some reflection, Jacob decided to join a church and began attending services for the first time in his life. Perhaps there was something to be learned and insight to be gained from the teachings of the Bible.

Despite all effort, it was growing more challenging to maintain balance, and made all the more conflicting with appealing offers now coming in from overseas for the 2021-2022 season. Although he had not trained anywhere close to the levels of prior seasons, Jacob still managed time to get ice time with OHP and was not that far removed from competitive hockey to close out the 2020 season. But he could also not shake the helpless feeling from being away from Harper and Nash. He was determined not to leave them again.

Jacob's strong sales and commission checks continued when his agent called in early December with a most enticing offer. The oil-rich country of the United Arab Emirates was hosting a major international hockey tournament in Abu Dhabi. Jacob was offered an all-expenses-paid trip with an opportunity to earn good money and gain exposure among teams competing from all across Europe and Russia. Several years earlier, Jacob would have jumped at this opportunity of a lifetime. But with the tournament occurring right around the holidays, he could not bring himself to spend another Christmas away from home. As much as he missed competing in the sport that he loved, he would not commit to again leaving his children.

The cold Cleveland winter came with an increased focus on earning money at Serpentini, balanced with his work for OHP and spending time with Harper and Nash. Nash was now in his second year of hockey at the Winterhurst Ice Rink, and Jacob could not hide the joy in watching his son take to the sport. He never put pressure on Nash to take up hockey and encouraged him to try whatever activity he enjoyed, but for now it was clear that Nash stood out and was a natural at the sport of his father. What was most rewarding to Jacob was not Nash's performance, but his love for the game.

Faced with all the demands, more sacrifices were being made. Jacob was missing more of Nash's games and often absent from activities with

Harper. One evening he was conducting paperwork with a customer at the car dealer when the realization hit him.

*What am I doing? I retired from hockey so that I can spend time with my kids, and here I am working late into the evenings, sixty hours a week, having to explain to them why I can't be more available.*

He also reflected on the mysterious conversation with a woman after church service just this past Sunday. Upon departing, she left with the words, "There is a gift waiting for you." The same message. Was a gift right in front of him and he was simply blinded? He knew something had to change.

Little could Jacob have realized at that moment that a conversation taking place far away would reveal that gift. A new professional hockey league was preparing to launch for the 2022 season. The league's founder, E.J. Johnston, had been working for years on the concept of 3ICE, a fast-paced three-on-three format that would bring creativity and excitement for the hockey world during the NHL's offseason. The league would be made up of professional hockey players not currently signed with an NHL team, although NHL experience was encouraged.

E.J. Johnston was on the phone with Greg Mauldin with the hope of recruiting the respected veteran for the league's inaugural season. Following the COVID lockout, Mauldin returned to the States and decided to retire after 17 years of professional hockey. When hockey resumed in late 2020, he was asked to serve as a coach for the USA Hockey National Team Development Program. The thirty-nine-year-old remained in such peak physical condition that he was lured back onto the ice and now closing the 2021-2022 season in Norway, returning to the Stavanger Oilers.

Johnston provided Mauldin with the new league's summer format. A fast-paced game designed for speed and creativity. Games to be played in Events on the weekends, moved to eight different cities featuring the league's six teams, with the championship game to be held in Las Vegas. Mauldin was well aware of Jacob's situation and desire to be with his children. He was also aware of Jacob's one regret that Harper and Nash never had the chance to watch their dad compete on the ice.

Greg Mauldin informed Johnston that his schedule would not enable him to compete for 3ICE, but he had just the perfect person for him to contact.

# Chapter Nineteen

## 3ICE Tryouts

### February – April, 2022

Reality TV Producer E.J. Johnston had a bold idea. And it came as no surprise to anyone who knew him that it centered around hockey. Hockey was always a part of E.J.'s life. His father Eddie Johnston was the last NHL goaltender to play every minute of every game, which he achieved while tending for the Boston Bruins during the 1963-1964 season. Eddie Johnston's professional hockey career would go on to span fifty-three years, with twenty-two of them coming as a player. During that span, he would win two Stanley Cups as a player and a third as senior advisor for hockey operations with the Pittsburgh Penguins. E.J. was born into the world of professional hockey.

During the 2015-2016 NHL season, the league experimented with a rule change to speed up play in overtime and reduce the need for shootouts. They introduced three-on-three hockey during overtime sessions, showcasing three skaters on each side plus the goaltender, replacing the normal five-on-five format. Fans loved the excitement that came with increased action from a more open style of play. E.J. took note and the seed for 3ICE was planted.

Johnston worked tirelessly on the concept, tinkering with rules, league structure, player selection, potential sites, and more. He discussed television deals with CBS Sports in the United States and TSN and RDS (Quebec) in Canada, pitching the concept to agents, players, entertainment executives, and investors. The league was formally announced on January 13 of 2020, formalizing TV deals and naming Hockey Hall of Famer Craig Patrick as the league's first commissioner.

COVID put the brakes on the project. Everything was shut down during 2020 and attendance restrictions for 2021 prompted the league to postpone play and launch in 2022. A formal announcement was finally made amidst much anticipation. A nine-week schedule beginning in June of 2022, with weekly Events culminating in a championship game to be held at the Orleans Arena in Las Vegas, Nevada.

Adding further enticement and attraction to the announcement, each team would be coached by notable names including legendary NHL players such as Larry Murphy, Joe Mullen, Bryan Trottier, and Ray Bourque. The players to be selected from a tryout of over 100 hockey professionals including former NHL skaters, minor league skaters, America's international standouts, and players at the cusp of an NHL career.

Everything was in place. The only thing left was for Johnston to finalize the list of names to be invited for a tryout, followed by a draft with six coaches selecting from the talent pool for the inaugural 2022 3ICE season.

It was mid-February when Jacob received an unexpected call. He was lounging on the couch and chatting with his mother and sister Beth. They had just recently moved to Cleveland and his younger sister Sarah was soon to follow. When Jacob's phone rang, his initial reaction was to ignore the call. It was an unfamiliar number but the 412 Pittsburgh area code intrigued him and the number did not come with a spam alert. Jacob answered the phone and was greeted by E.J. Johnston.

E.J.'s introduction was not necessary. Jacob was well aware of Johnston's involvement with 3ICE. He had first learned of 3ICE while in Norway. The coaches were all watching the Canadian sports channel TSN in the head coach's office when a story of the 3ICE league came on the air. "Hey Newts, come in here and take a look at this."

Joining the coaches, they were all captivated by the concept of a new league featuring the three-on-three format. Jacob also heard from Mauldin several days earlier, alerting him that he may receive a call from Johnston.

So, Jacob's heart began racing when Johnston introduced himself, inform-ing him of an invite to attend a tryout in Las Vegas on April 16. The tryout was invitation only. Over 100 hand-picked players were invited and a draft would follow with six coaches selecting seven players per team from the pool. In addition to the 42 selected, another group of players would be added and these players available to teams in case of injury, performance, or a selected player's unavailability.

Jacob was thrilled. The format was perfect. If selected, he would only be required to travel on weekends and could work out a schedule that would enable Harper and Nash to join him for some of the Events. There was also a chance to earn good money. All travel expenses were included and money was guaranteed, with bonuses for winning the weekly events and a grand prize of $1.1 million dollars to be split among the team that won the championship.

Jacob thanked Johnston for the opportunity, letting him know how excited he was to participate with 3ICE. After hanging up, he immedi-ately called Mauldin in Norway and thanked him for his role in making the invitation possible. Greg informed Jacob that a thank you was not necessary and he can repay him by making the cut and bringing home a championship.

There was work to do. It had now been over two years since he played at a competitive level on the ice. Fortunately, he remained heavily involved in the OHP program as a coach and personal trainer, and kept himself in good shape through diligent workouts and a healthy diet. But changes would have to be made if he was going to make the cut. He decided to quit the job at Serpentini and focus all efforts on hockey. He had two months to get himself back into hockey shape.

Over the course of the following weeks, Jacob began receiving more information about the league, the coaches, and the players involved. The lineup of six coaches was composed of a who's who among NHL elites. Hall of Famers who were considered legends of the game. One name stood out. Larry Murphy was the Detroit Red Wing's stellar defenseman who helped the team win two Stanley Cups in the late '90s. He proudly wore number 55, a number that Jacob would go on to wear when the number 5 was not available throughout his hockey career, both at the amateur and professional level. There were only a handful of seasons during Jacob's career that neither of those two numbers were available, and over time the number 55 became his preferred number. He immediately visualized himself skating for Team Murphy wearing number 55.

Another thing that stood out was the list of players. Jacob was familiar with virtually every name and many had some level of NHL experience. It was by no means a lock to make the final cut. He spent hours reviewing the list. Players who he had competed with and against, players who at one time performed with teams that he had skated with in Juniors, College, or the pros. There may be only a single degree of separation required to connect the tight-knit hockey fraternity. And there is a favored tool that players use to keep up with their peers.

Jacob pored over the stats of players using the Elite Prospects app. It was a tool that he and so many of his fellow skaters used daily. Via the app, it was somewhat of a ritual to keep up with players who he had performed with at one time over the years. And now he was gaining some sense of the players who made up the tryout pool. The vast majority were known to be offensive minded. Skaters known for their speed and scoring abilities. Relatively few defensemen, and Jacob suspected that he would be among the largest of the entrants. The league was clearly focusing on fast-paced scoring with quick players vs. defense with brawny defensemen. Jacob saw an angle that could work in his favor. He was always considered a skilled defender with good size and speed who stood out for his scoring ability and staying out of the penalty box. Even with a focus on scoring, teams would need some defense and he could bring both to a team if selected.

Preparation for the tryouts was going well. Freed from the long hours at the car dealership, Jacob was now getting plenty of time on the ice and in the gym. The local hockey community was also providing extra motivation. Skaters and their families with the Ohio Hockey Project were cheering him on to make the cut. Nobody was more excited than Nash. He was now six years old and hockey was his love. The idea of watching Dad competing with other professionals on TV in a large arena was almost incomprehensible. Harper was more subtle but no less thrilled for the chance to be a part of something special. The three sat at home on a Saturday evening discussing the possibilities. Jacob shared the weekly schedule and listed the dates where they could join him if he made the cut.

"Dad, you mean there is a city in Tennessee that is named after me and we can go there?"

"Well, Nashville has been around a bit longer than you, Jaakko. But yes, if I make the cut, we will all go to Nashville for the weekend."

Harper could only roll her eyes at her little brother before asking, "What number will you wear?"

Jacob smiled at the thought. With teams of only seven players the numbers of their choice should be readily available. "The same number I almost always wore. And the same number that Nash wears. 55."

The number 55 had recently taken on even more meaning. During a recent walk in the Metroparks with a college professor and book author who Jacob had gotten to know over the past year, the professor asked the exact same question and provided some reflection.

In the mystical field of numerology, numbers can take on a specific meaning or significance. The college professor looked up the meaning of the number "55" and shared the following. Numbers repeated in sequence are referred to in numerology as angel numbers, and seen as a positive confirmation that you are on the right path, supported by a higher power. Each number has a specific meaning, and 55 signifies upcoming positive changes, personal transformation, freedom, and growth. You are encouraged to embrace new opportunities and trust your inner guidance to achieve success.

The message was in sync with others that he had been receiving so often in the past year; signs of a gift that was awaiting him. It was up to Jacob to accept the gift and put in the work to make positive change. The following day, Jacob went out to purchase a whiteboard with some markers and an eraser. Just as he did in Kouvola, Jacob wrote on the board. Phrases like: "Be grateful" and "You are destined for success".

On the left half of the board, he wrote down exactly how he saw things take place at the upcoming tryout in Las Vegas.

"You are grateful to be playing on Team Murphy. You are performing at the highest level. You will make the final cut."

### Las Vegas, Nevada (April 15 – 17)

The big weekend finally arrived. In addition to a tryout for the players, the event was set up as a dress rehearsal for the upcoming season. All players were to report to the hotel on Friday, meet for dinner and an orientation, and prep for games to be played on Saturday. Television crews and announcers were also in attendance to film and broadcast the action, but games would not be televised. It was simply a practice run to fine-tune for the real thing. With the fast pace of multiple shortened games to be held in one showing and the need to provide sufficient time for advertisers, there were lots of things that could go wrong. E.J. Johnston wanted to make sure that everything was run to perfection. Players faced the pressure of performing on ice to make the final cut, and the crew and producers faced their own pressure to make sure that everything ran smoothly.

Following a day of non-eventful flights, Jacob checked into his room at the Orleans Hotel and Casino several miles off the Vegas strip. Before even unpacking his bags, he tore open the pamphlet received at the front desk to learn the team he would be competing with for Saturday games. His eyes went directly to the roster for Team Murphy. There, in green, the first name he came upon was "Jake Newton". WOW! Just as he visualized. Jacob was now more convinced than ever that he was destined to make the cut. *Just do what you came to do and don't screw up!*

Jacob enjoyed the Friday gathering and the family atmosphere that he could see the organizers were angling to promote for the league. It was good to see and catch up with players who he both knew in person and had a connection with. The weekend was made all the more enjoyable in that every player in attendance was provided with one thousand five hundred dollars and all of the weekend expenses, including flights, were paid for.

Just before the formal dinner was served, players were asked to take a few minutes and fill out a form with some personal information.

In anticipation of a delicious dinner which he could see being brought in by servers, Jacob quickly filled out the form before stumbling upon a question that caused some inner turmoil. "Did you receive the COVID vaccine?" He was struck with a sudden dilemma. If he answered truthfully and checked the "NO" box, could that be a factor in not making the final cut? He was able to secure a card which showed that he had been vaccinated in the event that it was needed for something like this, but seldom used the card and knew that if the organizers really checked, they would find no record of his receiving the vaccine. Jacob looked around and could see other players dropping off their completed forms. He was now among the last to complete the form and wondered, *What do I do?* After much consternation and hovering his hand for some time above the YES box, he made up his mind and answered NO. He recognized the importance of integrity. The same message he had been teaching for some time to Harper and Nash. If he was meant to perform for 3ICE, it would happen, regardless of his vaccine status.

The following day saw the Orleans Arena alive with activity. Teams of television crews, arena workers, and organizers arrived early to set up for the practice run but more importantly for the players, an audition for selection to a team. The day's game format would be slightly different from the regularly scheduled events, and even more chaotic. For the eight scheduled Events, teams would be paired to play three games where the winners would advance to the semifinals. The losing team with the highest scoring output would comprise the fourth team. Those four teams would then be paired, with the winners squaring off for the event final. The maximum number of games that any team would play on Event Day was three. That was not the case for the tryout.

To ensure that every player received sufficient ice time for a fair evaluation of all invitees, the day was made up of two sessions, one in the morning and one in the afternoon. The physical demands showed. The 16-minute games were designed with minimal stoppage in play. The only face-offs were to start each half, so the action was almost nonstop. By the afternoon session, the players were understandably exhausted. The day started with Jacob going all out on his first shift, eager to prove himself after over two years of non-competitive play. One minute later he skated off with the realization that the near-empty bench would require him to get right back out there before he could catch his breath. Keeping up this pace over two sessions was going to be a challenge.

The two eight-minutes halves with no stoppage seemed to last an eternity, and with Team Murphy racking up continual wins, they went into the locker room with the realization that they would soon be required back on the ice for their next game. The two teams skating on the ice following each game were almost immediately underway with their own contest.

Players were also required to adapt to a number of subtle rule changes. In an attempt to promote offense with crisp hockey skills, there was no body contact allowed. Players were not allowed to push, trip, or physically touch an opponent. Defenders must stop the puck, not the skater. The 3ICE rules aligned perfectly with Jacob's style of play.

In the event that a penalty was called, there was no player advantage with a power play. There was a jail-break in which the fouled player gets a head start and is chased by all other players *sans* the opposing goalie as he sprints to the net. The resulting play promised to offer perhaps the most thrilling seconds in all of sports. One skater, one goalie, and six others in wild pursuit to either stop or assist the shot on goal. If a goal was scored, the clock would not stop. The goalie would simply retrieve the puck, restarting play from the crease.

As the afternoon wore on, Jacob could see that the fast pace was taking a toll on a number of players. It was not uncommon to see a player bend over to vomit after returning to the bench following his shift on the ice. Jacob was thankful for the breathing work that he had so diligently practiced over the past few years, but found himself feeling a pain below his right buttock that would not go away. In addition to what appeared to be the beginning of sciatica pain, he felt a throbbing sensation in his foot. In normal circumstances he would have skated off the ice to check with a trainer, but this was not a normal circumstance. His mind raced back to the white board. "You are grateful to be here." This was his last shot at making a team that would enable Harper and Nash to join him. He was not about to blow this opportunity.

Following over six hours of nearly nonstop hockey with just one break between sessions, the play was finally winding down. It was obvious from the look on the skaters' faces that they welcomed the end in sight. It was also clear that lots of work was needed to clean things up for the 3ICE organizers. But they had two months to work out the kinks with knowledge that the normal events would be significantly simpler than the congestion of games that were conducted for the tryout.

Jacob slept soundly that night. He, like most of the players present, did not possess the energy to venture out to explore the Vegas nightlife after dinner. In addition to the physical exhaustion, there was another reason for Jacob's contentment that night. Before leaving the dining area after dinner, Jacob wandered around the room while workers were cleaning up the area and noticed a slip of paper sitting on the coaches' reserved table. On the paper were the names of players sorted under two columns: "Draft" and "Non-Draft". Listed under the "Draft" column, Jacob found the name: Jake Newton.

The players mingled over breakfast in the morning, saying their good-byes while reflecting on the unconventional day of hockey they had just experienced. E.J. Johnston thanked all those who were still in attendance for participating in the exciting 3ICE program. He informed them that a draft would take place the following Monday, and promised that every player would be contacted in the next few days regarding their status.

Jacob gathered his bags for the flights back to Cleveland. His confidence soared with knowledge of what he viewed from the coaches' table and the belief that he had accounted for himself quite well, but knew it would still be an anxious few days before the call actually came. He was well aware that anything could happen, and felt some lingering hesitation as a result of his COVID status. Taking a deep breath, he visualized the outcome of his dreams.

# Chapter Twenty

# The Awakening

April – August, 2022

Jacob sat down with a steaming cup of coffee at his dining table and logged onto the computer for a Zoom call. He arrived early, eagerly anticipating the chance to formally meet his new coach and teammates for the very first time. Setting up the camera, he waited for others to join in while reflecting on events over the past week upon his return from Las Vegas.

The call finally came from 3ICE Commissioner Craig Patrick on Thursday. Patrick congratulated Jacob for his outstanding play and informed him that he was selected by Team Trottier. "Coach Trottier will be calling you in the coming days. Great job and I look forward to seeing you at the first Event back in Vegas on June 18."

Coach Trottier called a few days later and his enthusiasm and excitement were contagious. He shared how thrilled he was with the team, stating that his players represented everything he was looking for with the skills and character to compete for a championship. He then provided some insight into his decision to select Jacob to the squad. "I just loved your spirit! So many were complaining and looking miserable, but the smile never left your face and you with such passion like you wanted to be there. That's exactly what I was looking for."

Jacob was ready to burst through the phone and lace up on the spot. This was exactly the type of coach he was looking to play for.

That was also the way that Trottier played the game. Bryan Trottier was a center who played 18 NHL seasons, winning four Stanley Cups with the New York Islanders and two with the Pittsburgh Penguins. He also won a Stanley Cup as an assistant coach with the Colorado Avalanche. Among his many personal accomplishments, Trottier shares the NHL record for most points in a single period (six points with four goals and two assists), and in 2017 was named among the "100 Greatest NHL Players" in history.

Glancing at the screen, Jacob could now see that more of his teammates were on the call waiting for the host to begin the meeting. Several names captured his attention. One was Chad Costello.

Costello began the 2013-2014 season skating with Jacob for the Ontario Reign. Jacob always viewed Chad as a highly skilled skater who was at his best when allowed to play to his strengths and do his thing. Unfortunately, that was not the way Smurf coached. Like Jacob, Costello walked away from the Ontario Reign that season. Chad, after just eight games. Freed from the constraints of playing under a controlling coach, he would go on to score an impressive 125 points for the Allen Americans during the 2014-2015 season, and top the 100-point mark for three consecutive seasons.

The name Bobby Farnham popped up on his screen. Farnham, who skated for three NHL teams, was a scrappy player who had a notorious reputation for his toughness and gritty play. During the 2012-2013 season skating for the Wilkes-Barre/Scranton Penguins, Farnham served a total of 274 penalty minutes. For comparison, Jacob never served more than 15 penalty minutes in a single season as a professional. Jacob was liking what he was seeing regarding the team makeup.

The dimly lit dining area suddenly came to life when coach Bryan Trottier appeared on the screen. The sincere enthusiasm conveyed by his smile and facial expression was unmistakable. A warm friendly face framed under his trademark cowboy hat. Jacob felt as if he was on a personal call with someone he had known for a lifetime. Trottier explained how excited he was to coach the group of men now on the call, and offered some of his expectations and coaching style for his new players.

The team was going to play to the players' strengths, and he wanted his players to go out and skate free and easy with a very simple motto that would go on to be heard frequently: "Skatin' legs and shootin' arms". Meaning, don't overthink; skate to a spot and get a shot on goal.

The players clearly enjoyed hearing the style of play that was in store for them. Coach turned the meeting over to his players to introduce themselves and share their own expectations for the upcoming season. Jacob was pleased for the chance to learn more of his new teammates.

Players representing a variety of backgrounds and stories of how they got to 3ICE introduced themselves. Canadians and Americans who had spent years playing hockey both on the North American continent and overseas. Only one player did not have professional experience.

Sean Dhooghe was a five-foot-three sparkplug, whose scouting report from the respected Hockeyprospect.com reads: "What he lacks in physical traits he certainly makes up for with his compete level being high and his hockey intelligence". The Chicago-area native, who had skated for the USA National U17 team, had just completed his fourth season of college eligibility with Arizona State University. He faced the prospect that his physical makeup may keep him from ever going pro, and was preparing for life after hockey with training to become an airline pilot. This was his one opportunity to prove himself among professional athletes and compete for a championship.

Jacob offered a brief synopsis of his own extensive background, and added the desire to have his children watch him compete on the ice for the very first time. The group brainstormed on how they would approach the season. Trottier guided the discussion which was free-flowing and constructive. They would play much the same way. Play the game with passion and joy.

The players couldn't believe how the time had flown by when Coach Trottier informed them that their meeting time was coming to a close. The group departed the call amidst much enthusiasm, eager to meet again, and even more eager to get together on the ice for the first time in just over one month.

Jacob clicked off the call and got up to refill his coffee. His mind was racing. On paper, Team Trottier would not be considered among the favorites. Far from it. He viewed the other rosters and there were some formidable teams. Teams with players who had extensive NHL experience and personal accolades. Team Trottier had only one player with NHL experience, and it came with a reputation for fighting and league suspensions. One undersized skater who would likely never play at any professional level. Another who had walked off a team with him. But one thing he noted was that everyone had something to prove. And everyone was excited to play for a coach who had picked the players to fit into his style of play and personality. Jacob was ready to get to work. He was liking this team.

### Event 1: Las Vegas, Nevada (June 17-19, 2022)

Jacob arrived early at Cleveland Hopkins International Airport for the flight to Denver. A four-hour layover would be required before arriving in Las Vegas, but he would still get there in plenty of time for the Friday evening dinner and meet up with players and coaches. The league's equipment managers were handling all hockey gear between events and locations, so Jacob was comfortable traveling lightly with only a travel bag, attired in his traditional shorts and t-shirt.

He met up with another player in Denver, a younger athlete who was on Team Murphy with Jacob at the tryout, and both headed to the gate for their early afternoon departure. Unfortunately, a series of weather delays across the region led to a cancellation of their flight.

Jacob's young traveling partner was in a panic. "What are we going to do? We need to get there in time for the dinner to learn the arrangements."

Jacob assured him that all would be fine and when they got to the airline's customer service desk, they managed to get the young man on standby for the next flight. Unfortunately, that was the last standby. Jacob saw his friend off and booked a late-evening flight. He searched for a suitable airport meal, reconciling that it would replace the event dinner.

Midnight was approaching when Jacob sat with other frustrated passengers wondering when their pilots would show up. When the crew finally arrived, the passengers' relief was short lived. Just as the plane was boarding, another announcement was made. The flight was cancelled. Word got around that the pilots were either too tired or unable to fly due to airline restrictions. He would need to book a hotel and catch the first flight to Las Vegas in the morning.

Jacob glanced at his watch and decided it was useless to get a hotel room for just a few hours of sleep, and besides that he was hearing from other passengers that many of the nearby hotels were booked. He decided to locate his gate and search out the most comfortable spot he could find. It was going to be a long night at the Denver International Airport.

The search was fruitless. Airports are not designed for comfortable rest, especially for a six-foot-three-inch 215-pound athlete. Jacob settled in a section where two seats were not connected with an arm rest and did his best to contort his body for some level of comfort. A light shone on him and the area was cold. Jacob had only t-shirts in the bag for extra cover, and added two pairs of underwear for a makeshift pillow. He was at least alone. That is, until a fellow passenger came by and chose to sit within ten feet of the lone customer at the gate to conduct a meandering phone call that seemed to Jacob would never end. It was a sleepless night.

When Jacob arrived at the Orleans Hotel the following morning, his first instinct was to lay in the bed and get some much-needed sleep. But a sudden urge and energy came over him. The reality of 3ICE was here; the excitement and anticipation built up over the past few months had finally arrived. He glanced at his phone and realized that he had time to make it to the nearby arena for the morning skate. Sleep could come later.

Jacob met up with his teammates and others on the ice, explaining his eventful evening, and couldn't get over the energy he was feeling. He skated freely and without effort. He only wished that they could lace up and go at it right then and there. He felt on top of the world.

Regrettably, the feeling did not carry over. The scheduled start time was moved up three hours so as not to interfere with the Stanley Cup Finals taking place between the Colorado Avalanche and Tampa Bay Lightning. Jacob tried but was unable to get any sleep at the hotel before needing to meet up with the team for the pregame meal. By the time they took to the ice, Jacob felt as if he was skating through slush.

Team Trottier was matched up against Team Fuhr. Jacob's play mirrored that of his teammates. They never got on track and showed little sign of life. Jacob clearly felt lifeless, and found himself in constant chase of Team Fuhr skaters on the attack, never able to get himself into good defensive position. The Trottier goaltender, Parker Milner, was facing constant pressure. Jacob remembered him from his days at Northeastern. Milner was a standout goaltender for Northeastern archrival Boston College. He would go on to win an NCAA championship two years after Jacob left college. But no goalie could withstand the barrage of shots on goal that Milner was up against. From time to time, Jacob could catch glances between his dejected teammates as if saying, "Are we really this bad?" Every time he skated off the ice, Jacob received encouragement and a pat on the back from Coach Trottier. It was helpful, but not enough to provide the energy needed. In fact, it only made Jacob feel even worse that he was letting his coach down.

Team Trottier skated off with a 5 – 0 loss. The truth is, the score probably should have been even more lopsided if not for some spectacular saves by Milner. There would be no more games for Jacob and his teammates on the inaugural 3ICE weekend.

Jacob met up that evening for dinner with his brother Andy, Andy's girlfriend Nicole, and their long-time friend Spanky. They made the drive from Utah to watch Jacob perform in the hope that they would all be celebrating in Las Vegas on Saturday night. Jacob did his best to put up a good front, but the overall mood was subdued. Andy, at least was energized watching his favorite team, the Colorado Avalanche, on the big screen above the bar. The Avalanche were going on for an impressive win to take a 2 – 0 series lead. Jacob took that as an opportunity to gracefully retire for the evening.  The one beer he drank over dinner had nearly wiped him out.  He thanked his guests for supporting him, apologized for not providing a better show, and promised that he would give them an opportunity to come back to Vegas for the 3ICE Finals.

### Event 2: Denver, Colorado (June 24-26, 2022)

Team Trottier was down, but not defeated.  Coach Trottier conducted another Zoom call and the players had much to share regarding the recent experience, what they had learned, and how they could approach the upcoming games to be better prepared.

They lamented the number of easy breakaway goals given up, putting their goalie in such a precarious position.  In a league designed for offense, they would take on a defensive identity.  Jacob was the only natural defenseman on the team, but everyone would help focus in that area, and they would always hold one skater in tow rather than have all three attack the goal in the initial surge.  Because of his gritty style of play, Bobby Farnham would also serve as the other defender on the team.  Either Jacob or Farnham would be on the ice at all times, acting as the first line of defense.

They also discussed the challenges of playing at the higher elevation for the Event Two games to be played in Denver.  The Mile High City is well known among athletes as a challenging place to play because of difficulty in breathing due to a loss in air pressure at the higher elevation.  Jacob had experience from playing at the Spengler Cup in Davos, and was now also a skilled trainer in breathing techniques.  He shared proven techniques to combat the loss of oxygen, and explained that their bodies would eventually adjust to the change in elevation.  Other players chimed in with helpful advice.  As always, Coach Trottier allowed his players to provide input as he masterfully guided the discussion.  The team would be better prepared for the upcoming games.

Jacob's arrival in Denver was much more uneventful than during the prior week.  There were no flight delays or layovers required.  But the Saturday morning skate presented the players with another challenge that they were not expecting. All weekend activities were moved to the University of Denver's campus due to the unavailability of the Ball Arena in downtown Denver. The Colorado Avalanche were on the verge of winning a Stanley Cup. They had just won their home game the prior night to take a 3–2 series lead over the Tampa Bay Lightning, so all 3ICE programs were moved to an alternate site to avoid any conflict in the use of facilities. And the University's Magness Arena hockey dimensions were larger than the standard NHL arena.

The standard NHL arena has dimensions of 200 feet by 85 feet. The University's rink was in line with the International Olympic/IIHF rinks. As Jacob learned from his years playing overseas, international rinks are designed 15 feet wider to encourage a more flowing, skill-based style of play. Conversely, NHL rinks encourage a more physical, hard-hitting style of play. For the 3ICE games to be played that Saturday evening, not only would players be subjected to lack of oxygen in the higher elevation, but now also faced with just three skaters competing in a larger rink. The players discussed how they could use this to their advantage. Every team would face the same challenges. Whoever was most prepared would have an edge.

Team Trottier came out an entirely different team from the prior week in Las Vegas. Going up against Team Carbonneau, they were much better prepared, playing in control and with a focus on defense. As the game wound down, their opponent appeared gassed and Team Trottier easily pulled away with a 6-1 victory. They were advancing to the next round.

That same play carried over into the semis. Another impressive showing with Team Trottier overcoming a 3-1 deficit against Team LeClair to notch a 5-4 win. They would now be going up against Team Mullen for the event championship. A chance for every player to earn a $7,000 bonus and guaranteed at least $4,000 for reaching the finals.

It was obvious to everyone by now that Team Mullen was the class of the field. They won the Event One championship and were piling up impressive wins for the second straight week. In the final game, Team Trottier was humbled in a 7-2 loss. The team of Joe Mullen stood alone at the top of the standings but Team Trottier was back in the race, knowing that they only needed to finish in the top four to reach the Championship series in Las Vegas on August 20.

The mood was much brighter for Jacob and his teammates during the evening's dinner, knowing they had put up a good show and were back in contention to reach the Finals. Their preparation during the week proved extremely helpful and Coach Trottier was visibly pleased with his team. As enjoyable as the dinner was, the time spent in the hotel bar following the meal was even more memorable.

It was a hockey junkie's dream. Sitting around a table with six of the game's most memorable legends, the stories and laughs flowed as smoothly as the drinks. With highlights from the Stanley Cup Finals visible on the big screen across the room, Jacob delighted in listening to colorful stories that could never be shared in print. The mood in the lounge was heightened even farther by the fact that many of the bar patrons were loyal fans of the Colorado Avalanche, who were on the verge of winning their third Stanley Cup. The eclectic mix of hockey fans, players, and legends all in one area created an atmosphere that smelled of hockey.

The coaches shared stories of their own playoff battles, and took note of some memorable playoff series between Colorado and Jacob's favorite team, the Detroit Red Wings. Jacob's ears perked up when John LeClair brought up the 1997 Playoffs. LeClair was skating for the Philadelphia Flyers, who had won the Eastern Conference and were awaiting the winner of the Western Conference Finals. To many, it was the Western Conference Finals which represented the true championship. The Colorado Avalanche and Detroit Red Wings were locked up in fierce battles, and the Flyers knew that the longer that series lasted, the more advantage Philadelphia would have to secure an upset. The Philadelphia organization tried to petition with the NHL to begin the Finals just days after the close of the Western Conference Finals. Their desperate attempt was denied. Allowed sufficient time to rest following a draining series against Colorado, the Detroit Red Wings would go on to win the 1997 Stanley Cup, sweeping Philadelphia in four games.

Jacob didn't want the night to end.  He felt a sense of contentment knowing that his team was back in the hunt and now surrounded by hockey legends in a relaxed environment sharing graphic stories of the game he loved.  As good as this was, it was about to get even better.  He closed his eyes and smiled, visualizing how the following week would play out.

### Event 3: Grand Rapids, Michigan (July 1 – 3, 2022)

Nash never stopped talking throughout the four-hour drive to Grand Rapids.  He had a million questions, and his excitement only grew with each response.  Harper was more reserved, but no less thrilled about being a part of something which they had heard so much about and watched on television for the past two Saturdays.  Now they were actually going to be a part of it.  It all seemed surreal.

From the moment that Jacob arrived with his kids at the hotel for check-in, the two were treated like celebrities.  One of the equipment managers, known to Jacob from his time with the Ducks, was the first to greet them.  Lounging in the lobby were the color and play-by-play announcers for the Pittsburgh Penguins who were also covering all event games.  They made a point of making Harper and Nash feel special, sharing how fun it was going to be to watch their dad in action.  More players and organizers stopped by to greet them. Jacob could only smile watching Harper blush at the attention and Nash's eyes grow in amazement upon meeting players whose moves he'd been studying from the TV screen.

The attention continued throughout the weekend, and when Coach Trottier joined them for breakfast the next morning it was like they were all family.  During the Saturday morning skate, Jacob brought them into the locker room and was overcome with emotion to see the faces of his beaming children.

Jacob also took the time to reflect on his own evocations while skating and wandering around the spacious Van Andel Arena.  The Grand Rapids Griffins compete in the American Hockey League (AHL), serving as the top-tier affiliate of the Detroit Red Wings.  So many of the players who

Jacob grew up watching and cheering for walked down these same halls as young players hoping to achieve their own dreams. The butterflies were growing. It was going to be special to compete on the ice with his children watching him skate for the first time in an arena that had produced some of hockey's biggest stars.

Team Trottier was matched up against Team Murphy in the opening round. The game was a hard-fought contest. Both teams came out wanting to prove themselves, and the atmosphere was thick with drama. The crowd was loving the action. Grand Rapids knows good hockey and the entire arena was on their feet as Team Trottier raced down for a final surge in hopes of breaking a 2-2 tie. Part of the 3ICE spectacle is loud music blaring over the speaker during live action, a sound that Jacob was not even aware of until watching a game in following weeks from the stands, but now even that could not be heard above the din of noise heard from the crowd.

Jacob skated across the blue line when the puck appeared into view between a jungle of legs. He approached and caught the puck square, a shot on goal which barely eclipsed a defender's stick. The shot also eluded the goalie, enabling Jacob to score his second goal of the game. The horn sounded with just 4.9 seconds remaining. Team Trottier survived an almost miraculous shot attempt as time expired and would go on to the next round.

Harper and Nash jumped in jubilation as they watched Dad mobbed by his teammates. Television cameras caught Jacob being interviewed as the Zamboni was readying to clean and smooth the ice for the upcoming game. Nash screamed in realization that they would be watching him play more hockey.

The semis featured a rematch against Team Fuhr, the team who had humiliated Team Trottier two weeks earlier in their opening game. Team Fuhr advanced despite a loss in the opening round, having scored the highest number of goals among the losing teams. This time the outcome was much different. Team Trottier was going to the finals for the second consecutive week.

There was extra excitement generated from a play going into the evening's final game. The crowd was still abuzz from an outlandish goal scored by Brandon Hawkins skating for Team LeClair. The goal, which came on a jail-break resulting from a penalty, was truly one of a kind. Even the Penguins announcers had difficulty describing it for the viewing audience, likening Hawkins to an "alien from outer space" and the shot on goal as, "never seen it before, don't know how to describe it".

On the play, Hawkins sprinted down the ice ahead of the pack and stopped on a dime just before reaching the net. He did a 360-degree spin, lifting the puck with his stick in the process, and turned to slap the floating puck past the startled goaltender's outstretched reach. Coach LeClair could be seen laughing in amazement as the entire crowd erupted. There was no question who would be receiving the three-thousand-dollar prize for shot of the night. And the play would go on to top ESPN Sports Center's Top 10 Sports Highlight.

Team Trottier faced off against Team Mullen for the Event championship. The same team who denied them first place money the prior week and who had won the first two Events. The game was also an opportunity to exact revenge and prove to his children the power of hard work and belief in oneself. A second consecutive chance to claim the seven-thousand-dollar first prize. This time, they skated off with a 6-4 victory, ending Team Mullen's eight-game winning streak to start the season. Team Trottier now held second place in the standings. It was going to be a celebratory Saturday with Harper and Nash joining him and his teammates in their exclusive hockey wonderland.

The trip back to Cleveland was much quieter than the drive up two days earlier. When not quietly reading a book or nodding off, Harper sat in the passenger seat calling her friends about the amazing weekend she just experienced. Jacob looked at the rearview mirror to view an exhausted Nash fast asleep. He smiled knowing full well the tenor of dreams that were spinning through his son's head.

### Event 4: Hershey, Pennsylvania (July 8 – 10, 2022)

Jacob had a trick up his sleeve as he prepared for the week four games in Hershey, Pennsylvania. Inspired by the Hawkins goal and recalling a move from former Red Wings star Pavel Datsyuk, Jacob practiced throughout the week on a play perfected by the Russian skater. The move, which can be equated to the crossover dribble made famous in basketball for leaving a defender helpless, was sure to allow a clean shot on goal. The trick was to perfect the difficult move and not take your own spill on the ice.

The charming city of Hershey, also known as "The Sweetest Place on Earth" because of its idyllic setting and connection with the chocolate company, has a rich hockey culture. The AHL Hershey Bears represent the longest continual membership of any club operating in the league, having represented the city since the 1938-1939 season. Gordie Howe, the Hall of Famer who was affectionately known as "Mr. Hockey", once remarked that "everybody who is anybody in hockey has played in Hershey". Jacob was hoping to execute the sweetest shot on goal at the sweetest place on earth.

Providing even more anticipation for the weekend, Jacob was hosting a special guest. He had recently added mental health coaching to his physical and hockey training repertoire. Beginning with his involvement in the OHP, Jacob was in demand to help others in personal one-on-one training sessions. Given his own experience in overcoming mental obstacles and a belief in balance between physical and mental awareness to achieve personal success, adding mental coaching seemed a natural fit.

One of Jacob's first clients was a former Secret Service agent who was suffering from post-traumatic stress disorder (PTSD). His client was from the east coast and, Jacob learned, also an avid hockey fan. He viewed an invitation to Hershey as a wonderful opportunity to meet in person for the first time. The family-friendly environment rich with hockey nostalgia also made for the perfect setting to open communication windows and relieve stress. Jacob's client arrived with the heightened anticipation of meeting up and spending an entire hockey weekend with some of the game's greats.

Team Trottier was matched up in round one against the team that was becoming their heated rival, Team Mullen. The local's love for hockey was readily apparent as the Hershey GIANT Center came alive for their introduction to 3ICE hockey. Jacob was on top of his game. He was making plays, seemingly always in the right place at the right time, and his goal put Team Trottier on the board. Was this the game in which he could execute the play he'd been practicing?

The opportunity came midway through the second half. In a tight game, Jacob had control of the puck with a defender hounding him just outside of the goalie crease. Moving left to right, he made a quick move before slamming on the breaks for a sudden stop. Ice flew in the air as the defender could not stop his momentum and fell backward on the ice. The goalie's eyes revealed panic behind his mask as he tried in vain to move into position, recognizing that a wide-open Jacob now had a clean shot on goal. Jacob only had an instant to flick the puck into the corner of the net and out of the goalie's reach or leg which was now desperately sticking out to provide any form of protection. Jacob took his shot and a photographer captured it perfectly. Striking for a shot on goal as his defender falls helplessly on the ice. Unfortunately, the puck hit the crossbar and spun upward rather than inside the net. The shot that was certain to win the three-thousand dollar "shot of the night", and possibly a place on ESPN's Top Ten Highlights, missed by a fraction of an inch.

Team Mullen survived the flurry and ultimately ended Team Trottier's chances of going on to win a second event title. Team Trottier would have to settle for a two-thousand-dollar payday, and their Saturday night games were over.

Jacob sat in the stands for the first time to experience 3ICE hockey as a spectator, joining his client after showering to take in the remainder of event games. He noticed for the first time the loud music blaring during action, and observed the excitement of fans enjoying the fast-paced action. His client, whose wide smile never disappeared throughout the entire weekend, could not stop talking about Jacob's shot on goal that just missed its mark.

Any disappointment from the team losing and out of the winnings for the weekend prize was quickly relinquished. Jacob enjoyed the conversation and recognized that if there was any week to lose your opening round and watch the action from the stands, it was that weekend.

### Event 6: Pittsburgh, Pennsylvania (July 22 – 24, 2022)

Excitement was building by the day inside the Winterhurst Ice Arena. Jacob picked up the intensity of his workouts with an extra week to prepare, given his unavailability to join Team Trottier for the Event 5 games in London, Ontario. Jacob's inability to travel inside Canada due to his COVID vaccine status enabled a replacement player to take his place. Jacob briefly allowed a concern to creep in that is shared with every professional athlete not under a major contract. Would his unavailability open the door for his eventual replacement? The thought was quickly laid to rest. He was a part of Team Trottier, driven to the team's success, and was only going to work even harder to make that happen. The young skaters and their families took notice.

Jacob's added visibility also brought to light the realization that Event 6 games were taking place in nearby Pittsburgh. More and more families were informing Jacob that they would be making the trip and spending the weekend in the Steel City to cheer him on. Not only the families of Nash's teammates, but others as well. Arena workers, skaters, their parents, it seemed that Jacob was going to have quite a cheering section for the upcoming games in the PPG Paint Arena.

Jacob made the two-hour drive to Pittsburgh on Friday morning, knowing that Annie would be driving Harper and Nash along with his sister Sarah and her family the following morning. Jacob detoured off the highway to enjoy the scenic drive along the Ohio River and foothills of the Allegheny Mountains. He was early, so no harm in adding time to the drive. He counted his blessings. To have family and friends join him in an environment that meant everything in the world to him was priceless. Who would have guessed going into the year that he would be in this position, competing for prize money in games televised across two countries?

His thoughts turned to Nash. The six-year-old was now competing for a team in organized games designed to utilize skills which he and his teammates had been learning for the past two years. Jacob smiled with memories of Nash badgering him relentlessly to sign up for the hockey program upon his arrival back to Cleveland. Nash took right to the ice, and Jacob could see that he was a natural. What was it that brought such joy in watching Nash skate? He clearly had the skill, but it was something else. Approaching a tunnel, the answer came clear. Nash loved the game. His love of hockey and a work ethic to continually improve his game were what gave Jacob the biggest level of joy and satisfaction. It made the reality of everything which he was experiencing with 3ICE and what he had to do even more meaningful.

Light from the tunnel's end was fast approaching. Jacob reached the opening and peered below to take in the panoramic setting before him. Three mighty rivers came into view, converging to form a scenic park alongside tall buildings and a string of sturdy golden-colored bridges in the heart of the city. Jacob's excitement grew. It was going to be a fun weekend of hockey in Pittsburgh.

Harper and Nash joined Jacob for breakfast the next morning, easily engaging in conversation with everyone around them as if they were a part of the 3ICE program. Jacob brought them into the locker room following the morning skate and Nash rapidly reeled off the names of Penguins' stars who called this same sacred place their home. Back at the hotel, the spacious lobby was teeming with familiar faces, resembling a joyous reunion. It seemed that Nash's entire team was present, and players from all across the youth league were running around the lobby and hallways proudly donning their jerseys.

Enthusiastic parents approached Jacob and wished him luck for the evening games. Everyone was in a joyful mood, and the energy was contagious. Now it was up to Jacob and Team Trottier to deliver a performance to match the support of their fans.

The team did not disappoint. From the moment they entered the ice for warmups, the Arena came alive with screams heard from the multitude of young fans in the stands. Nash led the cheers, surrounded by his teammates who had front row seats for the event, pounding the glass for added effect. Team Trottier picked up on the energy and easily won their opening game against Team Fuhr. They were advancing to the next round.

The noise and energy only grew with each appearance. And by the time the final game approached, the Cleveland contingent was in a frenzy. When the final horn sounded to close an impressive victory for Team Trottier's second event win, Nash and the young skaters were on their feet banging the boards in jubilation. Jacob led his teammates to the section housing the Cleveland contingent, bowing and raising their sticks to show their appreciation for the unprecedented support. It only raised the decibel level.

The evening's festivities were moved from the hotel and into an area seeped with Pittsburgh nostalgia. Tyler Murovich was a Pittsburgh native skating for Team Mullen. He rented out a restaurant that stood at the top of a hill which could be reached from a trolley. From that vantage point, the lit-up city sparkled below as Jacob was surrounded by family, friends, and the 3ICE hockey fraternity. With their win, Team Trottier now was assured a top-four seed for the August 20 Finals in Las Vegas. Harper and Nash sat nearby laughing with their friends. Even Annie was there to share in the celebration, perhaps feeling some sense of satisfaction in the knowledge that the many sacrifices made over the years were at least paying some dividends.

Jacob glanced around and spotted Coach Trottier with his trademark hat smiling in his direction, as if fully aware of everything that was going through his mind.  The coach raised his glass and Jacob returned the toast with a smile and genuine expression of gratitude.

### Event 8: Nashville, Tennessee (August 5-7, 2022)

The family was busy packing for the road trip.  Jacob's anticipation was further enhanced in that he was ready to get back on the ice following another break in action with the Week 7 games taking place in Canada. Jacob would have enjoyed going back to the arena in Quebec City where he competed as a twelve-year old skating in pee wee hockey.  Once again, his COVID vaccine status kept him out of action but watching the bustle of activity around him more than made up for the games missed.

Jacob's sister Sarah and her son Levi were joining Harper and Nash for the eight-hour drive to Nashville for a weekend of fun in the "Music City". Jacob rented a spacious SUV for the trip and booked an extra hotel room for Sarah and Levi.  It was not lost on Jacob that twenty years earlier, he and his brothers and friends packed the Chevrolet Suburban for an eventful trip to the Hockey Showcase held in Langley, British Columbia.  Mrs. Anderson was not available this time around to drive them, but the thrill was no less than what was felt in the stuffed Suburban twenty years earlier.

Talk of hockey and what awaited them in Tennessee was nonstop, and it was only when they crossed the bridge from Cincinnati to Kentucky that Jacob felt the need to take a break.  There was only one additional stop that was necessary before their arrival into Nashville. On a private Zoom call during the week, the players planned a surprise for their beloved coach.  Jacob needed to make a purchase, and at a gas station near the Kentucky-Tennessee border he found the perfect accessory to complete the required look.

By now, Harper and Nash were part of the 3ICE family, and Nashville provided the perfect setting to heighten their respective experiences with the program.  Harper delighted in the music scene that was visible all around them, and Nash remained convinced that the captivating city was named after him.  Jacob met with his teammates over Friday dinner and they decided to unleash their surprise on Coach not at the Saturday morning skate, but just before face-off for their evening game.

The Bridgestone Arena, located alongside Nashville's lively Music Center, was primed and ready for 3ICE hockey.  As Team Trottier came out to warm up for the first game to open the evening, the crowd came alive witnessing the unexpected display before them.  Laughter arose from the TV announcer's booth and Coach Trottier looked on in disbelief from his spot on the bench.  Six skaters and the goalie were skating in circles for warmups donning cowboy hats in lieu of hockey helmets.  A display of team unity which visibly pleased their coach as well as the cheering crowd.

*Team Trottier: from left, Bobby Farnham, Jacob, Sean Dhooge, Coach Trottier, Cam Brown, Chad Costello, Matt Salhany, and Parker Milner.*

The outcome of the game was almost secondary.  Team Trottier was not only assured of a spot in the upcoming 3ICE Championship Series, but they also secured the second seed.  Coach Trottier told his players in the locker room after the game that he loved each and every one of them and would never forget what they had done.  He closed his remarks with a challenge to be ready in two weeks to win the million-dollar prize.

The road trip was not over.  Jacob drove the following day to a rustic cabin in the Tennessee mountains.  Thoughts of the separation from his children while overseas were far removed.  Replaced with the joy in watching them running with their cousin Levi, all wearing cowboy hats purchased in Nashville, against the backdrop of the Great Smoky Mountains.

## 3ICE Championship: Las Vegas, Nevada (Week of August 14, 2022)

Team Mullen entered the finals as the clear favorite to capture the first-ever Patrick Cup and claim the $1.1 million prize. Their team ended the regular season accumulating 17 wins and four Event titles over the eight-week season. Team Trottier came in at second place with ten wins, finishing just ahead of Teams LeClair and Murphy with nine wins apiece. Coach Trottier's team had already surpassed the expectations that most had for the six-team field, but he and his scrappy bunch were not about to settle for simply an unexpected appearance to Vegas for the finals weekend. They had loftier goals.

Having two weeks to prepare, the team continued holding Zoom calls to discuss strategy while pushing one another to maintain their workout regimes. By the end of the week, they realized the Zoom calls weren't enough. They decided to meet up ahead of schedule in Las Vegas, book their own rooms, and arrange some practice time together at the Golden Knights practice facility.

Jacob arrived early in the week to meet up with his teammates. Harper and Nash would not join him on the trip. They would be watching with family and friends back home, enabling Jacob to focus all his energies for the Saturday evening games. When not practicing in the rink, the players found their own time to prepare for the finals. It did not come without incident.

Jacob awoke early one morning to conduct his daily visualization meditation ritual. He chose to go outside and beat the desert heat, soaking in the early morning rays to energize his mind. Stepping outside of the lobby, he found a place to sit around the corner of the front entrance. It seemed a peaceful place to gather his thoughts with minimal interruption. The shoeless Jacob sat down alongside the building and took off his shirt to use as a makeshift pillow to soften the concrete surface. Seated upright with hands outstretched, he closed his eyes and opened his mind.

Images of game action unfolded before him. Skating freely, stopping shots, finding open teammates, and scoring goals. He visualized the team in celebration and could hear the cheers from the crowd. People calling his name. The noise growing louder and more intense. Then he heard a crackling noise as if coming from a radio.

"We have a suspect who appears unarmed but should be considered dangerous."

"Sir! Sir! Can you hear me?"

Opening his eyes, Jacob was startled to look up and see a uniformed security officer nervously peering down above him. A crowd of onlookers looked on from behind, murmuring among themselves in wonder and anticipation.

Jacob fought to gather his senses in an attempt to assess what was happening. Then the realization hit him. Sitting alone half naked, he must have presented quite a sight to the arriving casino patrons just starting their day. Apparently, an elderly woman alerted security that a menacing-looking man appeared in a semi-conscious state and might be up to no good. What was even more alarming, other young men could be seen around the building in similar states. Apparently, Jacob was not alone among his teammates, who had taken his advice to conduct their own meditation sessions. But it was the bearded, shirtless, and strapping Jacob who seemed to pose the biggest threat. Perhaps he was the leader among this threatening gang who must be up to something nefarious.

Jacob tried to stifle his laughter, and explained to the officer that he was a professional hockey player preparing for games to be played on Saturday night at the adjoining Orleans Arena. A relieved security officer reported back on his radio that the situation was under control and the threat averted. The crowd of onlookers could be seen excitably gossiping amongst themselves over what they could make out before slowly retreating back into the casino. Jacob recognized that he needed to find another place to meditate.

Saturday evening arrived without further incident. Coach Trottier spoke to his team in the quiet locker room as Team Mullen was on the ice going up against Team Murphy in the evening's opening game. He shared how proud he was of the group, and how he would never forget the grit and determination that they displayed throughout the season. Distant cheers from the crowd could be heard as an Arena attendant opened the door to alert the team that their time on the ice was approaching. Team Mullen was wrapping up an impressive 5-1 win to advance to the finals.

Silence returned when the door closed. Coach Trottier finished his remarks with the words that he used to close every pregame speech. "I love you guys. Now let's go out there and get a win!"

Jacob could sense as soon as the team skated onto the ice for pregame warmups that they were all focused and ready to take care of business. The time spent together during the week heightened not only the team's physical preparation, but also their mental awareness and conditioning for the upcoming games.

Right on cue, Team Trottier got off to a quick start. And it was their smallest player, the lone amateur, who got the scoring started. Sean Dhooghe was awarded a penalty shot and skated ahead of the pack to put Team Trottier on the scoreboard. The scoring continued and soon the outcome was not in doubt. There was only one issue, and it posed a potential major problem for the team going into the final game.

The intensity of the game was clearly ratcheted up with knowledge of prize money on the line. As such, the play grew more physical, testing the boundaries of the 3ICE rules which do not allow contact. The referees did their best to control the action, but it finally happened. A fierce collision occurred between noted enforcer Bobby Farnham and T. J. Hensick skating for Team LeClair. Farnham scrambled back to his feet and went right after Hensick, who was expecting the charge. The two squared off, no doubt a follow-up of past skirmishes simmering between them throughout their NHL and AHL careers. The referees stepped in and immediately disqualified both players from the game. Team Trottier knew they would be playing in the final game, but were uncertain if the Farnham suspension would carry over.

The team sat quietly in the locker room following the win, awaiting to get back on the ice upon completion of the consolation game taking place between Teams Murphy and LeClair. Their silence and focus were magnified pending the uncertainty of Farnham's availability. If Bobby was unavailable to play, that would not only put the team down one man, but place Jacob as the lone defender on the team. They were already faced with a difficult challenge in stopping the potent Team Mullen attack, but doing so without one of their top defenders would prove an even larger obstacle.

League officials finally stepped inside the hushed locker room to deliver the verdict. Farnham was cleared to play the game. But make no mistake, the referees would be watching very closely and any further physical play would result in a player's immediate removal.

Buoyed by the news, Coach Trottier gathered his team for the pregame speech before sending them back on the ice. It was nearing showtime.

Jacob looked around the Arena as the team warmed up for the final game to determine the Patrick Cup winner and $1.1 million prize. The crowd was ready, the cameras were in position, and Jacob knew that Harper and Nash were sitting in front of the TV set back home with the family. This was everything that he had visualized and dreamed of. He was grateful beyond words. Jacob looked up to the rafters, offered a prayer, and joined his teammates on the bench for some final words before face-off.

Just as in the opening round, Team Trottier came out with focus and intensity. Every player skated as if their lives depended on it, continually stifling the attacks and constant pressure put on by their talented opponent. Then came a break. Chad Costello broke free and scored to put Team Trottier in the lead. Another goal put them up 2-0 at half.

Coach Trottier brought the team together on the bench, reminding them not to get complacent. "Skatin' legs and shootin' arms." Keep the pressure on.

Team Trottier came back out with the same intensity and halfway through the half they were up 4-1. Reality set in among the players that they were in position to win the Patrick Cup and prize money. That's when Team Mullen appeared to wake up. The team with a collection of outstanding skaters and the pride to match ratcheted up the pressure and quickly closed the gap. From 4-1 to 4-3, leaving enough time on the clock for at least a tie to send the game into a shootout, if not a win.

The crowd was now on their feet as the final minute saw Team Trottier facing relentless pressure. Goaltender Patrick Milner was making spectacular saves, but receiving no relief from the 3ICE rules keeping the puck in constant motion. The clock was winding down to the final minute, and both Jacob and Farnham were on the ice in a desperate attempt to help out their exhausted goalie. A final push with a fourth skater replacing the Team Mullen goalie forced heavy action to the right of the net. Just as the shot was taken, Jacob noticed an opening to his left. If the puck ricocheted in that direction, it could result in an open shot. He turned to his left, anticipating that the initial shot would be blocked. Sure enough, the puck ricocheted directly to the spot he envisioned and an offensive player had a final clean shot on goal. Jacob stuck out his stick in the nick of time to deflect the puck just as the final horn sounded.

Jacob raised his stick in jubilation, joined by his three teammates within arm's length and soon to be mobbed by three more teammates now charging them. The television cameras clearly captured him mouthing the words: "I love you guys!" Coach Bryan Trottier, winner of seven Stanley Cups, could not contain his excitement. He rushed onto the ice to celebrate with a team that he so easily identified with. A collection of players of whom he could not have been prouder.

** ** **

*A young boy with wispy blonde hair is surrounded by a mob of players, event organizers, and television cameras. He appears invisible to all around him, yet is able to soak in every ounce of emotion cascading through the pores of the entire throng within his reach. The noise rising above the distant crowd mystically fades away along with shouts that only moments ago were ringing in his ears. The silence is deafening.*

*The scene contrasts sharply with the recurring nightmare that for so long haunted him. A nightmare that miraculously ended on that day when Jacob came to his rescue and held him in his arms at the home in San Jacinto. The nightmare now a distant memory, yet its visual forever etched in his mind: Jacob is seen standing above a burning pit, trying desperately to escape from the chains that are holding him down. Far below, in the smoldering pit, nearly-lifeless children are barely visible. Their empty eyes convey helplessness, as if resigned to their fate. But the chains were broken during that visit. The child was freed. As were others.*

*Two thousand miles away, Harper and Nash are jumping up and down in front of the TV screen in the packed family room. Smiles light up the entire room. Dad kept his promise, just like he told them he would on that day of his baptism. The promise of living with faith and truth seemed vague at the time. But surely, this was the meaning.*

*The little boy smiles recalling the baptism. He was also there. The ceremony at the last moment was moved back a week to July 7. Seven and seven. Angel numbers that signify spiritual growth, divine guidance, and positive transformation. In a religious context, biblical passages relate the numbers with abundant forgiveness. The day was a further awakening. Also, a reminder that so many more need to be saved.*

*The noise gradually returns to the Arena. Joyful sounds blend into a musical hum emanating from the crowd. A large ceremonial Cup is placed in his hands. He is encouraged by all around to raise it. The boy holds the Cup high above his head. The crowd roars their approval. Unlike the chains which once held his protector down, the raised Cup now promises peace and clarity.*

*Tears roll down the little boy's cheek. He cannot conceal his smile. They are the tears of Happy Jake.*

*A camera from the rafters captures Jacob and Coach Trottier hoisting the Patrick Cup.*

*Clockwise from upper left: Jacob with his kids and Coach Trottier in Nashville. Team Trottier celebrating with E.J. Johnston. Post-game celebration. Jacob with his kids in Pittsburgh locker room.*

# Epilogue - Jacob's Words

Jacob Newton skated one more season with 3ICE, joining Team Fuhr for the 2023 season before hanging up the skates for good.

Since then, Jacob has focused his time and energy in helping others though his personal business, Newton's Mind, providing mental performance training for both athletes and non-athletes.

His list of clients for the athletes platform includes both professionals and amateurs, as well at teams in youth organizations. This training is geared towards improving mental performance, and focuses on athletes finding consistent competence, emotional control, and breathing techniques to be used for physical recovery and staying in the moment.

Newton's Mind also reaches out to non-athletes, particularly those individuals who have suffered from abuse and mental trauma. This training focuses on individual's emotional well-being, and is tailored to the specific goals and needs identified for each client.

Jacob remains devoted in his role as parent and mentor towards his children, Harper and Nash. Harper consistently maintains a 4.0 GPA, plays clarinet, and enjoys music and hanging out with her friends. Nash stars on the nationally ranked Cleveland Barons Junior Hockey Club as his love for the sport continues to grow. Jacob also serves as an assistant coach for Nash's Junior Baron's Club.

As an active public speaker, Jacob is increasingly invited to speak, particularly for men's organizations, offering motivational talks based upon his personal life experiences.

The following list of life lessons provides a general overview, in Jacob's words, that can be applicable for both athletes and non-athletes who aspire for emotional growth to achieve their maximum potential.

## Healing from my past

Reflecting back on my life, the choices I made and the immaturity I embodied, I realize that it was all deeply connected to the abuse I experienced as a 5- 7-year-old. For well over a decade, I subconsciously buried those memories away. I truly didn't remember them until that day my sister Bethanie brought them to the surface at my apartment in Anaheim. Until that day, my inner child was screaming for love and connection. The deeper parts of me needed attention, but I couldn't hear the screams because I was too often numb from alcohol and marijuana. The substances were an escape from the pain that I needed to feel.

I fell deeper with the first taste of alcohol, then came the first puff of a joint. Until these experiences, I was highly emotional and would experience mood swings that I couldn't possibly understand. Instead of searching for help, I turned to booze and weed. This allowed me to silence the inner scream and put a smile on my face. To make others laugh, smile, and want to hang out with me. It was a crutch, and eventually that crutch would crumble.

During my days of partying, I made decisions that deeply impacted those closest to me. My decision to have an affair forever left a mark on Annie and stained our marriage. Although she initially chose to stay with me, our marriage never recovered. The intimacy was lost, and our emotional connection was never the same. After she decided to end our marriage, I realized that I didn't want to feel that same pain again. I had been taking therapy for several years, but I needed more.

Playing in Finland and all alone, I became relentless in my pursuit to set myself free from the shadow of childhood abuse. In order to do so, I had to go back and relive those experiences. To go back both physically and mentally to where the abuse took place and remember the words, feelings, smells, and fear that I experienced. After reliving the memories, it was necessary to self-reflect without turning to substance to silence the pain.

After continual repetition, the pain slowly began to leave my body. I learned the value in giving myself permission to cry. Toxic energy and emotion were released from my body, at times coming out in the form of tears.

As a man in our society, it is deemed weak to be open and vulnerable. This is the biggest lie that men have been told. The true strength of a man is to confront his fears, wounds, and emotions to develop a deeper understanding of oneself. This is true strength, and enables the freedom to find inner peace, happiness, and a safety net for those who we love.

**Helping others: The importance of learning Grace and Compassion**

Through the inner work I've conducted with myself, a deeper level of grace and compassion for who I am has opened up. This has in turn allowed me to have more grace and compassion for others.

I now realize that I made a lot of mistakes and hurt a lot of people in the past because I was acting out based upon my previous life experiences. Most of my decisions were rooted in pain with a lack of understanding. These decisions weren't coming from a place of love, but from a state of trying to protect myself subconsciously. I didn't take ownership of my decisions because I was unable to be honest with myself. Once I took ownership of my pain, emotions, and wounds, I was able to begin the healing process for myself. But could I reach out to help others?

I was initially stuck in a mindset of: "If this is true for me, how can it not be true for others?" I failed to see others from a deeper level; they were often lost in their own cycles of victimhood or emotional neglect. I felt that judgment of others was, at some level, judgment of myself. However, when my judgmental mind turned off, doors opened to find compassion and a deeper understanding of others.

In our society, we too often fail to understand people's pain and actions because we choose to compare them to our own moral values. "If I were them, I would never do that." Well, we don't get to be them, free of all their life experiences that led them to choices which we are at odds with. When we choose to view people from a deeper lens, we learn empathy. We are able to meet them at their pain hiding below the surface.

When we only view the surface and become repulsed by their words or actions, we grow disconnected from truth and lose the ability to help others. That truth being, this person is internally in pain and needs love and connection. Not judgement and shame. Instead of calling them out, we should call them forward. Why not let them know we believe in their ability to make better and healthier choices? That simple belief may actually touch them at a level that will invoke change within them. Conversely, calling them out comes from a place of judgement and shame which only amplifies the internal chaos they are already experiencing.

Calling people forward creates connection vs. disconnect. It enables grace and compassion, which is the true catalyst for growth and change.

### For Athletes and professionals:
### A lack of identity outside of sports can lead to people-pleasing.

During my seasons in Texas, Lincoln, and Northeastern, as well as the first few years of my professional career, I had no identity outside of being a hockey player. All of my happiness was dictated by my on-ice success and obtaining my teammates' approval. The biggest enabler in continuing this unhealthy lifestyle was my high level of performance on the ice.

As a result of my success in hockey, I didn't see anything wrong with drinking and partying to excess. Why would I change when I was the go-to guy on every team I played on? What I didn't realize was that at some point, this lifestyle would catch up to me.

I worked hard off the ice on my physical abilities, but the partying never allowed me to play to my full potential. As a teenager, far from home, I didn't understand the power in saying no. If my teammates were happy with me, then I was happy with myself. I was the guy who had to be the center of attention at parties, and teammates always wanted to know where

I'd be after games. With no identity as a person, this acceptance became my source of happiness.

Looking back now, I realize that I was my own biggest obstacle. I should have spent more time gaining a higher level of awareness and confidence within myself off the ice. I was so afraid of how my teammates would react to a "no," and that fear led me to say "yes" all too often. Hockey was good to me with all the joy and experiences it brought into my life, but there is so much more I could have done had I been mentally and emotionally stronger.

Once I found my identity and became "Happy Jake", everything changed. I found the peace and happiness that I was starving for, and increasingly found myself surrounded by positive energy. This would go on to create opportunities that otherwise would never have arisen, and the pinnacle was reached when I raised the trophy as champions of 3ICE.

**Viewing yourself as "the victim" stunts growth and opportunities.**

From the time I left home at the age of 15 until my pro career started, I was a skilled defenseman with an uncanny ability to score and skate just as good, if not better than, forwards. This was my role on every team I played on. I had a relentless work ethic and God-given skills that I worked very hard to maintain and build upon. When I signed my contract with the Anaheim Ducks, I was expected to step into the same role: a defenseman who could score and contribute on powerplays.

When I was sent down to the AHL, I was asked to play a different style. To play with more physicality and use my 6'3 frame as a defensive force. I was resistant to this and didn't understand why I had to change from what gave me success in signing an NHL contract.

What I failed to realize was had I brought the same work ethic I used to become the player I was, I could have cultivated other areas of my game. I was lost in being a victim and lacked a growth mindset. This was my opportunity to reach the NHL, and it was my lack of maturity that ultimately closed the door to hockey's highest level. I was asked to change my style for reasons that I did not agree with or felt were beyond my control, but the coaching staff believed I could do it. Once again, I was my biggest obstacle at the most important time of my career.

Finally, remember that opportunities do not come with luck, but arise as a result of our own making. Often unexpectedly. So many positive events came into play once I cleared my mind which created an opportunity to compete for 3ICE and culminated with raising the championship trophy. And more doors continue to open to this day.

**Become more human than athlete**

For anyone who competes in sports, you will always be more "human" than "athlete". Every athlete will spend far more time away from the field than on the field. This is why it's so important to take care of your mental health and your life away from the sport. For me, I was struggling in my personal life and because of my unwillingness to seek help, my on-ice performance became a symptom to my personal life. At first, I was good at shutting it off and just being present with hockey, but that didn't last too long.

My first season away from home in Oregon, I often experienced extreme mood swings. During these periods, I was overly emotional, quick to cry, and would get extremely nervous before games to the point of throwing up. I didn't understand why and where that all came from. I needed support and someone to talk to about my personal life.

During my second season in Lincoln, I got so intoxicated one night that I faceplanted on the pavement. The next day we had a breast cancer walk and I showed up with bruises and bloody scars all over my face. The coach's wife approached me with a fan and said, "There's Jake Newton, the troublemaker." If only people knew the pain I was feeling, perhaps they could have looked beyond the surface and recognized my screams for help.

During my second season in Finland, I switched teams towards the end of the season and that meant continued separation from my kids for eight more weeks. This was crushing for me and it was difficult to show up to the rink and still perform at a high level. I spoke with the team's sports psychologist and all he wanted to talk about was hockey. In that moment, I didn't care about hockey, the father in me was grieving and needed space to talk about the guilt I felt in being away from my kids.

In the end, it's up to us as individuals to be the best person that we can be and to recognize the need for help when we experience inner pain. There is nothing wrong in seeking and asking for help. Likewise, we should also be vigilant in recognizing the subtle screams for help from our teammates and/or loved ones.

For parents:

### Remove your baggage and embrace your inner child

One of the hardest pills to swallow as a parent is knowing I can't save my kids from everything. Knowing that with each struggle and setback they face, there's a lesson for them to learn that I rob them of if I step in. Sometimes, being a parent means letting go and simply providing a safe support system, almost like a friend. When I get lost in the role of parent, I often find myself in teacher mode and try to guide my kids through lessons that I've learned. At times, though, they don't need another lesson; sometimes they just want a friend to listen and hold space for them.

When my children are feeling pain, it will cause me to reflect on my own. But that is mine to feel and not to project on them. I can't allow my pain and story to become theirs. So, I save my kids from carrying emotional baggage that isn't theirs to carry, and allow them to experience their own, understanding that pain is necessary at times to evolve and mature.

An interesting reality I've learned is that my kids are able to teach me just as much about life as I do for them. As parents, if we take a step back and tune in to our kids, we see imagination, curiosity, presence, joy, love, compassion and grace. All things that have the capacity to bring so much more fulfillment into our lives. As I continue on my journey, I've learned to focus on my inner child, thereby enabling my kids to grow and live their own lives free from the negative projections of my past and filled with a connection that brings us even closer together and makes me a better person.

# About the author

*The tears of Happy Jake* is Andrew Bajda's second published book. Bajda is the former president of Cleveland's Polish-American Cultural Center and a retired assistant professor at Cuyahoga Community College in Cleveland, Ohio, where he was a Bessie Award winner for teaching excellence and the lead faculty member for the Small Business (Entrepreneurial) program. Today, Bajda devotes his time to writing, public speaking, travel, enjoying life with his wife, and spending time with his close-knit family and friends.